THE SENTIMENTAL TOUCH

THE SENTIMENTAL TOUCH

The Language of Feeling in the Age of Managerialism

AARON RITZENBERG

Fordham University Press

NEW YORK   2013

Fordham University Press has no responsibility for the persistence or accuracy of URLs for external or third-party Internet websites referred to in this publication and does not guarantee that any content on such websites is, or will remain, accurate or appropriate.

Fordham University Press also publishes its books in a variety of electronic formats. Some content that appears in print may not be available in electronic books.

Library of Congress Cataloging-in-Publication Data

Ritzenberg, Aaron.
  The sentimental touch : the language of feeling in the age of managerialism / Aaron Ritzenberg. — 1st ed.
      p. cm.
  Includes bibliographical references and index.
  ISBN 978-0-8232-4552-9 (cloth : alk. paper)
  1. American literature—19th century—History and criticism. 2. American literature—20th century—History and criticism. 3. Emotions in literature. I. Title.
PS217.E47R58 2013
810.9'353—dc23

                                                                    2012027757

Printed in the United States of America

15 14 13   5 4 3 2 1

First edition

THE
AMERICAN
LITERATURES
INITIATIVE
A book in the American Literatures Initiative (ALI), a collaborative publishing project of NYU Press, Fordham University Press, Rutgers University Press, Temple University Press, and the University of Virginia Press. The Initiative is supported by The Andrew W. Mellon Foundation. For more information, please visit www.americanliteratures.org.

For my parents and my brother

Contents

ACKNOWLEDGMENTS

It gives me great pleasure to acknowledge the many people who helped me write this book. Caren Irr, my dissertation adviser at Brandeis University, helped me shape this project from its earliest stages and has been a brilliant, generous mentor. I am grateful to Michael T. Gilmore for reading my work carefully and for sharing his deep knowledge of American literature. I am fortunate that Gregg Camfield and Mary Louise Kete read the entire manuscript and offered many helpful suggestions. Special thanks to Ian Cornelius, Cathy Nicholson, Caleb Smith, and Ryan Wepler, who read multiple drafts of this work and helped refine some of its central ideas.

I would like to acknowledge the many friends and colleagues who offered crucial support and made important contributions to my thinking. I want especially to thank John Burt, Mary Jean Corbett, Elizabeth Dillon, Andrew Eastwick, T. J. Filip, Walter Foery, Karin Gosselink, Alfie Guy, Briallen Hopper, Hsuan Hsu, Shannon Hunt, Tom King, Michelle Komie, Sharon Komorow, Laura Korobkin, Wendy Lee, Paul Morrison, Elsa Olivetti, Mark Oppenheimer, Lisa Pannella, Phil Perilstein, Justin Reich, Brandon Stafford, Susan Staves, and Eric Tars.

Working with Helen Tartar and Tom Lay at Fordham University Press has been a pleasure. I appreciate the careful work of many people who helped with the final stages of this book, especially Robert Burchfield, Will Cerbone, Kate O'Brien-Nicholson, Kay Peterson, Tim Roberts, and Katie Sweeney. I thank Johns Hopkins University Press and Peter Lang Press for permission to print the portions of this book that have appeared previously as articles. Material from the introduction and third chapter was published as "Holding On to the Sentimental in *Winesburg, Ohio*," in *Modern Fiction Studies* 56.3 (Fall 2010): 496–517. Material from the first chapter was published as "Touching the Body, Training the Reader: Emotional Response in *Uncle Tom's Cabin*," in *The Hand of the Interpreter: Essays on Meaning after Theory*, ed. Mena Mitrano and Eric Jarosinski, 267–89 (Oxford: Peter Lang, 2008).

I am thankful for my teachers at Haverford College who first introduced me to the pleasures and rewards of close reading: Kim Benston, Steve Finley, Richard Hardack, Joanne Hutchinson, Jim Ransom, Debora Sherman, and Tina Zwarg.

My indebtedness to Jon Willis is long standing and deep; he has improved my writing and my thinking immeasurably. I am profoundly grateful for his wisdom and his friendship.

I am lucky to have a family that is endlessly supportive. I would like to thank my parents, Ken and Susi, whose powerful hearts and minds are the deep inspiration for this book. Finally, I dedicate this book to my brother, Dan, who has taught me what matters most.

THE SENTIMENTAL TOUCH

Introduction

The most poignant moments in *Uncle Tom's Cabin* are moments of touch. When characters in Harriet Beecher Stowe's 1852 novel experience profound emotions, they are silent, but they are able to share their feelings through bodily contact. With a sentimental touch, characters and readers alike imagine they are experiencing unmediated emotion. For instance, after the runaway Eliza eludes slave-catchers by carrying her child across the icy Ohio River, she finds unlikely help from Senator and Mrs. Bird, who aid in her escape:

> Mr. Bird hurried her into the carriage, and Mrs. Bird pressed on after her to the carriage steps. Eliza leaned out of her carriage, and put out her hand,—a hand as soft and beautiful as was given in return. She fixed her large, dark eyes, full of earnest meaning, on Mrs. Bird's face, and seemed going to speak. Her lips moved,—she tried once or twice, but there was no sound,—and pointing upward, with a look never to be forgotten, she fell back in the seat, and covered her face. The door was shut, and the carriage drove on.[1]

Words elude Eliza. We know by her touch, though, that she conveys heartfelt gratitude to Mrs. Bird and that the two women share an earnest sympathy. There is no difference between the hand of the slave and the hand of the senator's wife; both are "soft and beautiful," equal in value, exchanged freely and easily. Stowe does not describe Eliza's thoughts, but rather narrates her bodily actions. We know only by her movements that Eliza is overwhelmed with emotion. Though Eliza and Mrs. Bird are on opposite sides of a defining racial divide, a touching moment can overcome the power structure that would bring the nation to war. For the sentimental author, the body reveals a surpassingly deep truth. The most authentic, transparent mode of communication occurs with the touch of hands. In a perfect sentimental touch, meaning is produced instantly and unproblematically.

I would like to examine another sentimental touch, this time in a novel that is rarely, if ever, discussed alongside *Uncle Tom's Cabin*. Sinclair Lewis's *Babbitt* (1922) is known mostly for its satirical depiction of modern business life and its critiques of conspicuous leisure and consumption.[2] George Babbitt, a forty-six-year-old real estate agent, lives in a dismal world of fetishized consumer objects. In modernist style, the text is punctuated with advertisement slogans and newspaper clippings. Babbitt realizes the falsity of "zip and zowie" consumer culture, but finally conforms whimperingly. Caught up in his own psychological crisis, he slips back to his ailing wife:

> Instantly all the indignations which had been dominating him and the spiritual dramas through which he had struggled became pallid and absurd before the ancient and overwhelming realities, the standard and traditional realities, of sickness and menacing death, the long night, and the thousand steadfast implications of married life. He crept back to her. As she drowsed away in the tropic languor of morphia, he sat on the edge of her bed, holding her hand, and for the first time in many weeks her hand abode trustfully in his.[3]

Babbitt's revelation—the sudden revaluation and recentering of a life that seemed out of control—is made manifest through abiding hands. Even in a drugged haze, Babbitt's wife acknowledges and trusts the silent return of her husband. Babbitt's circumstances could scarcely be more different than Eliza's—Babbitt suffers the middle-aged alienation of white-collar mediocrity, while Eliza represents the purest victim of the vilest institution. Sinclair Lewis's figuration of transcendent touch is different than the pure version of emotional profundity that we see in *Uncle Tom's Cabin*. Yet, strikingly, Lewis deploys a sentimental trope to signal a tight emotional union. Though George Babbit and his wife are silent, readers understand that he has changed. The touch of a hand secures what was a collapsing bond between George and Myra Babbitt. Critical discourse has separated *Uncle Tom's Cabin* and *Babbitt*: Stowe's nineteenth-century sensibility—marked most of all by a deep sincerity—sits in opposition to Lewis's modernist irony. But in the sentimental touch we find an uncomfortable alliance between these two radically different texts. The utopianism of the sentimental touch has transformed from a vision of overcoming social barriers to a promise of intimacy in an anonymous world.

The touch in *Babbitt* is surprising not because of what happens in the narrative (readers may have guessed that George Babbitt would return to his wife) but because of what kind of language Lewis uses to describe Babbitt's emotional redemption. When touching hands resonate deeply and silently even in the face of catastrophe, it would seem that we are in the world of sentimental novels, not twentieth-century satire. An earnest sentimental trope should not fit in the thoroughly unsentimental world of Babbitt. While the sentimental touch seems to rely on bodies that can communicate straightforwardly without words, Babbitt exists in a world where bodies are alienated from each other and alienated from themselves. After all, the domestic bonds that undergird sentimentalism are absent from Babbitt's world. As Lewis writes, "there was but one thing wrong with the Babbitt house: It was not a home" (18). Babbitt's living conditions are emblematic of a world of houses and not homes, where disaffection runs deep. The source of alienation, for Lewis, is a deeply embedded business culture. Babbitt is an eminent capitalist who "made nothing in particular" (6), who lives in a world that has "standardized the beauty out of life" (100). Managerial culture—in which personhood becomes swallowed by standardization, in which human relationships are rendered abstract—seems the very opposite of sentimental culture. What, then, is a sentimental touch doing in this modernist novel? How does a communication based on personal feeling survive in a fully mediated culture? What is the fate of sentimentality in an age that seems more and more impersonal?

Literary critics have commonly asserted that sentimentalism lost its force with the hardening of a dehumanizing economic structure. Indeed, realist authors at the end of the nineteenth century sought to abandon sentimentalism, and modernist authors at the beginning of the twentieth century held sentimentalism in contempt as they endeavored to make a new art for the machine age. Surprisingly, though, as exemplified by *Babbitt*, sentimental language persisted in American literature even as a culture of managed systems threatened to obscure the power of individual affect. This book examines the various ways that a single literary convention of sentimentalism—the sentimental touch—was used, reused, and disfigured during the rise of managerialism. I explore the strange, lingering power of sentimental language, especially in literature whose authors avowedly distanced themselves from sentimentality in the face of a rapidly changing culture. Sentimental language has an afterlife, enduring in American literature long after authors and critics declared it dead, insisting that human feeling can resist a mechanizing culture, and embodying, paradoxically, the way that literary conventions themselves become mechanical and systematic.

Literary sentimentalism first emerged with the rise of a mercantile economy. Cultural authority was no longer entirely a function of birth, as in the aristocracy; in an emerging marketplace, members of the newly consolidated mercantile hegemony needed a new means of showing their legitimacy, of embodying their authority.[4] The sentimental emphasis on manners indicated that outward deportment could correspond to an inner consciousness. Stowe's sentimentalism, her insistence on the legibility of bodies and the accuracy of moral judgment based on aesthetics, makes perfect sense for her time and place.

The cultural force of sentimentalism, though supremely powerful in mid-nineteenth-century America, declined precipitously in the late nineteenth and early twentieth centuries.[5] Authors and critics began to see sentimentalism as disreputable and unserious, as too reliant on cultural assumptions that did not fit with a new age. Between 1850 and 1940, the organization of the American economy shifted in a fundamental way. Businesses grew to such an extent that they could no longer be owned and controlled by individuals or even families; complex bureaucracies took over, becoming themselves sources of permanence and power.

A new figure emerged in the American economic landscape: the career manager. The manager did not actually buy, sell, or move products, but "monitored and coordinated" production and distribution, and soon monitored and coordinated other monitors and coordinators.[6] As many theorists have remarked, the steady bureaucratization and dehumanization of business culture took its toll on the psyche.[7] Max Weber, speaking in 1909 to colleagues in the Verein für Soziopolitick, declared:

> Imagine the consequences of that comprehensive bureaucratization and rationalization which already to-day we see approaching. . . . [T]he performance of each individual worker is mathematically measured, each man becomes a little cog in the machine and, aware of this, his one preoccupation is whether he can become a bigger cog. . . . [I]t is still more horrible to think that the world could one day be filled with nothing but those little cogs, little men clinging to little jobs and striving towards bigger ones. . . . This

passion for bureaucracy, as we have heard it expressed here, is enough to drive one to despair.[8]

Weber's nightmarish vision is of a culture in which business bureaucracy not only atomizes workers but also contributes to a broadly alienated society.[9] As networks grow, the "little men" who make up the bureaucracy become increasingly myopic, and anonymity threatens to replace community. "Passion for bureaucracy" is a jarring phrase, "enough to drive one to despair" because an emotional investment in bureaucracy promises no returns. Passion, in fact, seems the opposite of bureaucracy. Weber foregrounds the incongruity between deep feeling and dispassionate organization, but he also shows the way that emotional language lingers in descriptions of the most inhuman phenomena.

For Weber, as for Adam Smith and Karl Marx, changes in the organization of capitalism signaled not just economic change, but changes in social relations.[10] Though literary critics have rarely considered the growth of massive business bureaucracies as a revolution, business historians have long recognized the movement's centrality to U.S. cultural development. The historian Louis Galambos writes, "The single most significant phenomenon in modern American history is the emergence of giant, complex organizations."[11] To focus on managerialism is to examine the deep structural change that sits beneath industrialization, urbanization, and the revolutions in transportation and communication. Large-scale systematization not only influences a narrowly defined business culture, but changes the most fundamental ways that Americans think of themselves and their relationships.[12] When capitalism emerged as a massive ruling order whose hierarchical structures outlasted any human, when individuals organized their lives around divisions of labor above all else, Americans became increasingly atomized and alienated. The figure of the manager became widespread in American society, and American literature reflected a growing cultural anxiety about the systematization of personal relationships.

A defining feature of managerial capitalism is the complex web of relationships that constitutes a managerial network. Managers have an abstract relation with other managers in a giant hierarchical flowchart of operations. The network itself becomes more powerful than its constituent members. The hierarchy takes on a logic of its own, forming a web that becomes increasingly vast, complex, and inescapable. Managerialism spread quickly at the end of the nineteenth century, as thinkers such as Frederick W. Taylor brought the administrative structure that originated in the railroad industry into the factory. Pondering the management revolution in 1954, Peter Drucker wrote, "Scientific management is all but a systematic philosophy of worker and work. Altogether it may well be the most powerful as well as the most lasting contribution America has made to Western thought since the Federalist papers."[13] An all-pervasive managerialism is not the capitalism that Adam Smith envisioned in *The Wealth of Nations*. For Smith, market fluctuations lie beyond the influence of any individual actor; in a managerial system, however, managers can manipulate production and distribution in such a way that economic forces are no longer beyond the reach of human influence. As Chandler says, "the visible hand of management replaced what Adam Smith referred to as the invisible hand of market forces."[14] As the forces of management become more prevalent in American culture, sentimental literature declines in its cultural status: as the visible hand rises in capitalism, it sets in literature. The sentimental touch does not, however, disappear altogether from the American novel; indeed, as its appearance becomes rarer, its correspondence with a specific utopian ideal becomes more pronounced.

As the language of Adam Smith and Alfred Chandler exemplifies, the hand is a common metaphor in the field of capitalism.[15] According to the Oxford English Dictionary, "hand" was defined as "a person employed by another in any manual work; a workman or workwoman," as far back as 1655. As a synecdoche for a laborer, the hand diminishes the worker's identity to a mere function of labor—"human beings reduced to working parts," as Janet Zandy puts it.[16] Yet the very linguistic associations that allow the hand to be a reductive metaphor also enable the hand to be an expansive metaphor. The hand is the physical link between the self and the environment—the site of tactile engagement between an individual and the world. As Aristotle wrote, "So the soul is like the hand. For the hand is an instrument of instruments."[17] If the hand is the primary site of work, it is also the primary site of touch.

My interest in bringing together two fields—studies of capitalism and studies of emotion—hearkens back to the common roots of both fields, theories of which emerged together in the eighteenth century. Though today Adam Smith is most widely known for his 1776 treatise *The Wealth of Nations*, it was *The Theory of Moral Sentiments* (1759) that first brought him acclaim as a thinker. As a moral philosopher, Adam Smith posited that we know virtue and vice not through reasoning, but through feeling; Smith was fundamentally interested in bodily responses to the world. Moral sense philosophy is the intellectual underpinning of sentimentalism; the way to effect social change, for the sentimentalist as for the moral philosopher, is through manipulation of a body's feeling. Philosophers have recently recognized the tight link between Smith's two major texts, asking us to remember that Smith is a foundational thinker both for capitalism and sentimentalism.[18] It is significant that a philosopher equally interested in economic production and sensory perception coined the term "the invisible hand" for what would become our most famous metaphor of economic forces.[19]

The resonances between the hand in economics and the hand in sentimentalism become even more pronounced when we focus on managerialism. The word "manage" comes from *manus*, Latin for hand.[20] As the etymological root of "management," the hand stands for the control that a manager exerts over workers. The sentimental hand, by contrast, is the hand of the moral sense; the power of this hand does not come down from a bureaucratic system, but seems to rise up spontaneously from within the subject. We do not question the feeling we get from the sentimental touch, precisely because it *is* a feeling.

In tracing one of the hallmark tropes of the sentimental novel—the human touch whose meaning surpasses all language—through literary works that were written during a massive cultural change, I chart the increasing American anxiety about the relationships between bodies in a society where the body may be defined by its organizational status above all else. If the sentimental body was transparent, legible, and intimate, the managerial body is opaque, mysterious, and unlocatable.[21] As a marker of intimate human contact, the sentimental touch represents a literary desire to resist a cultural change in which human closeness gives way to corporate organization.

I am not suggesting that the literary portrayal of humans touching is restricted to a certain period; humans have always touched each other, and writers have always portrayed the human experience. Nor am I suggesting that the profundity of the human touch is a function only of sentimental literature. In the final lines of Milton's *Paradise Lost*, when Adam and Eve "hand in hand with wandring steps and slow, / Through *Eden* took their solitarie way," we understand that the touch signifies a source of hope in the midst of expulsion, the deepest sympathy during the gravest tragedy.[22]

This study explains what makes the sentimental touch a unique, pervasive trope throughout American sentimental and romantic literature, and—most strikingly—through American modernism. The sentimental touch, like Milton's use of the touch, conveys a psychological depth via a gesture involving only surface contact. Unlike Milton's figuration, though, the sentimental touch is a stylized, conventional trope that carries with it a set of literary historical associations. As June Howard explains in "What Is Sentimentality?":

> Most broadly—when we call an artifact or gesture sentimental, we are pointing to its use of some established convention to evoke emotion; we mark a moment when the discursive processes that construct emotion become visible. Most commonly—we are recognizing that a trope from the immense repertory of sympathy and domesticity has been deployed; we recognize the presence of at least some fragmentary element of an intellectual and literary tradition. Most narrowly—we are asserting that literary works belong to a genre in which those conventions and tropes are central.[23]

I show that the sentimental touch is a unique, identifiable trope and that its use extends beyond sentimental literature. The sentimental touch invokes not only a specific figuration of the body but also a specific relationship between bodies that corresponds to premanagerial economic practices—practices that involved craftsmanship and face-to-face interaction as opposed to sharp divisions of labor and highly mediated communication. Howard illuminates the systematic qualities of sentimentalism: evoking emotion relies on "established convention." Evocations of feeling are powerful insofar as they feel personal; but to be felt as personal, evocations of feeling rely on impersonal "discursive processes." Put another way, the fact that emotions feel like they rise up within our bodies is testimony only to the power of an impersonal structure that governs the very way we conceive of our bodies.[24] Sentimentalism forces us to confront the fact that what we experience as our own most intimately—emotions—may in fact be programmed, mechanical responses to convention. This is not to say that feeling is not important or powerful. Rather, when we think about feeling, we should think about the intricate relationship between our notions of the body and the economic and social structures in which our bodies reside.[25]

Capitalism and the body are not strangers. As Adam Smith and Karl Marx would agree, capitalism needs the body. The controlled body, in the form of the worker, serves capitalism. But the body, in its apparent naturalness, can also seem to ground the individual outside the system of capitalism. As Terry Eagleton explains in *The Ideology of the Aesthetic*:

> Society as a whole, given its fragmented condition, is increasingly opaque to totalizing reason; it is difficult to discern any rational

design in the workings of the market place. But we might turn nevertheless to what seems the opposite of all that, to the stirrings of individual sensibility, and find there instead our surest incorporation into a common body.[26]

Bodily relations seem to be the antidote to an alienating culture. Moments of the sentimental touch are often silent, as if signaling that language cannot be trusted, especially in proximity to the site of an ostensibly natural, transparent truth. To shift our attention away from the market and toward bodily senses, to turn from the inscrutable system of capitalism toward feeling, suggests that we can find security in the thing that exists beyond the reach of capitalism—the natural body. However, this book shows that the body is never only natural and that conceptions of the body, as Terry Eagleton would agree, change as economic practice and culture change. I take seriously Roland Barthes's injunction to "scour nature . . . in order to discover history."[27] What seems most natural—the direct communication between two bodies—can in fact reveal deeply embedded cultural assumptions. To study the formal changes in the trope of the sentimental touch, then, is to track historical changes in the way that culture understands meaning and the body.

The sentimental touch can counter the repression of the manager by granting authority to personal sensibility in the face of impersonal rule. However, its use as a literary trope is not entirely subversive. The very presence of the sentimental trope in the writings of authors who set out to be antisentimental shows the fine line between cultural inheritance and cultural resistance. Literature is simultaneously a response to changes in capitalism and a function of those changes. As Michael T. Gilmore writes, "the relationship between literature and economic change is neither wholly disabling nor empowering but a complex combination of the two."[28] Literature is a product of culture, but it is also a producer of culture; literature simultaneously registers social change and responds to social change.[29] In *The Incorporation of America*, Alan Trachtenberg explains that fiction at the turn of the twentieth century became political; realism "became nothing less than the extension of democracy into the precincts of fiction."[30] Trachtenberg locates the site of cultural resistance at the level of subject matter: the representation of low figures, of slang and dialect, signified a populist response to gentility and corporate control. *The Sentimental Touch* shows that literature registers social change not only on the level of subject matter but also on the level of trope.[31] The trope of the sentimental touch is not merely the site of cultural resistance; it is also the site of cultural anxiety and cultural power.[32] The sentimental trope, brought beyond the world of the sentimental, carries with it a utopianism that changes according to cultural conditions.

Many literary critics have examined American sentimentalism in the nineteenth century, charting its heights and subsequent decline.[33] Jane Tompkins examines sentimentalism in its historical context to "account for the enormous impact of works whose force escapes the modern reader."[34] Like Tompkins, I am interested in the political work that sentimentalism can embody and unleash. But a number of scholars are skeptical that literature grounded in personal affect can have positive political force. Lauren Berlant has argued in her important book *The Female Complaint* that sentimentalism causes politics to become "privatized," pushing women to feel a vague sense of redemptive belonging rather than working to fix the social world that continues to exploit and subordinate them. For Berlant, sentimentalism mobilizes "a fantasy scene of collective desire," but does not actually change everyday life; in this view, the humanizing force of sentimentalism is insidious, since it obscures and thereby enables an unjust ruling order.[35] As my study demonstrates, realist and modernist authors who use sentimental tropes are cautious about sentimentalism for some of the very reasons that Berlant articulates. Even with a keen awareness of the dangers of sentimentalism, though, novelists continue to deploy sentimental tropes to signify and suggest the ways that humanity can overcome an inhuman regime.

I remain more optimistic than Berlant about the restorative energy that sentimentalism contains. My aim is not to redeem or repudiate sentimentalism, but to demonstrate how language can both respond to and reinforce a systematic, mechanical culture. The trope of the sentimental touch marks a genuine engagement with humanity by infusing a potentially soulless society with emotion. But if the sentimental touch disrupts mechanical culture, if it generates utopian energy, it does so only by capitalizing on the coglike workings of a literary device. To recognize the machinelike aspects of literary convention is not to disavow sentimentalism, but rather to see how emotion in literature endures in a depersonalized society.

This book identifies a trend in American literature not through an exhaustive study of the huge number of books published during the rise of managerial capitalism, but through a study of several major canonical texts and constellations of works that surround these texts. I look at novels (rather than, say, poetry or drama) because of the novelistic ambition to depict the full complexity of being human in a specific historical moment.[36] *Uncle Tom's Cabin, Adventures of Huckleberry Finn, Winesburg, Ohio,* and *Miss Lonelyhearts* progress from the highly sentimental to the high modern, from a world in which bodies are legible to a universe of mystified, opaque bodies. I focus on these four books not to reassert their importance or greatness, but to use texts that are commonly held as representing a trend in American literature (the movement from sentimentalism to realism to modernism) to identify another corresponding trend (the curious retention of the sentimental touch). I also examine texts that were written in the same periods as the four primary texts to show that conceptions of the body in American literature follow an identifiable trend; the pattern I am examining is not simply the unlikely accident of a few moments in a few novels.

There are, of course, other ways to explain the endurance of sentimental language into the age of American modernism. Sentimentalism might be understood as a defensive reaction against the irrational and turbulent forces of modernity. From this perspective, a sentimental worldview—valorizing steady, peaceful bodies in a secure domestic space—would promise to stabilize civilization against the volatility of desire and the unpredictability of the market. For Stowe and her philosophical precursor Francis Hutcheson, sentimental sexuality offered a way to perpetuate a stable family that would serve as the foundation of a moral society; feminine passionlessness might counteract masculine licentiousness, which could otherwise break apart families and corrupt society.[37] A sentimental view of women—as moral beings rather than sexual beings—was appropriated by an emerging consumer culture at the end of the Victorian period. As T. J. Jackson Lears points out, sentimental notions of sexuality were deployed in the early 1900s by advertisers who peddled "the maintenance of domestic harmony through intelligent consumption."[38] The advertised image of domestic bliss was a commercialized version of the sentimental sexuality espoused by Stowe and Hutcheson. Along the same lines, the steadiness of a sentimental family might appeal to modern society as a way to guard against the erratic fluctuations of the financial world. After all, this period of American history witnessed a series of economic panics, recessions, and depressions.[39] Stowe, Twain, Anderson, and West were each touched by the unpredictable and often devastating oscillations of the business cycle.

Yet, as I hope to make clear, the trope of the sentimental touch is not always reducible to a harnessing of sexuality. Nor is authorial wariness toward business culture and economic structure purely a function of market instability. In important ways, the opposite is true. The inscrutable forces that threaten individual agency in the late nineteenth and early twentieth centuries are not just the mad pulls of sexuality and the marketplace but are also, crucially, the mechanical, logical, and inflexible constraints of bureaucracy. Novelists who use the sentimental touch may be responding to a society that is immoral and unpredictable, but, more significant, they are responding to a new bureaucratic order whose members feel increasingly anonymous, alienated, and bound by inhuman structures. The novels I examine do contend with sexual drives and economic forces that are irrational, but, more important, the novels wrestle with a deep, threatening sense of impersonality wrought by a managerial system that presents itself as utterly rational.

A looming threat of impersonality led John Dewey to write a series of articles in the *New Republic* in 1929 and 1930 in order to articulate and analyze how an "outwardly corporate" civilization resulted in "a submergence of the individual."[40] Dewey declares, "The tragedy of the 'lost individual' is due to the fact that while individuals are now caught up into a vast complex of associations, there is no harmonious and coherent reflection of the import of these connections into the imaginative and emotional outlook on life" (81). When Dewey pits "a vast complex of associations" against an "imaginative and emotional outlook," he suggests that to be fully bureaucratic is to be less than fully human. According to Dewey, the "quantification, mechanization, and standardization" that define corporate America have "invaded mind and character, and subdued the soul to their own dye" (52).[41] The result is a bewildered society made up of individuals with fractured loyalties and unstable notions of selfhood. I am interested in the ways that novelists respond to this sense of individual discord and personal incoherence created by an emerging and often impenetrable managerial culture. When authors like Twain, Anderson, and West continue the sentimental work of Stowe—even as they declare they are writing against the sentimental tradition—they participate in a literary culture that is grappling with the diffusion of identity. To use the sentimental touch in this world is to demonstrate literary "mechanization and standardization," but it is also to assert that individuals matter, that persons have an emotional center, that "mind and character" can be restored.

Chapter 1 attends closely to Harriet Beecher Stowe's *Uncle Tom's Cabin* (1852) as an example of the premanagerial American sentimental novel. The narrative sustains an appeal to the sentiments of the reader through descriptions of the emotional sensitivities of the characters. For Stowe, sentimentalism is a utopian force—powerful enough to destroy slavery. Stowe's text trains the reader to respond to sentimental bodies:

when we see a body in unjust pain, we are not only moved emotionally, but we should be moved to act in the world as well. The most highly sentimental scenes in the novel feature moments of tactile power. The gentle hand engaged in a sentimental touch is the antidote to the brutalizing hand of the overseer; even in its early form, the sentimental touch critiques the hand that is misused to serve economic interests. Stowe's sentimentalism is rooted in the moral sense, the shared feelings of right and wrong that, according to the moral sense philosophers, hold society together. Stowe's sentimental bodies are politically effective because they resonate with society's moral sense and therefore with the cultural and economic climate. Indeed, Stowe's portrayals of bodies in her text are typical of American textual bodies in the mid-nineteenth century. The apparently unproblematic use of the sentimental trope during the 1850s does not imply that all human relationships before managerial capitalism were utopian ideals characterized by universal legibility and full transparency. The narrative of the American economy is not one in which the single ugly force of managerial capitalism overthrows a humble hometown utopia. But even as goods were traded over vast distances in the 1840s, there was not a complex system of administrative networks. Owners were managers; positions within the economy, even as it grew to a national level, were easily identifiable. Personal relationships characterized by the sentimental touch—a transparent, unmediated mode of communication—are compatible with a premanagerial economic system.

Chapter 2 examines *Adventures of Huckleberry Finn* (1885) in terms of the changing economic structure of Twain's time.[42] Twain's novel is framed by episodes in which Tom Sawyer adheres to the codings of romance novels to absurd and potentially devastating effect. Most critics read the Tom Sawyer sections of the novel as critiques of an earlier age's literature. However, the sections of the novel that seem to be most embedded in the past actually display a fierce anxiety about Twain's contemporary culture. As the casuistic leader of a boy's gang and mastermind of the final escape plot, Tom Sawyer is a parody of the manager of Twain's age. Tom personifies a culture so deeply embedded in system management that it has lost the moral sense. In a culture with no moral sense, sentimentality is fraudulent, and manipulation, as the Duke and the King prove, is easy. Huck and Jim, in the center of the text, develop a sensibility that is deeply sentimental. For the runaway orphan and the escaped slave, the sentimental touch is not a sham, but is a restoration of the moral sense and a vindication of sentimentalism. *Adventures of*

Huckleberry Finn warns against the emotional excess of sentimental literature, but the text endorses sentimental values.

The final chapters focus on American modernism to show how the sentimental trope unexpectedly retains power even as the culture of the manager becomes increasingly dominant. The third chapter examines Sherwood Anderson's *Winesburg, Ohio* (1919), a text that was written when managerial capitalism was in full emergence, and when the literary influence of the American sentimental novel seemed to be in full decline. Managerial culture had penetrated sectors of life far away from cities and factories. Anderson himself was a businessman before he became an author, and he was obsessed with creating an innovative art that reflected the modern age. In *Winesburg, Ohio*, what seems to be at first a full repudiation of the sentimental tradition becomes an appropriation of sentimental form. Even in a society where bodies appear to be isolated beyond resolve, the sentimental touch remains the only successful mode of communication. Moments of the touch, though, are anxious, as if the characters themselves know that sentimental contact is incoherent with a modernist sensibility. Anderson's deployment of the sentimental trope shows us that American modernism—despite its aspirations—is not a full rupture from the past. Indeed, the persistence of the sentimental trope in an unsentimental world signals the ossification of literary structure alongside the hardening of bureaucratic frameworks. This is not to argue that Anderson is less formally innovative or less socially engaged than previously thought. Rather, I argue that Anderson's use of an atavistic trope marks his vexed relationship with one of the dominant social forces of his age—the pressures of managerialism. Anderson's response to a new form of capitalism looks to an old form of literary representation.

In Nathanael West's *Miss Lonelyhearts* (1933), the subject of chapter 4, we are in the world of modern, urban misery. The dark side of early twentieth-century capitalism yields a city of universal alienation, devoid of human contact. Like the narrative of *Winesburg, Ohio*, the form of West's novel is managerial: each episode is like an interchangeable part. The newspaper where Miss Lonelyhearts works signifies not an intellectual climate, but the overt breach of bureaucracy into the realm of culture. There is, however, a brief, surprising moment of sentimental contact: Miss Lonelyhearts and Peter Doyle clasp hands silently and share a deep sympathy that we see nowhere else in the text. The sentimental touch in West's novel typifies the way that the trope has changed in the eighty-one years since *Uncle Tom's Cabin*. West's utopian moment does not offer the possibility of an understanding that may change the world, but is instead a quickly disappearing, tiny glimpse of a personal redemption. Few critics seem to have noticed this sentimental moment in *Miss Lonelyhearts*. The sentimental touch is powerful in spite of—indeed, because of—its disjuncture with a fully ruptured culture. West's work is important not just for its depiction of a New York City that exemplifies the darkness of an economic era but also for the way that its very language and form respond to a deep shift in the organization of daily life in the United States. West's unexpected use of a sentimental literary figuration becomes a gauge by which we can measure his response to a civilization that seems to be failing. The sentimental touch is not merely the moment when characters overcome a crisis of personal alienation; the sentimental touch becomes the moment when West both demonstrates and resists the social changes that have rendered moments of unmediated bodily expression so fragile and unlikely. The human touch seems to be lost in the world ruled by the manager, but might be gained in literature.

The epilogue notes the scarcity of the sentimental touch in the middle and end of the twentieth century. I argue that the vanishing trope continues to imagine the utopian possibility of unmediated communication, even as I point out that literary use of the sentimental trope is not entirely defiant. I offer a short consideration of David Foster Wallace's *Infinite Jest*, arguing that what seems to be a reclamation of sentimental values in recent fiction is not entirely a rejection of modernist thought, but rather a continuation of the overlooked ethical concerns of the modernists. When writers use the sentimental touch in an unsentimental universe, they are engaging in a utopian literary fantasy, offering an apparently natural body in an attempt to soothe the capitalist alienation embodied by the manager. *The Sentimental Touch* explores the ways in which literature reflects a cultural anxiety, offering an imaginative compensation for what is lost in social life.

In *The Principles of Scientific Management* (1911), Frederick Taylor wrote, "In the past the man has been first; in the future the system must be first."[43] Taylor's triumphant declaration invokes a new world of productivity and efficiency, but a world potentially devoid of a full emotional life. I hope that this study complicates Taylor's notions of both "man" and "system." The personal sentiments that make us feel human are in fact social; our feelings have always been subject to economic and cultural systems. If this means that "man" was never quite first, it also means that humans can still assert their humanity, even in a fully bureaucratized network. The system, perhaps, can be touched by sentiment.

1 / Touching the Body, Training the Reader

Uncle Tom's Cabin is centrally concerned with the human body. Indeed, any novel about slavery—about the buying, selling, and controlling of the body—will be fundamentally interested in the relationships between physical bodies. Stowe writes that at a slave auction, the trader Haley "forced his way into the group, walked up to the old man, pulled his mouth open and looked in, felt of his teeth, made him stand and straighten himself, bend his back, and perform various evolutions to show his muscles."[1] Just before he feels a slave's body, the slave trader makes his own body felt, pushing his way into the throng of slaves. Stowe reminds us of the musculature of the market. The slave economy depends on physicality—on bodies that dominate other bodies, and on bodies that are valuable insofar as they can perform physical labor "on plantation" (195). The novel's interest in the body, though, is not just a function of the subject matter, but is a function of the narrative form. In other words, *Uncle Tom's Cabin* is obsessed with the body not just because it is a novel about slavery, but because it is a sentimental novel. As a sentimental text, Stowe's work adheres to a specific literary tradition that carries with it a set of inherited aesthetic codes. Under sentimentalism, bodies are legible—not just to other characters, but to readers as well. Characters and readers alike view the exterior of a body to draw conclusions about interior character. Sentimental works show us the feelings of characters to manipulate our own feelings; as we watch bodily interactions between characters, our own bodies are affected.

Sentimentalism, then, always has a certain political charge insofar as it is engaged in manipulating the real bodies, the actual lives, of its readers. Sentimentalism desires to change the life of the reader and by extension the entire world beyond the text; as a literary form, sentimentalism is well suited for a utopian sensibility. As is well known, Stowe wrote *Uncle Tom's Cabin* in 1852 with the deliberate intention of changing her society; the way to change society, for Stowe, was to first change her readers' bodies—to make them cry, to make them feel. The text's deployment of sentimental literary codes comprises the central attack on slavery. It would be a stretch to say that, for Stowe, slavery must be abolished because it does not adhere to the aesthetics of sentimentalism. We can say, though, that the ways in which the system of slavery does not adhere to sentimental aesthetics awakens us to the precise reasons, for Stowe, why slavery must be abolished.[2]

To focus on aesthetics is not merely to consider the text as a work of art. Rather, I am centrally concerned with the way in which the book interacts with bodies reading the book. As Terry Eagleton explains, Alexander Baumgarten's original formulation of the term "aesthetics" refers "to the whole region of human perception and sensation, in contrast to the more rarefied domain of conceptual thought."[3] Aesthetics is the world of the physical, the realm of the human body. For Stowe, there is not a distinct boundary between the work of art and the world beyond the text. Karen Sanchez-Eppler explains that there is a physical interaction between readers of sentimental works and the texts themselves:

> Reading sentimental fiction is . . . a bodily act, and the success of a story is gauged, in part, by its ability to translate words into pulse beats and sobs. This physicality of the reading experience radically contracts the distance between narrated events and the moment of their reading, as the feelings in the story are made tangibly present in the flesh of the reader.[4]

Stowe compounds the narrative presence in the body of the reader by frequently (and often didactically) addressing the reader and occasionally vouching for the authenticity of her portrayals. The formulaic, coded qualities of sentimentalism foreground the fact that sentimental texts are not a true mimetic copy of the world (even if they claim to be); but it is exactly in their mechanical, predictable—and therefore eminently legible—way of rendering the world that sentimental texts are able to move readers. This chapter examines the specific ways that *Uncle Tom's Cabin* portrays bodies being influenced by each other and thus the way that the mere portrayal of bodies attempts to influence readers' bodies. When sentimentalism works most powerfully, the description of bodies interacting without speaking—the portrayal of hands physically touching—becomes the most potent, and most utopian, way of touching the reader.

The earliest critics of the novel were concerned with the most touching aspects of the book. At its publication, contemporary critics tended to focus on the text's aesthetic qualities—how beautiful was the prose, how moving was the narrative, how deeply felt were the emotional descriptions. Leo Tolstoy and Henry James were among many early literary admirers. The text is famous for being a hugely successful best seller, outselling all books besides the Bible in the nineteenth century. However, in the first half of the twentieth century, critics rarely considered best sellers, especially sentimental works written by women. The critical silence of the early twentieth century suggests that critics began to lose touch with the sentimental codings of the text.[5] In the mid-twentieth century, critics of the text were primarily concerned with its racial representations. James Baldwin famously and viciously attacked the novel in 1949 for its stereotypical and dehumanizing representation of black figures and for its naive optimism based in empathy. "Uncle Tom" became "a byword of racist complicity."[6] Stowe's racial depictions continue to be a central concern for many critics, who ponder the political implications of a text written by a white woman that became America's most famous representation of a black man, and that was written to help black slaves (and to entertain white readers), but argues vociferously for emigration and has racist depictions of blacks that have endured in harmful and repugnant ways. In the late twentieth century, a fertile source of critical controversy arose out of the debate between Ann Douglas and Jane Tompkins. Both critics argued for a revival of critical interest in nineteenth-century American sentimental literature. For Douglas, sentimental literature revealed the insidious ways in which female authors rationalized the new economic order, praising virtues of femininity and passivity, but conceding any political power. Tompkins, on the other hand, argued that sentimental texts were actually political; for Tompkins, the hallmark of the sentimental text was its desire to change the social order. Much recent criticism follows in the groundwork of Tompkins and Douglas, arguing to what extent *Uncle Tom's Cabin* is complicit with or resistant to nineteenth-century power structures.[7]

A strand of recent scholarship that has arisen in reaction to what Laura Wexler calls the "Douglas-Tompkins debate" examines the ways that Stowe's aesthetic sensibility follows in the tradition of Scottish Common

Sense philosophy.[8] Gregg Camfield, in particular, challenges twentieth-century academic antisentimentalism, arguing that sentimentalism is central to the philosophies of Lord Shaftesbury, Francis Hutcheson, and John Locke. For Camfield, the sentimental aesthetic is a serious philosophy, as opposed to a feminized anti-intellectual indulgence. While Camfield argues that Stowe deliberately changed some sentimental devices to spread the doctrines of Scottish philosophy, I focus on the ways in which even Stowe's most typically sentimental representations are crucial to her aesthetic.

To examine the aesthetics of the text is in some ways to return to the earliest critical concerns with *Uncle Tom's Cabin*. Nineteenth-century reviewers tended to focus on how the book moved its readers. In 1852, George Sand wrote for the French publication *La Presse*, "This book is in all hands and in all journals. It has, and will have, editions in every form; people devour it, they cover it with tears. . . . She is far from us; we do not know her who has penetrated our hearts with emotions so sad and yet so sweet."[9] In 1868, Reverend E. P. Parker declared, "And all the while the power of her own intense sympathy for the oppressed millions whose cause she pleads, is felt throbbing in every line of the narrative."[10] Almost fifty years after its publication, in 1896, Charles Dudley Warner wrote that *Uncle Tom's Cabin* "is still read, and read the world over, with tears and with laughter."[11] Each critic attests to the immense popularity of the book, but, more important, each critic points to the way that the text affected the bodies of readers. Though these critics wrote over a span of fifty years and across two continents, their responses are remarkably similar. When we look within the text itself we see that readers are prompted to react in a specific manner.

Stowe's text trains the reader to read productively. Stowe uses the legibility of the sentimental body as a counterforce to the illegibility of the slave body—the body that, even when it appears white, is treated as black. Placing a sentimental system of reading the body against the system of slavery, Stowe pits legibility against opacity, domesticity against patriarchy, sensibility against detached rationality, and sympathy against abstract moral calculus. The political edge of Stowe's text is not predicated on her depiction of the brutalizing effects of slavery, though her text is famous for portraying the evil inherent in the slave system, even in its comparatively mild Kentucky manifestation. Instead, the foundation of her political critique is her sentimental aesthetic. This chapter focuses on a single literary trope—the sentimental touch—to show that for Stowe, finally, sympathy can defeat slavery. The sentimental touch is effective not only because it taps into a solidly established literary tradition but also because in tapping into sentimentalism, it resonates powerfully with the cultural and economic conditions of America in the 1850s.

Sentimental Aesthetics

The roots of sentimentalism as a distinguishable type of literature are nearly coeval with the origins of the English novel. The earliest English novels—the first long prose works that explored the deep psychology of everyday individuals—helped to establish sentimentalism as a distinct, recognizable literary form. One of the hallmarks of the sentimental novel is the text's treatment of the body. As John Mullan writes in *Sentiment and Sociability: The Language of Feeling in the Eighteenth Century*:

> In the novels of the mid-eighteenth century, it is the body which acts out the powers of sentiment. These powers, in a prevailing model of sensibility, are represented as greater than those of words. Tears, blushes, and sighs—and a range of postures and gestures— reveal conditions of feeling which can connote exceptional virtue or allow for intensified forms of communication. Feeling is above all observable, and the body through which it throbs is peculiarly excitable and responsive.[12]

In the sentimental novel, bodies are eminently legible; indeed, as Mullan explains, bodies can mean more than words. Excising language is stripping away a layer of interpretation, casting off a level of mediation that is likely to distort the message. I want to stress Mullan's point that "feeling is above all observable." What we think of as most internal and ineffable—our emotions—are made manifest to the external world. Bodies are revelatory.

The hand, since it is the site of a body's interaction with the world, requires special consideration. An 1848 technical book entitled *The Hand Phrenologically Considered: Being a Glimpse at the Relation of the Mind with the Organisation of the Body* testifies to the cultural weight of reading meaning through hands:

> But the hand not only affords us characters by which the age and sex may be determined, it is likewise an index of the general habit of body, of the kind of temperament, and of the mental tendency and disposition. . . . A soft, thick hand, loaded with fat, denotes little energy of character, and a soft, yielding, inactive disposition;

while, on the contrary, a thin, bony, or muscular hand indicates a rough, active, energetic nature.[13]

The hand, because it discloses what otherwise may be hidden qualities, is the key for unlocking the truth of an individual's character. In sentimental literature, scenes in which characters interact solely through their bodies, especially with their hands, are moments of the deepest profundity for the characters, and are moments that are intended to move the reader emotionally. The touch is touching.

The sentimental touch is especially prevalent in eighteenth-century British novels. In Samuel Richardson's *Clarissa* (1747–1748), Clarissa relies on touch to convey her most heartfelt emotions: "She paused again, her breath growing shorter; and, after a few minutes: And now, my dearest cousin, give me your hand—nearer—still nearer—drawing it towards her."[14] Clarissa dramatizes the triumph of the body over speech. When words do not come easily, when language fails, the body will overcome the inadequacy of oral communication. In Laurence Sterne's *Tristram Shandy* (1759–1768), Uncle Toby is "not eloquent," but communicates deep love through his body.[15] For Sterne, as for the sentimental novelists, the touch is powerful: "The youth took hold of my hand, and instantly burst into tears."[16] Holding hands leads to crying: the touch yields the most intense emotion. Sterne conveys the emotion not through a description of feeling, but through a narration of action. Just as the youth is moved by the body, readers are moved by the youth's body. We know the depth of the youth's emotions not because they are articulated, but in fact because they are not articulated, because they are only apparent in a somatic reaction.

The prevalence of legible bodies in eighteenth-century British literature corresponds to British cultural and social conditions of the time. A new commercial culture arose in opposition to and alongside the established aristocratic style. Cultural authority was no longer fully dependent on inherited social status, as in the aristocracy; in an emerging marketplace, members of the newly consolidated mercantile hegemony developed a new means of displaying their legitimacy and thereby embodying their authority.[17] The eighteenth-century British emphasis on manners was the recognition that outward deportment could signify an inner consciousness; in this case, the well-mannered gentleman showed his political and social commitments through his behavior. Lawrence Klein explains that Lord Shaftesbury's commitment to mannerliness grew out of political and moral convictions: "When he advocated the hegemony of gentlemen and gentlemanliness in society, he was reacting against those agencies with which gentlemen had traditionally shared the various forms of hegemony, namely, the Church and the King."[18] Shaftesbury challenged the dominance of godly and courtly power by asserting the power of the public gentleman. Klein continues:

> In Shaftesbury's central project of forming "character," the modeling of an outward self was as important as constructing the inward one. . . . Thus, far from confining himself to the motions of the mind, Shaftesbury was concerned with sheer physicality and considered such aspects as the pose of the body, the gestures of the limbs, and the mien of the face.[19]

For Shaftesbury, as for Stowe, the aesthetic world registers the moral universe. Shaftesbury writes, "Will it not be found that what is beautiful is harmonious and proportionable; what is harmonious and proportionable is true; and what is at once both beautiful and true is, of consequence agreeable and good."[20] Terry Eagleton explains, "Such is the celebrated 'moral sense' of the British eighteenth-century moralists, which allows us to experience right and wrong with all the swiftness of the senses, and so lays the groundwork for a social cohesion more deeply felt than any mere rational totality."[21] Social and moral rules are powerful because they are sensed from within rather than imposed from without. Morality can be felt in the body.[22] The virtuous is beautiful; the vicious is ugly.

Adam Smith, in *The Theory of Moral Sentiments* (1759), writes:

> Human society, when we contemplate it in a certain abstract and philosophical light, appears like a great, an immense machine, whose regular and harmonious movements produce a thousand agreeable effects. As in any other beautiful and noble machine that was the production of human art, whatever tended to render its movements more smooth and easy, would derive a beauty from this effect, and, on the contrary, whatever tended to obstruct them would displease on that account: so virtue, which is, as it were, the fine polish to the wheels of society, necessarily pleases; while vice, like the vile rust, which makes them jar and grate upon one another, is as necessarily offensive.[23]

Smith uses the concrete image of the machine to explain the abstract notion of moral sensibility. The emotional world is not opposed to the mechanical world, but is constitutive of it. Sentimental literature grows from this philosophy, in which "human art" produces a "beautiful and noble machine"; in the sentimental literary aesthetic, formulaic and codified tropes in a book produce mechanical and emotional reactions in a reader. It is no accident that Adam Smith also laid the groundwork for modern economic theory in *The Wealth of Nations*. For Smith, the material realm is coextensive with the moral realm; the rise of a complex commercial society occurs alongside the rise of moral sense philosophy.

The Wealth of Nations was published in 1776; the foundation of modern thought on capitalism corresponds to the founding of the United States of America. The Scottish moral philosophers, who like America's founders challenged the long-standing rule of the aristocracy, would remain influential in the United States well into the nineteenth century. Gregg Camfield writes:

> American historians have had no difficulty discovering the influence of the Scottish philosophers on American culture. According to Perry Miller, for example, the Scots gave America its "official metaphysic" for over half of the nineteenth century. This should come as no surprise considering that America's cultural conditions so closely resembled those that gave rise to the Scottish school in the first place.[24]

Camfield reminds us of the close connections between economic conditions and cultural beliefs. According to Elizabeth Maddock Dillon, who compares eighteenth-century political development in Europe to that in the United States (a movement from autocracy to liberalism), "sentimentalism has its roots in the same concerns with autonomy that define aesthetic theory of the eighteenth century."[25] Stowe's sentimentalism, her insistence on the legibility of bodies, on the accuracy of a moral judgment based on aesthetics, makes perfect sense for her historical moment.[26] Literary production is tied directly to social history; writing is always mediated by culture.[27]

In the case of Stowe, her literary treatment of the body bears the marks of a culture at the premanagerial stage of capitalism. Society still holds the anti-aristocratic aesthetic beliefs of an emergent British mercantile class, but culture is not yet overtaken by large-scale managerial capitalism, in which the body will be rendered abstract and ultimately illegible. The first fifty years of the U.S. economy were marked by increased specialization. With this specialization, the general merchant of colonial times was replaced with the commission merchant; the world of commerce grew increasingly impersonal. The economy was not yet a vast system of hierarchical managerial networks, but the strings of economic relationships had grown to a point where a full economic transaction was no longer a single face-to-face experience.[28] Bodies, though, could still locate themselves within the chain of the economy; even if the number of people that made up a single transaction had grown, the economy still depended on relationships between individual bodies. In the slave economy that Stowe depicts, even as the slave sellers rarely know the eventual buyers, the system is based on a series of personal economic relationships.

In fact, changes in the early nineteenth-century business world more clearly defined some personal relationships. In the colonial era, the family produced goods, educated children, transferred craft skills, and cared for the elderly. With the rise of commerce, the family lost its central role in production and was no longer united in a kinship network held together by common tasks.[29] A shift in the economy caused a shift in values; the family itself turned from a unit of production to a unit of domesticity and the foundation of social order. The family was held together not by work, but by sentiment. Places within the emerging system were determined by bodies; men worked outside the home while women were responsible for raising children and managing the house. Dillon explains that "while women certainly performed domestic work in the nineteenth-century household, including the work of child rearing, this labor was represented as sentiment or love rather than work."[30] Men's bodies were seen as public, while women's bodies—even as they performed household labor—came to be defined as domestic.

Stowe's bodies are eminently material; that is, our introduction to characters throughout *Uncle Tom's Cabin* are almost always a vivid physical description. When introducing Eliza, the heroine who flees Mr. Shelby's Kentucky plantation, the narrator explains, "these natural graces in the quadroon are often united with beauty of the most dazzling kind, and in almost every case with a personal appearance prepossessing and agreeable" (54). When grace is a "natural" attribute rather than a learned trait, character is a function of biology. The body thus is transparent, revealing the deep truth of character. As Herbert Ross Brown explains in *The Sentimental Novel in America 1789–1860*, "Novelists strove to draw the faces of their men and women with the hope that, as in *The Children of the Light*, 'To the student of expression, the characteristic, the individuality of each of these persons, might easily be discovered from a glance at their countenances' (C. Chesboro, *The Children of the Light* [New York, 1853], p. 44)."[31] For Stowe, as for Chesboro, as for Lord Shaftesbury, external features mark internal qualities. In the sentimental worldview, the physical body is the ultimate authority.

Reading the Body

When introducing Uncle Tom, the narrator declares, "At this table was seated Uncle Tom, Mr. Shelby's best hand, who, as he is to be the hero of our story, we must daguerreotype for our readers" (68). "Hand," here, is a reductive metaphor; for Shelby, Tom is important insofar as he is an appendage of work. Stowe continues, "He was a large, broad-chested, powerfully-made man" (68), and reminds readers that slavery relies on sheer physicality above all else. The description that follows is less a physical picture, though, than a characterization: his "truly African features were characterized by an expression of grave and steady good sense, united with much kindliness and benevolence" (68). Stowe's daguerreotype is an emotional and moral X-ray, unproblematically asserting an internal truth even as it claims to be describing the physical nature of the body. Stowe's description of Uncle Tom corresponds with what George Fredrickson terms romantic racialism: "Although romantic racialists acknowledged that blacks were different from whites and probably always would be, they projected an image of the Negro that could be construed as flattering or laudatory in the context of some currently accepted ideals of human behavior and sensibility."[32] Fredrickson's use of the word "image" to signify character traits acknowledges that, for romantic racialists, in the age of "sensibility," behavior is inextricably linked to the body. Stowe, speaking of *Uncle Tom's Cabin*, declared: "My vocation is simply that of a painter, and my object will be to hold up in the most lifelike and graphic manner possible Slavery, its reverses, changes, and the Negro character, which I have had ample opportunities for studying. There is no arguing with *pictures*, and everybody is impressed by them, whether they mean to be or not."[33] Stowe's painting is not merely the image of an object, even as she purports to describe "the Man that Was a Thing" (the original subtitle, replaced by "Life among the Lowly"). Stowe herself makes no distinction between image and interiority; graphic "pictures" will only better display "the Negro character."

The body's legibility, in the sentimental tradition, allows the narrator to draw moral conclusions alongside physical pictures. A look at other works from mid-nineteenth-century America shows that Stowe's text treats the human body in ways that are representative of both sentimental and romance literature. In James Fenimore Cooper's 1826 *The Last of the Mohicans,* for example, there is a direct link between character and physicality. Hawkeye declares of the treacherous Magua, "I knew he was one of the cheats as soon as I laid eyes on him!"[34] In his 1850 *The Scarlet*

Letter, Nathaniel Hawthorne writes of Pearl, "This outward mutability indicated, and did not more than fairly express, the various properties of her inner life."[35] For Hawthorne, as for Cooper, there is no distinction between outwardness and inward character. Stowe's treatment of the body, then, is not a function of the subject matter of her book but of the cultural conditions of writing. Unlike the romance novelists, however, Stowe deploys the legible body in order to engage directly in politics.

Stowe dramatizes the irrationality of American slavery by showing that bodies within the slave system, even as the sentimental tradition renders them legible, are not legible by the standards of the slave system itself. In other words, slavery in the South authorized itself on the premise of a binary truth, where black equals slave and white equals free. Stowe shows us, though, that bodies within the system do not actually correspond to a binary division. Stowe writes of Eliza, "As she was also so white as not to be known as of colored lineage, without a critical survey, and her child was white also, it was much easier for her to pass on unsuspected" (107). Eliza's body attests to the irrationality and falsity of a system that insists on a binary code. Her ability to pass as nonslave within a culture that insists on her position of slavery signals a body that is unreadable. For Stowe, the mystified, unreadable body does not signal an aberration in the signifying power of the individual body, but points to a problem of the system of signification itself.[36] Sentimentalism and slavery are two competing and mutually exclusive modes of representation. Within sentimentalism, the body is legible; within slavery, the body is not.[37]

Eliza's husband, George, can also pass for white. The narrator declares, "We remark, *en passant*, that George was, by his father's side, of white descent. His mother was one of those unfortunates of her race, marked out by personal beauty to be the slave of the passions of her possessor, and the mother of her children who may never know a father" (182). Inscribed upon George's body is the history of sexual violence; he is a living testament to his mother's rape, a breathing relic of his father's cruelty. His body is false to slavery—his skin is not black, even though he is black in the eyes of the slaveholder; but his body is true to sentimentalism—his skin is an accurate marker of the degradations of slavery. The narrator's remark *"en passant"* is a remark *in* passing, but it is also a remark *on* passing (that is, *about* passing).[38] George's very ability to pass for white is the deep, physical proof that slavery does not adhere to sentimental truth. The figurative *"in passing"* can quickly and subtly shift to the literal *"on passing"* as if signaling that even linguistic idiom will not interfere with the narrative's insistence on physical, material legitimacy, on the rule of the literal body. Even in the phrase "the slave of the passions of her possessor" we can see the valorization of the literal over the figurative. A "slave of the passions" is usually a figurative slave—one who is completely ruled by the influence of his or her own emotions. But for the narrative, a "slave of the passions" is a literal slave; George's mother is the "property of her possessor." Stowe uses figurative language to signify a literal position. Even the impositions of metaphor will not detract from the authority of the literal word and the physical body.

Stowe continues to describe George:

> From one of the proudest families in Kentucky he had inherited a set of fine European features, and a high, indomitable spirit. From his mother he had received only a slight mulatto tinge, amply compensated by its accompanying rich, dark eye. A slight change in the tint of the skin and the color of his hair had metamorphosed him into the Spanish-looking fellow he then appeared. (182)

As with the description of Eliza, there is no distinction between physical traits and character attributes. While Stowe attacks the binary codification of race, she reveals her own racist beliefs. Fredrickson writes of such nineteenth-century attitudes, "Notions of white or Anglo-Saxon superiority were common even among critics of the slave system."[39] Romantic racialists subscribed to the notion that races were distinguished not just by biological, physical traits, but by character attributes; antislavery crusaders often "acknowledged permanent racial differences but rejected the notion of a clearly defined racial hierarchy."[40] Stowe's description of George simultaneously values European blood and condemns slaveowner bloodlines. "Fine European features" and "a high indomitable spirit" go hand in hand. Yet the narrative subtly equates Kentucky pride with a heritage of sexual atrocity; presumably, many genetic members of "the proudest families in Kentucky" are slaves. George's body is the abominable historical record of slave rape just as it is the physical proof that the South wrongly enslaves humans whose roots are truly white. In a position that can be reconciled only with romantic racialism, the narrative simultaneously indicts slavery for the violence it bestows upon the black body *and* for slavery's insistence that European bodies be treated as black. Slavery is not only cruel, but unnatural—the South's binary law of black and white goes against the immanent truth of George's physique, and, by extension, George's character.

The direct relationship between the physical body and a character's emotional and psychological interior is crucial for the sentimental text to operate forcefully. The narrative sustains an appeal to the sentiments of the reader through descriptions of the emotional sensitivities of the characters. For Stowe, emotional outpourings of characters should produce emotional upwellings within the reader. The very description of textual bodies racked with emotion will influence the body of the reader.

The reader, though, may not have the same emotional sensitivities as the characters and may not even exist in the same cultural field of emotional and moral sentiments as the author. As Neal Oxenhandler points out in "The Changing Concept of Literary Emotion: A Selective History," critics since Descartes have questioned the "ontological status of affectivity."[41] That is, an emotional response to text seems so dependent on the subjective experience of the reader (itself seemingly dependent on the reader's own cultural context) that interpretations founded on affectivity seem doomed to obscurity and critical failure. Oxenhandler argues, though, that "the fact of the matter is that in all ages readers have applied affective terms to literature without rendering their responses fatally private and hence incommunicable."[42] Indeed, as we have seen, critics in the fifty years following the publication of *Uncle Tom's Cabin*, despite writing from different cultural circumstances, had similar responses to the text. One reason for this, as Oxenhandler shows when he points us to reception theory, is that texts prompt readers to react in a specific way. As Hans Robert Jauss explains in "Literary History as a Challenge to Literary Theory":

> A literary work, even if it seems new, does not appear as something absolutely new in an information vacuum, but predisposes its readers to a very definite type of reception by textual strategies, overt and covert signals, familiar characteristics or implicit allusions. It awakens memories of the familiar, stirs particular emotions in the reader and with its "beginning" arouses expectations for the "middle and end," which can then be continued intact, changed, re-oriented or even ironically fulfilled in the course of reading according to certain rules of the genre or type of text. The psychical process in the assimilation of a text on the primary horizon of aesthetic experience is by no means only a random succession of merely subjective impressions, but the carrying out of certain directions in a process of directed perception which can be comprehended from the motivations which constitute it and the signals which set it off and which can be described linguistically.[43]

Even the most emotional, apparently subjective experience of reading is less a function of the reader than a function of the text itself. Readers who feel emotion are being managed by a textual system, "carrying out . . . certain directions." Reception of a text is never arbitrary, but is a directed experience, a response to specific instructions.

Jauss does not argue that all responses to a text are predetermined; indeed, Jauss is interested in the changing responses of readers over time. "The horizon of aesthetic experience" changes over time, as later readers are influenced both by the text and responses to the text. A changing "horizon" of aesthetic and linguistic expectations can explain the consistency of critical responses for the half-century following the publication of *Uncle Tom's Cabin*, and can also explain the conspicuous absence of critical inquiry for the first half of the twentieth century. Most important, we must recognize that an emotional response is not utterly personal and therefore incommunicable. What seems to be most personal—the emotions that well up from deep within the reader—can in fact be most impersonal, a programmed response to a carefully crafted set of directions. As in Althusser's theory of interpellation, what we recognize as originating from deep within us is in fact an imposition from outside ourselves.

Jauss's theory is well suited to sentimentalism; the sentimental aesthetic is strong because it operates through personal sentiments and affections instead of absolutist power.[44] As the moral philosophers argue, the bourgeois social order maintains its power through the daily habits, customs, and desires of its subjects. Eagleton explains, "The aesthetic is in this sense the relay or transmission mechanism by which theory is converted to practice, the detour taken by ethical ideology through the feelings and senses so as to reappear as spontaneous social practice."[45] What seems a spontaneous, personal response, as Jauss and Eagleton would agree, is in fact a reaction based on the law of aesthetics—"this law which is not a law."[46] For Jauss, the text directs the reader by tapping into a set of literary expectations and by subtly manipulating the narrative and the language to create a specific response. Stowe's text, as we have seen, taps deeply into the sentimental tradition; but besides depicting a sentimental narrative, the text also depicts the proper sentimental reception of a narrative. Chapter 9, "In Which It Appears That a Senator Is But a Man," is emblematic of the way that Stowe trains the reader. By depicting the persuasiveness of bodies to characters within the narrative, by manipulating the intratextual sympathies of characters, and by anticipating the sympathies of projected readers, Stowe guides even the most unemotional reader. In fact, the text aims its aesthetic instruction at the reader who claims to be ruled by intellect rather than passion.

After her tense escape across the icy Ohio River with her child in her arms, Eliza finds brief shelter in the home of Senator and Mrs. Bird. The comfortable couple had been discussing the Fugitive Slave Act. The narrator explains that "it was a very unusual thing for gentle little Mrs. Bird ever to trouble her head with what was going on in the house of the state" (142), but the Fugitive Slave Act so troubles the "timid, blushing little woman" (142), that she must confront her husband.[47] Mrs. Bird is four feet tall, "with mild blue eyes, and a peach-blow complexion, and the gentlest, sweetest voice in the world" (143). We know that this ostensible description of her body serves to describe her character; her eyes, complexion, and voice all point to a deep identity that is mild, gentle, and sweet. The peach portrait underscores her fierce reaction to the news of the Fugitive Slave Act: she "rose quickly, with very red cheeks, which quite improved her general appearance, and walked up to her husband, with quite a resolute air" (143), to declare that he ought to be ashamed. Her voice is rendered powerful not through her words, but through her body. The blush appears to carry the weight of nature and the indisputability of biological truth. As Mary Ann O'Farrell explains in *Telling Complexions: The Nineteenth-Century English Novel and the Blush*: "By means of its attentions to blushing as a perceived event of the body, the novel suggests that—in seeming involuntarily and reliably to betray a deep self—blushing assists at the conversion of legibility into a sense of identity and centrality."[48] The novel, in O'Farrell's explanation, grants the blush accuracy and reliability, as if portraying a depth of truth that mere words cannot reach. The narrative suggests that even if her mind will not produce convincing logic, Mrs. Bird's somatic reaction will be persuasive.

Indeed, the senator, though not fully convinced of his wife's position, realizes that the argument no longer exists solely in the realm of logic. He responds, "we mustn't suffer our feelings to run away with our judgment" (144). He exposes the masculine etymological roots of "senator" (*senex* means "old man"), as he pits *his* rationality against *her* sensibility.[49] As they continue to argue, Mrs. Bird soon replies, "I hate reasoning, John,—especially reasoning on such subjects. There's a way you political folks have of coming round and round a plain right thing; and you don't believe in it yourselves, when it comes to practice. I know *you* well enough, John" (145). Mrs. Bird knows the deep truth of her position, but it is not through the workings of abstract thought. More important, she knows the deep truth of her husband. She distinguishes between "reasoning" and "*you*"—between an enlightenment knowledge based in logic and a more profound truth based on feeling and a sentimental identity. As Gregg D. Crane explains, "Stowe's belief in the merit of an individual's critique of law through his or her moral sensitivity positions her legal theory squarely within the natural rights tradition of Hugo Grotius, John Locke, the Scottish Common Sense philosophers, and the founding fathers."[50] Stowe speaks through the voice of Mrs. Bird as she argues that feeling should be the primary consideration in questions of politics.

Right on cue, old Cudjoe announces the arrival of the runaway slave. The senator is "amazed" at the vision before him:

> A young and slender woman, with garments torn and frozen, with one shoe gone, and the stocking torn away from the cut and bleeding foot, was laid back in a deadly swoon upon two chairs. There was the impress of the despised race on her face, yet none could help feeling its mournful and pathetic beauty, while its stony sharpness, its cold, fixed, deathly aspect, struck a solemn chill over him. He drew his breath short, and stood in silence. (146)

The sudden presence of Eliza's body cuts short the senator's debate. It is not the sight of Eliza that chills the senator, but it is the "feeling" of her "mournful and pathetic beauty." In the sentimental world, feeling supercedes all other senses. Like the blush, feeling is experienced as an internal bodily reaction, unquestioningly accurate and reliable. The very word straddles emotion and touch; the physical body and the emotional world are inextricably linked in "feeling." Reasoning clearly will not do in the presence of a tortured body. The senator cannot even speak. The senator's silence is not a function of reasoning or logic, but is itself a somatic reaction; the senator's lungs react to Eliza's presence.

When Eliza recovers from her "deadly swoon," she tells the story of her escape. She explains that her master had been kind but was planning to sell her son. Two of her children have already died, so she decided to risk her life in escape rather than bear the loss of another child. The brief, poignant story inspires a crowd of sobbing:

> The two little boys, after a desperate rummaging in their pockets, in search of those pocket-handkerchiefs which mothers know are never to be found there, had thrown themselves disconsolately into the skirts of their mother's gown, where they were sobbing, and wiping their eyes and noses, to their hearts' content;— Mrs. Bird had her face fairly hidden in her pocket-handkerchief; and old Dinah, with tears streaming down her black, honest face, was ejaculating, "Lord have mercy on us!" with all the fervor of a

camp-meeting;—while Cudjoe, rubbing his eyes very hard with his cuffs, and making a most uncommon variety of wry faces, occasionally responded in the same key, with great fervor. (150)

The two little boys are, of course, stand-ins for the children that Eliza lost. Presumably they are sobbing partly because of the frightening realization that someone of their age and size has died; death is suddenly close and real. The weeping underscores the humanity of each child, the depth of emotion that each boy contains. Sobbing is not entirely painful, though; the boys wipe their faces "to their hearts' content." We glimpse a clue to the overwhelming popularity of the sentimental text. Unleashing deep emotion in the safety of domestic garments can be pleasant. Responding to a sentimental story, as it exposes our emotional vulnerabilities, forces us to find solace in a domestic setting that is ultimately comfortable. It may take the wiping of our tear-stained faces to realize the softness of our mother's gown.

Weeping, like blushing, is a deep somatic response. The spilling of tears, the literal overflow of emotion, is the quintessential sentimental reaction to a world both tender and cruel. As Herbert Ross Brown explains, "Of all the cherished tokens of sensibility, the tear was at once the most common and the most precious. . . . In this language of the heart, tears were the most eloquent pleaders. They were infallible signs of grace in the religion of the heart."[51] The scene in *Uncle Tom's Cabin* of unabashed weeping draws forcefully on the sentimental tradition. We know, now, that the Bird family is truly one of sensibility, that the Bird family lives in a world of sentimental values. Most important for the narrative, the two sobbing boys allow Mrs. Bird, and by extension the (presumably white) reader, to fully sympathize with Eliza.[52] Her two sobbing boys surely remind Mrs. Bird of what might have been lost, just as they remind Eliza of what might have been.[53] For Stowe, sympathy is made powerful not just by the invocation of lost sons, but by the actual presence of weeping boys. The narrative maintains its insistence on the authority of the physical body.

The narrative continues:

Our senator was a statesman, and of course could not be expected to cry, like other mortals; and so he turned his back to the company, and looked out of the window, and seemed particularly busy in clearing his throat and wiping his spectacle-glasses, occasionally blowing his nose in a manner that was calculated to excite suspicion, had any one been in a state to observe critically. (150)

Stowe simultaneously asserts the senator's dignity and his sensibility. The decorum of statesmanship and the propriety of sentimentalism are at odds for the senator. But the authority of his body supercedes the authority of his lawmaking self. The senator soon decides that Eliza must be led to the safety of the Quaker Von Trompe family and that he is the only one able to take her. Mrs. Bird articulates the fullness of the senator's change in the course of a single scene, declaring, "Your heart is better than your head, in this case, John" (153). The senator is a fully converted man of sensibility, trusting the immediacy of experience over the strain of ratiocination, his wife over his congressional colleagues, his body over his mind, his emotions over his intellect.

Senator Bird's conversion from intellectual, detached defender of the Fugitive Slave Act to emotional, righteous actor on behalf of Eliza seems at first glance to be rather sudden, but the senator's change takes place over the course of a scene that carefully displays the techniques of sentimental persuasion. The senator is convinced by a progression of bodies that grows steadily more persuasive. We watch as he reads a series of bodies: first he responds lightly to a blush as he watches his wife react to a discussion of the Fugitive Slave Act; then he sees the actual, tortured body of a fugitive slave when Eliza is carried into the scene; soon he reads the bodily reactions of the small crowd that listens to Eliza's story; finally he recognizes his own bodily reaction—a response both to Eliza's story and to the sobbing characters listening to the story. The scene is a parable of sentimental reading—even if we are as insensitive as a senator who has voted for the Fugitive Slave Act, we can be persuaded by the structure of sentimentalism. It is important that the senator does not merely respond to the sickening spectacle of a slave's beaten body, or even to the pathos of her brutal, eloquent (though typical) family narrative; instead, the senator's greatest response is to the tearful reaction to the story. Emotion begets emotion.

If Mrs. Bird is a stand-in for Stowe, then the senator stands in for the reader. In fact, before he sees Eliza, the senator "began to read the papers" (146); when Eliza enters, he "laid down his paper, and went into the kitchen" (146)—substituting an act of intellect for an act of domesticity. After Eliza falls asleep but before she relates her story, the senator "pretended to be reading the paper" (147). As readers, we are always more like the senator than Mrs. Bird. That is, reading is a necessarily intellectual, abstract exercise, seemingly more suited to the slow ruminations of abstraction and conceptualism than to the emotional immediacy of physical presence. Stowe demonstrates, though, that this need not be the case—indeed, that this *should* not be the case. We should be careful not to infer that her argument therefore lacks the truth of logic; we should instead realize that the cold calculations of logic can mislead. The antirationalism exhibited by Stowe should not be taken for a lack of philosophical seriousness, but rather for an engagement with the moral sense philosophers. Camfield explains that Stowe's text exhibits the fundamental beliefs of the Scottish philosophers,

> that human beings can objectify their reactions to the external world by comparing them with the reactions of others, that is to say, human beings can rest assured of the accuracy of their empirical knowledge if it's gained through the senses common to most human beings; and . . . that human beings have a moral sense in addition to their physical senses.[54]

When everyone around Eliza "was, in some way characteristic of themselves, showing signs of hearty sympathy" (150), the senator himself begins to show similar "signs" of sympathy. When the senator shows sympathy, "readers can rest assured of the accuracy of their empirical knowledge," and we can show sympathy.[55]

More important, when the senator acts, we can act. The scene is crucial because Senator Bird chooses to take an active role in helping Eliza. Sympathy leads to deed.[56] Political action is not the strained debate, the "tiresome business, this legislating" (142), that takes place in the halls of Congress. Rather, political action is the perilous nighttime ride to transport a fugitive slave to safe haven. The senator, once a figure of the dispassionate mind, becomes a figure for a full bodily investment into politics, as he "tumbles over into the mud" (158) to aid the carriage that transports Eliza and Harry. As Catherine O'Connell says, the "description of the terrible roads in Ohio and the discomfort of the carriage trip seem digressive, but the point is driven home that true sentimental sympathy consists not solely of weeping but of acting on the feelings for which those tears are the visible sign."[57] Stowe clearly shows her desire to close the gap between sentiment and politics; in *Uncle Tom's Cabin*, the sentimental is the political.

Touching Politics

The text was written with the idea that sentiment can affect politics. Many critics have maintained that sympathy, in fact, may limit involvement in politics. Lauren Berlant argues that sentimental literature believes that "crises of the heart and of the body's dignity produce events that, properly publicized, can topple great nations and other patriarchal institutions."[58] Berlant warns, though, that sentimentalism, in its very reliance on emotions, can be depoliticized as it dissociates the personal from the political. But for Stowe and the moral sense philosophers, personal sentiment—especially as manifested in the body—is quite political. *Uncle Tom's Cabin*, in fact, did affect politics.[59] As Eric Sundquist writes:

> its instrumental role in the abolitionist cause is beyond question. . . . It added an entirely new dimension to a campaign that had often bogged down in internecine quarrels and useless theorizing. By giving flesh-and-blood reality to the inhuman system for which the Fugitive Slave Law now required the North, as well as the South, to be responsible, it became a touchstone for antislavery sentiment.[60]

The "flesh-and-blood reality" that Sundquist describes is, of course, not constructed out of flesh and blood, but is made from words.

Paradoxes emerge when we ponder a world constructed of text that valorizes the deed and the body more than the word and the dispassionate mind. Gilmore examines the "word-action dynamic" in "*Uncle Tom's Cabin* and the American Renaissance," where he declares that "real presence alone can awaken readers or listeners out of their sleep of law and custom and rouse them to act in the name of conscience."[61] Since the text, mere words on a page, offers no real presence, no actual flesh and blood, Gilmore argues that Stowe can offer real presence by tapping deep into the Christian sensibility—"the spiritual reality" of Stowe's readers.[62] The Word is made flesh through the Bible. This chapter has already suggested another way in which Stowe's text can at least create the same effect as flesh-and-blood reality: since we cannot respond to the physical presence of actual bodies, the text shows us the proper response to a sentimental narration.

But Stowe's insistence on the authority of the physical body (her moral sense philosophy) still seems at odds with her belief in the authority of the text (her notion that a book can change lives). We have seen the senator respond to bodies who are themselves racked by the power of words. An even fuller development of Stowe's aesthetic sensibility occurs when bodies respond merely to other bodies, when there are no words within the narrative. The "flesh-and-blood" reality, the "real presence" that Stowe strives for, is most acute when characters communicate only through their bodies. These moments are utopian not only for their emotional impact and political implications but also for the suggestion that it is possible—indeed, that it is desirable—to have a world in which bodies can communicate without words. At its utopian heights, Stowe's text imagines a world where text is not necessary.

In a world in which bodies are the site of deepest truth, moments of bodily contact are packed densely with meaning. After the senator has been inspired by a scene of weeping to fully invest himself in aiding Eliza, Stowe writes:

> Mr. Bird hurried her into the carriage, and Mrs. Bird pressed on after her to the carriage steps. Eliza leaned out of her carriage, and put out her hand,—a hand as soft and beautiful as was given in return. She fixed her large, dark eyes, full of earnest meaning, on Mrs. Bird's face, and seemed going to speak. Her lips moved,—she tried once or twice, but there was no sound,—and pointing upward, with a look never to be forgotten, she fell back in the seat, and covered her face. The door was shut, and the carriage drove on. (155)

In the midst of life-saving haste, time stops for an instant, just long enough for Eliza and Mrs. Bird to touch hands. Language is not necessary; indeed, speaking is impossible for Eliza. When emotions run too deep, language will not do. Stowe herself does not describe the thoughts of Eliza and Mrs. Bird, but instead narrates their movements. Like Eliza and Mrs. Bird, readers have deep access to feelings only by way of bodies. Only hands can convey the deepest sense of gratitude; only touch can confirm the sympathy of two mothers each of whom has lost children. We cannot differentiate between the hands, both of which are "soft and beautiful." With the free, transparent exchange of "earnest meaning," the bodies are—for a single utopian moment—equal. In a moment of sympathy, the slave and the senator's wife shatter the political and racial structure that defines and cripples a nation. With this sentimental touch, Stowe suggests not only that a perfect exchange of sympathy is possible but also that the perfect transmission of feeling can lead to a perfected world.

The sentimental touch is commonly used in American sentimental literature to signify moments of extreme pathos. In Susan Warner's *The Wide, Wide World* (1850), the tearful Ellen is comforted by hands when language will not suffice: "Better than words, the calm firm grasp of his hand quieted her."[63] Romance literature, too, uses the sentimental trope to herald profound emotion. In the last scene of *The Last of the Mohicans* (1826), "Chingachgook grasped the hand that, in the warmth of feeling, the Scout had stretched across the fresh earth, and in that attitude of

Friendship, these two sturdy and intrepid woodsmen bowed their heads together, while scalding tears fell to their feet, watering the grave of Uncas, like drops of falling rain."[64] The novel ends with a final, peaceful acknowledgment between races—a display of sensibility as natural as the weather. In *The Scarlet Letter* (1850), Pearl asks her mother about the minister, "Will he go back with us, hand in hand, we three together, into the town?"[65] We, along with Pearl, know that "hand in hand" will be an unspoken but fully legible public expression of acceptance. In one of the most famous scenes of touching hands in American literature, Ishmael describes the manipulation of sperm in "A Squeeze of the Hand," chapter 94 of *Moby-Dick* (1851):

> Squeeze! squeeze! squeeze! All the morning long; I squeezed that sperm till I myself almost melted into it; I squeezed that sperm till a strange sort of insanity came over me; and I found myself unwittingly squeezing my co-laborers' hands in it, mistaking their hands for the gentle globules. Such an abounding, affectionate, friendly, loving feeling did this avocation beget; that at last I was continually squeezing their hands, and looking up into their eyes sentimentally; as much as to say,—Oh! my dear fellow beings, why should we longer cherish any social acerbities, or know the slightest ill-humor or envy! Come; let us squeeze hands all round; nay, let us all squeeze ourselves into each other; let us squeeze ourselves universally into the very milk and sperm of kindness.[66]

Melville explicitly invokes the sentimental, even as his text is in some ways a response to the femininity and domesticity of the sentimental novel. In mid-nineteenth-century American literature, the sentimental touch is a fully loaded trope that speaks to the height of feeling and the insufficiency of language. Words can never fully express emotion; bodies are indisputable.

For Stowe, the indisputable bodily presence of Eliza and her husband, George, is the primary evidence of their humanity—a humanity that slavery refuses to acknowledge. George, as a runaway, pleads for help from the manufacturer Mr. Wilson, demanding, "Look at me, now. Don't I sit before you, every way, just as much a man as you are? Look at my face,—look at my hands—, look at my body" (185). Face and hands are the sites of interaction between the body and the world and are thus the concrete proof of deep identity. Hands, though, possess even more authenticity than the face. Only the hand can offer tactile proof; only the hand can touch. Here, though, George's hand does not touch, at least not yet. Instead, George narrates his life story; the scene is not one of instant understanding but of slow conversion. The narrator explains:

> This speech, delivered partly while sitting at the table, and partly walking up and down the room,—delivered with tears, and flashing eyes, and despairing gestures,—was altogether too much for the good-natured old body to whom it was addressed, who had pulled out a great yellow silk pocket-handkerchief, and was mopping up his face with great energy. (187)

Again the presence of the body, more so than the narration itself, most greatly affects Mr. Wilson. Wilson himself becomes "the good-natured old body," suggesting that affective speech appeals to the body above all else. Sentimental listeners, like sentimental readers, are bodies first and foremost. The speech is made authentic through the body, and tears beget tears.

The episode with Mr. Wilson reminds us not only that bodies are essential to sentimentalism but also that they are essential to slavery. George's past displays the fierce anxiety over bodily control that courses through the slave economy. The narrator explains that George

> had been hired out by his master to work in a bagging factory, where his adroitness and ingenuity caused him to be considered the first hand in the place. He had invented a machine for the cleaning of the hemp, which, considering the education and circumstances of the inventor, displayed quite as much mechanical genius as Whitney's cotton-gin. (54)

George's move from laborer to machine inventor is a transition from field hand to craftsman and suggests progressive economic development. The invention of a labor-saving device shifts George's importance from his body to his mind. As David Montgomery explains in *Worker's Control in America*, "The functional autonomy of craftsmen rested on both their superior knowledge, which made them self-directing at their tasks, and the supervision which they gave to one or more helpers."[67] But slavery cannot exist with slave autonomy. Harris, George's owner,

> was waited upon over the factory, shown the machinery by George, who, in high spirits, talked so fluently, held himself so erect, looked so handsome and manly, that his master began to feel an uneasy consciousness of inferiority. What business had his slave to be marching round the country, inventing machines, and holding up

his head among gentlemen? He'd soon put a stop to it. He'd take
him back, and put him to hoeing and digging. (55)

George's newfound autonomy is manifested in his body—"erect . . . hand-
some and manly." Harris, in response, will assert his control over George
by moving him from mind work back to body work. Soon George is "put
to the meanest drudgery of the farm" (56). If the owner cannot control
the slave's mind, he can control the slave's body.

When George takes off his glove in front of Mr. Wilson, he reveals
"a newly-healed scar in his hand," and declares, "That is a parting proof
of Mr. Harris' regard" (189). The hand, though, quickly moves from a
mark of human chattel (even as it suggests the stigmata) to a mark of
equality. The "parting proof of Mr. Harris' regard" was a scar, but the
parting proof of Mr. Wilson's regard is a handshake: "George stood up
like a rock, and put out his hand with the air of a prince. The friendly
little old man shook it heartily" (190). George's very body registers his
movement from slavery to freedom; the handshake seals his rising status. George's rise from hand-scarred slave to hand-shaking freeman (as
he declares himself) mirrors the rise of the handshake in Western culture. Prior to the eighteenth century, touching was carefully regulated
in terms of class; most rules of etiquette pertained to showing respect
for higher rank. Keith Thomas explains that the handshake as a normal
way of greeting was "part of the move to a more egalitarian, less deferen-
tial, ethic, for the handshake superseded the habit of bowing, kneeling,
or curtsying."[68] Herman Roodenburg tells us that Quakers in the sev-
enteenth century greeted each other with the handshake because "this
particular gesture connoted friendship and brotherhood, just as they
addressed each other as 'friends' thereby eliminating all hierarchy and
class distinctions among themselves."[69] The handshake became a common form of greeting only in the nineteenth century, with the softening
of social hierarchies that came with the rise of a commercial society and
the decline of aristocracy. A clasp of hands, then, is the erasure of hierarchy, at least for the brief moment of contact.[70]

Just as George declares that his hand is the marker of his manhood,
Stowe insists that hands are the marker of humanity. We know that the
delicate, cherubic Eva St. Clare is deathly ill when her "little hands had
grown thinner" (382). She still, though, is able to use her hands to offer
love to Topsy, the neglected, mischievous slave-child: "'O, Topsy, poor
child, I love you!' said Eva, with a sudden burst of feeling, and laying
her little thin, white hand on Topsy's shoulder" (409). Eva is the first
person able to touch Topsy in love and is thus the first person to reach

Topsy's heart. Richard Brodhead writes, "Diagnosing Topsy's maternity deficiency, Eva offers her the flow of affection and the primitive tactile *sign* of affection withheld from Topsy in her faultily constructed origin. . . . Touched by Eva's love and so penetrated by Eva's moral vision, Topsy at once begins 'trying to be a good girl.'"[71] The touch not only conveys love but actually spreads morality.

Eva's tactile power is at its height when she is on her deathbed—the most highly sentimental scene in the novel. Eva demands that her hair be cut, so that those whom she loves (presumably everyone around her) will still be touched by a vestige of her material presence, even when she is no longer on earth. Stowe writes, "It is impossible to describe the scene, as, with tears and sobs, they gathered round the little creature, and took from her hands what seemed to them a last mark of her love" (419). The narrator foregrounds the limits of language in a scene that relies fully on the sense of touch. Language can deceive, words can be misinterpreted; the physicality of hands, though, can always be trusted. While language mediates meaning between two bodies, touch conveys meaning directly.

Stowe repeats the scene of silent touch when St. Clare is on his deathbed, about to join Eva in the afterlife. Tom, seated next to St. Clare, offers a prayer whose authenticity is verified by the fervor of Tom's somatic response—"strong crying and tears" (456). After the prayer racks Tom's body, there is silence: "When Tom ceased to speak, St. Clare reached out and took his hand, looking earnestly at him, but saying nothing. He closed his eyes, but still retained his hold; for, in the gates of eternity, the black hand and the white hold each other with an equal clasp" (456). St. Clare passes over language for the more immediate senses of touch and sight. He then closes his eyes and further narrows his sensory perceptions. His sensory awareness, though, deepens; fully concentrated on touch, he is closer than ever to Tom, and closer than ever to heaven. The silent touch becomes a fully utopian moment. On the threshold of the kingdom of heaven, the slave and the slaveholder have "an equal clasp." The progression from voice to vision to touch signals the height of sentimental feeling. In the transparent, unmediated mode of communication, not only are bodies intimately aware of their relationship, but they are able to transcend social and cultural boundaries to realize a fullness of humanity that lies beyond speech and vision.

Touch and Utopia

Stowe's utopian project is to inspire the abolition of slavery.[72] But in doing so she picks up another utopian project—one closely associated with sentimentalism—to represent feeling in its most unmediated form. In the final chapter, Stowe famously writes:

> But, what can any individual do? Of that, every individual can judge. There is one thing that every individual can do,—they can see to it that *they feel right*. An atmosphere of sympathetic influence encircles every human being; and the man or woman who *feels* strongly, healthily and justly, on the great interests of humanity, is a constant benefactor to the human race. (624)

Stowe has not set out to change our minds, but to change our bodies. The novel, of course, can only describe touch; the text can only enter our minds. Stowe's aesthetic, though, allows readers to acknowledge the supreme power of unmediated bodily communication. We realize the full legibility of bodies; we have been trained to respond to sentimental bodily cues. The sentimental touch is the literalizing and mechanizing of sympathy. The trope signifies not only that characters can communicate in a fully transparent fashion but also that readers can recognize and experience unmediated emotion.[73]

The sentimental touch lies at the heart of Stowe's politics. The depiction of unmediated emotion is a full development of the influence of moral sense philosophy and is well suited for bodies in the premanagerial stage of capitalism. Stowe's writing fits smoothly in her time and place. The touching trope is emblematic of a moment in literature when bodies and interactions between bodies are legible, just as it is symptomatic of a moment in capitalism when direct negotiations between bodies are common. The relationship between the market and bodies will never be closer than in the age of the slave economy. As the economy shifts, as gaps grow between the market and bodies, and between bodies within the market, literature's treatment of the body will reflect an expanding depersonalization in American culture. The sentimental touch will persist, but its utopian overtones will carry new significance.

2 / Managing Sentimentalism in *Adventures of Huckleberry Finn*

In the final paragraph of *Adventures of Huckleberry Finn*, Huck tells us that Tom has recovered from being shot in the leg during the escape: "Tom's most well, now, and got his bullet around his neck on a watch-guard for a watch, and is always seeing what time it is."[1] Tom's wishes seem to have come true: his exhaustingly elaborate plans for Jim's rescue have been executed, and he has been dramatically (though not dreadfully) wounded in the process. His bullet is a keepsake that he can glance at regularly, reminding himself of his romantic exploits. But Tom's bullet-watch does not merely remind him of a glorious past; connected to a timepiece, it promises to track the future.[2] The ending of this novel suggests that the days of the raft are over. One does not drift aimlessly with a bullet-watch. Indeed, the watch crystallizes what Huck already noticed: "Tom superintended. He could out-superintend any boy I ever see" (240). Tom is a young manager, eager to control the work around him, eager to systematize and mechanize his world. Tom has become the arbiter of official measurement, and slow intimacy is to be replaced by speedy efficiency. America's most famous book about seeking freedom closes in an era of system management.

Twain would develop the character of the superintendent more fully in his next novel, *A Connecticut Yankee in King Arthur's Court*. Hank Morgan, the Yankee, is the "head superintendent" of a massive arms factory that makes "guns, revolvers, cannon, boilers, engines, all sorts of labour-saving machinery."[3] When the Yankee finds himself in Camelot in the sixth century, he quickly becomes known as "the Boss" and

industrializes a country stuck in the "ungentle" codes of medieval aristocracy (91, 29). Twain's mockery of an absurd chivalric culture becomes
an apocalyptic critique of a brutal Taylorized system in which the Yankee—who has declared himself "nearly barren of sentiment" (36)—lays
waste to tens of thousands of men. Many critics have written about the
ways that *A Connecticut Yankee* grapples with the emergent industrial
and bureaucratic culture of the late nineteenth century.[4] Rather than
focusing on Twain's frontal assault on managerial culture in *A Connecticut Yankee*, I concentrate on Twain's subtler and more deeply embedded
critique in *Huckleberry Finn*. In *Huckleberry Finn*—published four years
before *A Connecticut Yankee*—Twain criticizes managerialism without
actually staging scenes of industrialization or factory work. Twain's anxieties about bureaucracy and emotion reveal themselves not on the level
of content, but on the levels of form and trope. Instead of a "Man-Fac-
tory" (130), we get the coercive powers of managerial leadership; instead
of mechanized violence in a world of time-travel, we get a bullet-watch.

Tom's bullet-watch is the emblem of a personal triumph, but it also signals the cultural triumph for a specific mode of temporal consciousness. A
uniform standard of time in the United States did not emerge until 1883—
two years before Twain published *Adventures of Huckleberry Finn*—when
railway networks became sufficiently large and complex to warrant a
single timetable. Punctuality and precise timekeeping were functions, first
and foremost, of the needs of the earliest corporations. National and inter-
national systematization quickly influenced the most fundamental ways
that individuals conceived of their days.[5] As Eviatar Zerubavel writes,
"What seems to have replaced nature as a temporal referencing anchor is
the principle of rationality, long viewed as one of the key characteristics
of modern civilization."[6] Huck's raft, the vehicle that propels Twain's plot,
spins and eddies, moving with the currents of the Mississippi River; Tom's
bullet-watch imposes a rational schedule on what had been an erratic and
natural flow.

When notions of time become tied to mechanical timepieces rather
than to the sun and the stars, it becomes possible to organize days with
a new precision. The symbolism of Tom's bullet-watch resonates not only
with newly standardized time but also with the emerging field of scientific management. Though Frederick Taylor did not write *The Principles
of Scientific Management* until 1911, his work ushering in the scientific
management movement began in the 1880s.[7] Taylor wanted to end the
"wastes of human effort" that came from the "awkward, inefficient, or ill-
directed movements of men."[8] His solution was to break every work task

down to its simplest elements and optimize the worker's performance of each element.[9] Managers sought to create systems of labor that were all-encompassing, in which every work detail was controlled. Watches became a crucial emblem of scientific management, since managers measured the elapsed time for each component of a work task.[10]

Mark Twain's notorious speculation in the Paige Typesetter suggests his interest in time-saving, money-making techniques.[11] He admitted his own money-lust and was famously connected to patrons in the world of business.[12] *Adventures of Huckleberry Finn*, though, is far from a celebration of new economic developments. Rather, we should be suspicious of Tom Sawyer, whose petty governance relies on a false expertise, and whose obsession with rules comes at the expense of a humane sensibility. With the bullet-watch standing for the coming reign of standardized clocks and corporate time management, and Tom himself standing for the superintendent who controls but does not participate in the labor process, the final chapters of Twain's novel offer a forceful critique of managerialism.

I am suggesting, in other words, that Twain critiques the age in which he wrote *Huckleberry Finn* just as much as he critiques the age in which the novel is set. Twain published *Adventures of Huckleberry Finn* in 1885, thirty-three years after Stowe's *Uncle Tom's Cabin*. Twain writes, though, that the novel takes place "forty to fifty years ago" (27)—before *Uncle Tom's Cabin*, before the Civil War, before emancipation. The novel was written in the age of post-Reconstruction and literary realism, but it takes place in the age of slavery. Critics have often examined the ways that Twain's text condemns the age in which it is set. In this view the Tom Sawyer episodes, which open and close the book, are critiques of the literature of Twain's predecessors; the gang segment and the evasion chapters are examples of a ludicrous bondage to the romantic imagination. More recently, critics have suggested convincingly that Twain's text criticizes the failures of Reconstruction. Victor Doyno explains, "scholars have increasingly come to view the last portion of the novel, in which a free Black is in effect reenslaved, as a direct commentary on what was happening to Blacks in the South when Twain was writing the book."[13] For Doyno, the episode that seems to be most embedded in the past actually addresses Twain's contemporary culture.[14] Indeed, the ending is certainly a rebuke of the racial politics of Reconstruction, but it is also a critique of the major economic change happening in Twain's lifetime. When we pair the evasion chapters with the gang episodes that open the book, we find a text framed by Tom Sawyer, and we find a fierce condemnation of the managerial culture that Tom Sawyer's rule exemplifies.

Put another way, if we read the novel from the beginning with Tom's bullet-watch in mind, we see that Twain's concern with a culture moving quickly toward systematization and mechanization pervades the entire work. The fears that we see in *Adventures of Huckleberry Finn* reflect the dawning of a depersonalized capitalism: loneliness in a world where everyone else seems to know their precise place; the loss of personal relationships; the anxiety of looking after new wealth; and the fear of not being in full control, of literally being managed by elaborate, incomprehensible schemes. The historian Robert H. Wiebe explains, "As the pace of industrialization quickened early in the eighties, the incomprehensible ways of the corporation were also alienating a multitude of wage earners. Rapidly losing control over their working lives, they knew only that decisions made somewhere else pushed them about like so many cattle."[15] In addition to financial distress, American workers experienced social and cultural disorientation. Economic conditions at the end of the nineteenth century led to the crystallization of highly systematized, regulated social forms. The anxieties of cultural change were not limited to those directly involved in new economic ventures, but extended to individuals who at one time seemed to live beyond the reach of big business.[16]

If Tom Sawyer stands for the coming reign of corporate culture, Huckleberry Finn represents resistance to a civilization obsessed with time management. Huck tries to escape from all systems and regulations. The boy Huck exists before the massive bureaucratization of the American economy and American culture; his anxieties from "forty to fifty years ago," though, are also Twain's anxieties (indeed, a culture's anxieties) about the present. As Alan Trachtenberg says of the fiction of the 1880s and 1890s, "the major picture included a keen lament for the passing of an older, more secure and reliable way of life, one based on ingrained assumptions about the possibilities of freedom."[17] Twain's lament for the passing of an age is mirrored by Huck's search for security and reliability in a highly regulated world that has no place for him. After he explains Tom's fixation with the bullet-watch, Huck says, "I reckon I got to light out for the Territory ahead of the rest, because Aunt Sally she's going to adopt me and sivilize me and I can't stand it" (265). Instead of a false, manufactured consciousness, Huck promises an unfettered earnestness. The final words of Twain's book are: "The end. Yours truly, Huck Finn." It seems that the remedy to an alienating culture exemplified by Tom Sawyer is the cultivation of a consciousness that relies on a truthful, personable sensibility. In his final invocation of the truth, perhaps Huck Finn offers a release from the pressures of a managerial culture that is most interested in manipulation. Perhaps we can rely on an intimate sensibility grounded in truth. Perhaps we can rely, in other words, on a sentimental worldview.

But, as Huck warns from the very beginning, truth is elusive in this book, and sentimentalism is not to be trusted blindly. The opening sentences of chapter 1 read, "You don't know about me, without you have read a book by the name of 'The Adventures of Tom Sawyer,' but that ain't no matter. That book was made by Mr. Mark Twain, and he told the truth, mainly. There was things which he stretched, but mainly he told the truth" (32). Beware, says Twain's creation, of my creator; the author may not be entirely trustworthy. Read warily—not because books are powerless, but because they are so powerful. If *Uncle Tom's Cabin* taught us to be sentimental readers, to read right so that we may "feel right" so that we may act right, *Adventures of Huckleberry Finn* teaches us to be careful readers. Reading right is a tricky business. And feeling right, as we will see, may not always lead to acting right.

For the sentimentalist, truth lies in the realm of the body—tears cannot lie, and the touch can express meaning beyond the realm of language. By questioning the very possibility of truth, Twain questions the political potential of sentimentalism. *Adventures of Huckleberry Finn* takes place in a world of manipulation, where the truth is bent easily, where bodies can mislead, and where a politics based on sentimentalism may be destructive. Huck's adventures feature a series of manipulative schemes in which characters use each other, often for undisclosed, insidious purposes. As Huck makes clear when he invokes "Mr. Mark Twain" as a character who tells "stretchers," the text itself is interested in manipulation. Twain's concern with manipulative power reflects a culture where literary manipulation—in the form of sentimentalism— has been a dominant force, and where economic manipulation—in the form of managerial capitalism—is a rising force. *Adventures of Huckleberry Finn* ties an unquestioning acceptance of literary inheritance to an unquestioning acceptance of social conditions and shows the danger of unexamined cultural legacies.

While Huck Finn flees from the systematized culture that surrounds him, Mark Twain is keenly aware of the systematized textual forms that surround his own work.[18] As many critics have shown, Twain's work is a response to the highly popular sentimental and romance novels that had dominated American writing. As this chapter shows, though, *Adventures of Huckleberry Finn* is not merely a repudiation of sentimentality and romance fantasies. Even as Twain explicitly derides the emotional excesses of sentimentalism, even as the Walter Scott is a broken, sinking ship—a hulking danger clogging the Mississippi—Twain does not fully reject his cultural inheritance.[19] The text, in its very critique of sentimentalism and romance, uses sentimental tropes. The sentimental touch is not always true for Twain; indeed, under a managerial regime sentimentalism has soured. When intimate relationships give way to business structure, when the law of the manager replaces the law of the heart, society loses the moral sense. Sentimentalism with no moral sense is a literature with no philosophical center; what is left is an empty set of gestures whose meaning can be manipulated by hucksters and schemers. Twain's ambivalence about sentimentalism is tied directly to his concerns with managerialism. At their worst, both turn humans into mechanical objects who respond automatically and predictably to rote instruction. It is not emotional language, per se, that Twain satirizes. Rather, Twain rails against standardized, machinelike figures of speech that appeal to emotion just as they cancel any deep human subjectivity.

Yet even as he is worried about the mechanization of emotion, even as he shows us that the sentimental touch can be Taylorized, Twain does not entirely let go of the sentimental. True emotion in *Adventures of Huckleberry Finn* is still marked by bodily reactions and interactions. Huck and Jim, as we will see, develop a moral sense that epitomizes a sentimental worldview. Huck and Jim learn to trust their own bodies, to listen to their moral sense, even as they come to distrust a culture that judges and condemns based on physicality—where crying equals sincerity, where black equals slave.[20] Their deep anxieties about trusting their bodies and their culture in a world rife with untrustworthy characters align with Mark Twain's own anxieties about using sentimental tropes in a world where sentimentalism is easily put to crooked use. Put another way, anxieties of form recapitulate anxieties of subject matter. The text, Twain warns us, can deceive, especially if we are sentimental readers eager to cry, but it is only through text that we can recognize deception, and it is still through text that we can experience real emotion. Twain's ultimate restoration of the moral sense is not only a vindication of sentimentalism gone awry but is an antidote to a managerial culture in which bodies are increasingly controlled by impersonal forces.

Inheriting Sentimentalism

Acts of reading pervade *Huckleberry Finn*, and as Twain makes clear, acts of reading are always acts of interpretation, and often acts of misinterpretation. From his opening invocation of Tom Sawyer's books, Twain alerts us to the fact that text and textual interpretations are a pervasive influence in American life. The affecting power of text was not new for Twain's America. The premise of *Uncle Tom's Cabin* was that a popular text could influence politics. But after the Civil War, American culture was no longer eager to accept the wide-eyed optimism of a sentimental politics. Louis J. Budd writes that before the Civil War, "the promise of romantic democracy to set all wrong matters right for whites still sounded believable. After the Civil War, however, many of those matters not only looked but felt different; the age of Henry Clay, Daniel Webster, and even Abraham Lincoln seemed almost quaint. Overriding a chaotic increase in population, modernization crunched onward without a pause."[21] The most enduring literary response to post–Civil War American culture was realism.[22] Realists sought mimesis through "the serious treatment of everyday reality," as Erich Auerbach wrote.[23] Leading literary spokesman William Dean Howells declared in "A Call to Realism," "let fiction cease to lie about life; let it portray men and women as they are, actuated by the motives and the passions in the measure we all know."[24] For the realists, the teary manipulations of sentimental narratives and the outrageous plotlines in romance literature did not fit with American social reality.

Adventures of Huckleberry Finn is an ideal vehicle for Twain to critically examine his textual inheritance—a legacy that fully employed sentimental tropes. In *Huckleberry Finn*'s direct predecessor, *The Adventures of Tom Sawyer*, Twain himself uses the sentimental touch to signify deep sympathy after Becky and Tom emerge unharmed after being lost in the cave: "During the first half hour a procession of villagers filed through Judge Thatcher's house, seized the saved ones and kissed them, squeezed Mrs. Thatcher's hand, tried to speak but couldn't—and drifted out raining tears all over the place."[25] The passage is tinged with satire but is also filled with the physical signs of sentiment, and we cannot doubt that the characters in the scene are deeply affected.

Twain is an eccentric realist—his deployment of the sentimental trope signals an outmoded form, but can also signal an authentic, trustworthy form. Like many of the realists, he points to the outdated absurdity of sentimental gestures. But unlike Chopin, Norris, and Dreiser, for instance,

Twain's sentimental moments do not always point to the failure of an earlier generation's literary imagination.[26] Though criticism traditionally pits sentimentalism against realism, it makes sense that Twain would deploy sentimental tropes. After all, sentiment has an important position in the American natural rights tradition. As I discussed in chapter 1 of this study, America's founders were deeply influenced by the Scottish Common Sense philosophers, the intellectual progenitors of sentimentalism. The language of sentimentalism is also the language of the Declaration of Independence—the language of humanism, of social promise, of moral sense philosophy. A full indictment of sentimentality would be at odds with progressive realist literature—a literature, to use William Dean Howells's phrase, "not only of delightfulness but of usefulness."[27] So instead Twain offers a careful deployment of sentimentality—at once displaying its ill effects and its moral power. Twain's careful use of sentimental tropes is a literary opposition to slavery and moral abjection within the text, but is also a counternarrative to Twain's contemporary cultural situation—not just the failures of Reconstruction, but the looming cultural anxiety brought about by a major shift in the economy.

If one of the hallmarks of the new economy is a strict adherence to clocks, the phrase "forty to fifty years ago" is a willed inexactitude. The antidote to a culture of rationalized control where bodies are connected through abstract networks is a drifting space where bodies are close. The raft is no place and the good place, outopia and eutopia. On the raft, Huck's and Jim's bodies become increasingly legible, their touch becomes progressively more meaningful, and their unspoken connections become ever deeper. In short, when the raft is utopian, bodies on the raft are sentimental. The novel, of course, does not take place entirely on the raft; as Trachtenberg puts it, the text charts "the incursions of history on the idyll of Huck and Jim on their raft."[28] As history interferes with the raft—when social forces interrupt the journey, when Huck and Jim must leave the raft—figurations of the body change. Tracing the various ways that bodies are figured over the course of this novel is a way of mapping Twain's vexed relationship with sentimentalism and his simultaneous consideration of cultural change.

The Seriousness of a Boy's Book

A discussion of bodily representation and interaction in the text at first seems to be out of place in the main debates that have kept *Adventures of Huckleberry Finn* at the center of critical controversy for much of its 125 years. Morality, not the body, has been the focus of the critical discussion.[29] But we should remember that an examination of the body, especially in terms of sentimental aesthetics, is fundamentally concerned with morality. In the realm of sentimental aesthetics, morality can be felt in the body; just as we can judge an object to be ugly or beautiful by our felt response, so can we judge actions to be good or bad, moral or immoral, based on our feelings, our body's immediate reaction.

Twain criticism has remained split between detractors and defenders for much of the twentieth century.[30] Until recently, even as they invoked morality, critics have tried to purge Twain of sentimental associations.[31] Recently, though, critics have shown how Twain endorses sentimental values, even as he remains wary of excessive emotion. Gregg Camfield declares that "Twain often attacked sentimentalism on utilitarian grounds, but he often endorsed sentimental conventions by using them straight."[32] Mary Louise Kete argues that Twain deploys authentic sentimentalism to combat sham sentimentalism.[33] Both Camfield and Kete point to a deep ambivalence in Twain's writings: Twain struggles to fully trust sentimental language, for while it addresses morality through emotion it easily deceives.[34]

Twain's attack on the harmful effects of sentimentalism begins with Tom Sawyer. Before we are on a raft with Huck and Jim, we are in a cave with Tom Sawyer's gang. Each member takes an oath that Tom proudly declares "was out of pirate books, and robber books" (37). Tom never questions his own authority or the authority of the texts. In his unyielding adherence to literary conventions, Tom becomes a ridiculous, comical figure. Tom's obstinate tie to the romance novel is not a tie to rebellion, even if he would like to think so. Instead, Tom's supposed social revolt actually secures the bonds of domesticity by holding fast to the sentimental conception of the family. Huck explains that after he tried to run away from the Widow Douglas: "Tom Sawyer, he hunted me up and said he was going to start a band of robbers, and I might join if I would go back to the widow and be respectable" (32). For Tom Sawyer, the romance of rebellion is a game, one that must abide by the "respectable" rules of sentimentalism. The romance does not oppose sentimentalism but works under a cloak of insurgency to uphold the laws of sentimentality.

Even when Tom Sawyer's gang seems to be plotting its most antisocial behavior, the gang works to forward a sentimental ideology. Twain writes, "Some thought it would be good to kill the *families* of boys that told the secrets. Tom said it was a good idea, so he took a pencil and wrote it in" (37). Huck is almost kicked out of the gang for not having a family—his mother is dead and his alcoholic father is missing. Luckily for Huck, the gang agrees that they could kill Miss Watson. The gang secures a surrogate mother; rebellion actually tightens family bonds.[35] But while romance is a fantasy, the sentimentalism that comes with it has actual effects. Tom's raid on "Spaniards and A-rabs" and a fleet of camels and elephants is of course fake, nothing more than the bullying of a Sunday-school picnic (41); but the domesticity that must adjoin the romance fantasy is real. Tom is the town's favorite rebel, since his is a saccharine rebellion. "Boys will be boys," as Uncle Silas declares, especially because boys, rebelling properly, will "turn up . . . all sound and right"—will become proper, respectable men (257).

Tom is in a management position from the beginning. Using authority gained from his own unquestioned (though obviously dubious) research, he rules his gang with paternal power. His coercive, managerial treatment of his boys resonates with relationships in an adult workplace. In *The Principles of Scientific Management*, Frederick Taylor wrote:

> Under scientific management the "initiative" of the workmen (that is, their hard work, their good-will, and their ingenuity) is obtained with absolute uniformity and to a greater extent than is possible under the old system; and in addition to this improvement on the part of the men, the managers assume new burdens, new duties, and responsibilities never dreamed of in the past. The managers assume, for instance, the burden of gathering together all of the traditional knowledge which in the past has been possessed by the workmen and then of classifying, tabulating, and reducing this knowledge to rules, laws, and formulae which are immensely helpful to the workmen in doing their daily work.[36]

In the eyes of management, managers are a beneficent force working for the good of underlings who are incapable of understanding the complexities of the labor process. Laborers are valued insofar as they adhere exactly to the guidelines of a bureaucracy that claims to have science on its side.[37] Managers never treat workers as adults; as Robert Franklin Hoxie explains in his 1915 *Scientific Management and Labor*, "the worker is no longer a craftsman in any sense, but is an animated tool of the management. He has no need of special craft knowledge or craft skill, or any power to acquire them if he had, and any man who walks the street is a competitor for his job."[38] Like children in the eyes of an adult, workers are tools to be molded and put to good use. Tom's workers are actual boys—ideal subjects for a manager ready to activate his fantasy of productivity. Tom does not invoke the laws of scientific management, but he does invoke the laws of literature to a similar effect. With Tom Sawyer, Twain aligns the coercive use of literature with a culture of management. Romantic notions that cultivate sentimental ideologies go hand in hand with a managerial system that cultivates helplessness.

Weak Sentimentalism

In his posthumously published *Letters from the Earth*, Mark Twain writes that the moral sense is the "secret" of man's "degradation. It is the quality which enables him to do wrong. It has no other office. It is incapable of performing any other function. It could never have been intended to perform any other. Without it, man could do no wrong."[39] Twain's attack on the moral sense seems to be a strike at the heart of sentimentalism. Moral sense philosophy—grounded on the notion that we can determine right from wrong with the quickness of aesthetic judgment (that is, that morality can be felt in the body)—is the philosophical basis of sentimental literature. For the Scottish Enlightenment philosophers, the moral sense was the source of society's cohesion. For the sentimental author, the moral sense was the key to a politically effective literature. For Twain's satirical narrator in *Letters from the Earth*, the moral sense justifies evil. Twain's vicious condemnation suggests a disappointment in a once-promising philosophy and perhaps an even more profound disappointment in humanity. Twain's ideas seem to have been borne out by the decay and swift corruption of sentimental literature.

As we saw in the age of *Uncle Tom's Cabin*, a sentimental worldview corresponds to a distinct form of capitalism. Domestic bonds tightened in the mid-nineteenth century when work moved away from the family; the family defined itself through emotional ties rather than through its role in production. Sentimentalism thrived precisely when *Adventures of Huckleberry Finn* takes place. But as the world became increasingly defined by money, as systems of capital management and ownership grew more and more rigid, the cult of domesticity declined. According to Susan Harris, "by the mid-nineteenth century . . . sentimentality had become an intertextual construct, pointing to other texts rather than to action in the world. The decadence of sentimental language resulted from its loss of political intent; its valuation of feeling as an end in itself."[40] In other words, in an age of social rigidification and the hardening of business networks, sentimental language itself succumbed to the reification of systems. The power of sentimental aesthetics came from the tight bond between the body's interior life and the material world—feelings would spurn the body to action in the physical world. But as the physical world seems less and less responsive to human intervention, sentimental feeling becomes separated from the political world. What was once a revolutionary aesthetic becomes antirevolutionary; authors evoke feeling not for the sake of effecting social change, but for the pleasure of feeling. The pleasure of a sentimental text in the face of an emerging bureaucratic economy lulls readers into gentle acceptance of the increasingly inflexible capitalist world.[41] Twain is aware of this critique. In fact, before he shows the morally redemptive power of sentimentalism, and before he uses sentimental tropes to counter a looming bureaucratic society, Twain lampoons a culture in love with feeling good and in which sentimentalism has lost its moral force.

Huck's hometown, St. Petersburg, is a town infatuated with sentiment; the culture is eager for emotion, keen to be touched. The sentimental trope is dangerous in such a place. Here on the shore, we should not trust sentimentalism, for sentimentalism blinds, deceives, and corrupts. When Pap tries to get money from Huck, Judge Thatcher and the Widow Douglas try to protect Huck. Huck explains, "the judge and the widow went to law to get the court to take me away from him and let one of them be my guardian; but it was a new judge that had just come, and he didn't know the old man; so he said courts mustn't interfere and separate families if they could help it; said he'd druther not take a child away from its father" (48). The new judge seems to offer an enlightened law—a law that values the strength of domestic ties over the tempting pull of economic considerations. This is the kind of sentimental jurisprudence that Stowe would have liked. When Pap gets out of jail, the "new judge said he was agoing to make a man of him" (48). The new judge is perfectly sentimental; after all, he is a "new judge," progressive and sensible. The judge brings Pap to his house, clothes him, feeds him, and "after supper he talked to him about temperance and such things till the old man cried" (48). A conversation about "temperance and such things"—about sentimentalism—brings tears. Huck's characteristic deadpan delivery works perfectly: what would undoubtedly be tears of boredom for Huck are, for the new judge, a sign of success. Pap's tears are a somatic response; crying, in the sentimental worldview, signals sincerity.

When Huck's Pap insists on his newfound temperance, he offers his hand as physical proof, announcing: "Look at it gentlemen, and ladies all; take ahold of it; shake it. There's a hand that was the hand of a hog; but it ain't so no more; it's the hand of a man that's started in on a new life, and 'll die before he'll go back. You mark them words—don't forget I said them. It's a clean hand now; shake it—don't be afeard" (48–49). The town drunk knows the rules of sentimental aesthetics. He demands a sensory progression—from look, to touch, to shake; an increasing bodily intimacy will secure a trusting relationship. Words are important—indeed, should be pressed into memory—but the body trumps all. Pap's use of words teeters on the edge of bathos; his hand, he proudly declares, was "the hand of a hog." But anatomical idiocy becomes sentimental metaphor, as Pap secures his sincerity with his body. The clean hand marks a clean interior life.[42] In adherence to the rules of a sentimental novel, the scene of a body moved is moving for the spectators; they gather and kiss the hand and cry. The touch should be touching.

But after being tucked in by the judge and his wife into a beautiful bedroom, Pap

> got powerful thirsty and clumb out onto the porch-roof and slid down a stanchion and traded his new coat for a jug of forty-rod, and clumb back again and had a good old time; and towards daylight he crawled out again, drunk as a fiddler, and rolled off the porch and broke his left arm in two places and was most froze to death when somebody found him after sun-up. (49)

Genre shifts quickly: the sentimental swiftly turns slapstick. Pap's almost-frozen self is a body without feeling; a body that signaled the triumph of sentimentalism is suddenly senseless. Pap's nearly numb body points to the culture's lack of a grounding moral sense. In a culture with no moral sense, a masterfully sentimental body does not correspond to a sensible interior. As Camfield notes, the judge perceives "reality through the medium of ideal stereotypes," but "ignores particulars to the detriment of all concerned."[43] The judge is eager to place Pap into a sentimental narrative. Jane Tompkins argues that sentimentalism draws its power from stereotypes, and that stereotypes should be embraced as "the instantly recognizable representatives of overlapping racial, sexual, national, ethnic, economic, social, political, and religious categories; they convey enormous amounts of cultural information in an extremely condensed form."[44] For Tompkins, stereotyped characters are crucial for the success of sentimental narratives; stereotypes instill a community of readers with common aesthetic and linguistic expectations. In other words, stereotypes train the sentimental reader.

Twain warns us, though, that stereotypes can cloud vision and obscure judgment. The new judge, himself an unnamed stereotype for the ideal sentimental reader, saw what he wished to see—an ideal stereotype of the converted sinner. Indeed, Pap brilliantly played the part of the converted sinner, but only until sundown. The text is not only a critique of the sentimental aesthetic but is also a strike at sentimental readers. A reader steeped in sentimentalism believes that a politics of emotion is enough to change the world, that feeling right leads directly to acting right since the body is the conduit for both feeling and action. The new judge and his wife would like to be living in a sentimental world but are stuck in a world where the body is not always reliable—hands do not unproblematically reveal the truth. The touch can mislead.

If the text cannot trust touch to communicate directly, it certainly cannot trust language to convey meaning fully. Huck, narrating his escape from Pap's cabin, declares, "Everything was dead quiet, and it looked late, and *smelt* late. You know what I mean—I don't know the words to put it in" (58). At first Huck's keen synaesthetic awareness sounds like Stowe's belief that certain feelings are beyond the realm of language. Perhaps the ineffectiveness of language here is like the silence between Eliza and Mrs. Bird, marking a moment in which words cannot do justice to emotional profundity. But it is Huck, not Twain, who narrates this passage. The impossibility of conveying meaning may not be a function of language but might be the fault of the language user. Huck's inability to articulate a certain feeling may be a result of Huck's own struggles with English. Twain foregrounds the limitations of language just as he ironizes the sentimental sense that true depth of feeling resides outside the system of speech.

Yet Twain slowly and subtly aligns Huck with an earnest sentimentalism unlike that of St. Petersburg. Huck's matter-of-fact narration makes it easy for us to overlook his deep psychological trauma, but we should remember that his father, in Huck's words, "chased me round and round the place, with a clasp-knife, calling me the Angel of Death and saying he would kill me and then I couldn't come for him no more" (54). Escape, for Huck, is not a romantic game, but a drive to save his own life. While Tom Sawyer's adventures are a managerial fantasy aligned with a coercive sentimentalism, Huck's adventures are a realist narrative aligned with a moral sensibility. We can understand why Huck quickly attaches to Jim, who is stable and not a threat. Huck explains, "I warn't lonesome now. I told him I warn't afraid of *him* telling the people where I was. I talked along, but he only set there and looked at me; never said nothing" (64). Twain offers another version of silence when Jim "never said nothing." Silence here does not signify the deep connection of emotional profundity. Instead, silence contains an absence of understanding; Huck reveals the naïveté of a boy who does not fathom the seriousness of his situation. Jim's speechlessness, after all, is the strategic silence of a runaway slave.

The episode almost has a sentimental touch. Victor Doyno writes:

> In the manuscript version of this part of the novel, Huck is eager to hear why Jim is on Jackson's Island and promises to keep Jim's secret. After Jim admits that he has run away because he overheard Miss Watson talking about selling him downriver, Huck seems surprised, and Jim reminds him of this promise. Huck immediately offers to shake Jim's hand, a symbolic sealing of their agreement, as between two equals. But Twain decided to cancel that gesture of reciprocity, probably because the handshake would imply an interpersonal mutuality far too early in the novel. The relationship has to be earned through future shared experiences, and through Huck's struggle with himself in what Twain would later call a battle between "a sound heart and a deformed conscience."[45]

Twain is keenly aware of the symbolic power of hands; as Doyno makes clear, shaking hands is not only a physical contract but a social interaction that signifies intimacy. Herman Roodenburg explains about the history of the handshake, "shaking hands and other 'nonsensical minutieae' were indeed as important as matters of state. In diplomatic circles they even *were* matters of state. More generally, we may conclude that the body reflected even in its smallest gestures the value that society, this other body, attached to matters of hierarchy or equality."[46] Bodily gestures, especially in the company of silence, mean deeply. Twain avoids the sentimental touch here not because it is trite, but because it is powerful, not because it would mean too little, but because it would mean too much. Sentimentalism has to be earned.

Twain is careful to show us that the body carries meaning for the characters as much as for the readers. Jim's superstitions are rooted not just in the physical world, but in his body. He explains to Huck, "Ef you's got hairy arms en a hairy breas', it's a sign dat you's agwyne to be rich" (67). It is Jim, the slave, who most explicitly ties the body to capitalism. For the slave, who soon claims, "I owns mysef, en I's wuth eight hund'd dollars" (69), a discussion of the body quickly becomes a discussion of money.[47] Jim, as literal-minded as Huck, shows an attachment to materiality that is an absurd version of sentimentalism's quest for physical truth, for a philosophy that can be felt in the body.

The philosophy that can be felt in the body is the moral sense, whose corruption signifies a degraded culture. When Huck and Jim have a moral debate about whether "borrowing" food is actually stealing, they decide to continue borrowing as long as they stop borrowing certain items: "But towards daylight we got it all settled satisfactory, and concluded to drop crabapples and p'simmons. We warn't feeling just right, before that, but was all comfortable now" (83). Huck borrows Stowe's phrase—he and Jim "feel right." In Twain's world though, feeling right does not lead directly to moral behavior. For Huck, feeling right is feeling righteous and is a function of moral casuistry passed off as moral sense. Perhaps Twain was right to say that "No one, then, can be the better man for having the Moral Sense."[48]

Sentimentalism, so far, is small-mindedness—a narrowness of thought that is self-serving and self-congratulatory. Huck panics when he lands on the *Walter Scott*, declaring, "I catched my breath and most fainted. Shut up on a wreck with such a gang as that! But it warn't no time to be sentimentering" (87). Huck makes his own verb out of sentimentalism, as he experiences a panicky somatic reaction. But "sentimentering" is a weak verb—one of fainting, crying, and giving up hope. Sentimentalism, for Huck, is feminized inaction—an inward-looking excess of emotion that freezes the body. As we will see, though, Huck's adventures involve the recovery of a moral sense. The text will suggest that sentimentality can be redeemed.

Restoring the Moral Sense

Despite Twain's insistent degradation of sentimentalism, we can see a strand of true domesticity and earnest sentimentalism woven into what seems to be the ongoing attack on sentimentality. As in *Uncle Tom's Cabin*, hands sometimes reveal a deeper truth. Indeed, Huck's hands— or at least, his inability to properly manipulate his hands in a feminine fashion—give him away when he masquerades as a girl. Huck runs away from the stifling house of the Widow Douglas, and away from the nightmarish cabin of his Pap, but he does not run away from domesticity. The raft epitomizes a sentimental conception of domestic space; it has "a snug wigwam" (82) and is the site of safety and comfort, of intimate kinship ties.[49] For the slave and for the abused orphan, family cannot be defined by bloodlines—family is a function of intimacy, of closeness brought about by a shared moral sense.

The raft is a space defined in opposition to the world, beyond the wreck, out of contact with the shore. On the raft, Jim and Huck reflect upon the world's insanity. Jim adamantly opposes the wisdom of

Solomon, declaring, "I reck'n I knows sense when I sees it; en dey ain' no sense in sich doin's as dat" (93). Jim is not learned, but he is a moral sense philosopher, trusting the judgment of his body. Moments of earnest sentimentality begin to take place on the raft, where Jim and Huck's relationship is never ironized.

When Jim and Huck are reunited after a bewilderingly dense fog, we see that Jim's true sentimentalism has not yet fully aligned with Huck's budding moral sensibility. Jim declares, "It's too good for true, honey, it's too good for true. Lemme look at you, chile, lemme feel o'you. No, you ain' dead!" (98). Jim's joy is almost religious, as if Huck really has returned from the dead. He literally cannot believe his eyes, and must "feel" Huck. The touch is proof, securing Jim's love. Huck, in response, resists Jim's sentimentalism. In true Tom Sawyer style, Huck pretends that Jim is drunk or deluded. He wonders, "Gone away? Why, what in the nation do you mean? *I* hain't been gone anywheres. Where would I go to?" (98). Jim is baffled, "Well, looky here, boss, dey's sumf'n wrong, dey is. Is I *me*, or who *is* I? Is I heah, or what *is* I? Now dat's what I want to know?" (98). When the sentimental truth seems to have been a false epiphany, Jim calls his very being into doubt. For Jim, what lies beyond the sentimental realm is ontologically perilous. When love does not redeem, when touch no longer signifies truth, identity itself is threatened.

The moment begins to echo the new judge's disappointing sentimental experience with Pap—when the redeeming touch proved to be a lapse in reason, and when heartfelt emotion plunged into the low comedy of a drunken ass falling off a roof. Huck tries to extend the comedy routine, but soon the light of the clearing sky reveals physical proof of the journey through fog. Jim refuses to participate in the slapstick routine. Jim, "without ever smiling," tells Huck:

> When I got all wore out wid work, en wid de callin' for you, en went to sleep, my heart wuz mos' broke bekase you wuz los', en I din' k'yer no mo' what become er me en de raf'. En when I wake up en fine you back agin', all safe en soun', de tears come en I could a got down on my knees en kiss' yo' foot I's so thankful. En all you wuz thinking 'bout wuz how you could make a fool uv ole Jim wid a lie. (100)

Jim's words, containing the evidence of an authentic somatic response, ensure that the moment cannot descend into comedic farce. Jim, confessing his love in anger and humiliation, reveals a selflessness that is unmatched, a depth of love and commitment that Huck has never before encountered from anyone. On the raft, the sentimental is serious: Huck's emotions are deep, Jim's tenderness is real.

After Jim's outpouring, Huck "apologizes to a nigger," declaring, "I didn't do him no more mean tricks, and I wouldn't done that one if I'd a knowed it would make him feel that way" (100). In a moment that signals Huck's earnest sentimental convictions, Huck is concerned, above all, about Jim's emotions. Soon Huck is caught in a deep philosophical problem: "Then I thought a minute, and says to myself, hold on—spose you'd a done right and give Jim up; would you felt better than what you do now? No, says I, I'd feel bad—I'd feel just the same way I do now" (104). Huck's moral dilemma seems to lie beyond the realm of Stowe's sentimentalism. There is no way that Huck can "feel right." As postbellum readers, we can recognize that Huck's moral dilemma is a choice between his own feelings for Jim (what we recognize as the right choice) and his adherence to the standards of his society (clearly the wrong choice). Such is the gift of hindsight, of critical reflection outside the moment. In the moment, though, it is difficult to parse how one's own feelings are structured by society. Indeed, moral sense philosophy lays the groundwork for a tightly cohesive society in which the social norms of right and wrong are felt in the body, in which society's judgments are experienced as personal taste. Huck, with Twain, drifts headlong into the central problem of a society held together only by sentiment. What if society's standards of morality are, viewed from a critical distance, morally reprehensible? What if feeling right is wrong?

Huck's solution is pragmatic: "So I reckoned I wouldn't bother no more about it, but after this always do whichever come handiest at the time" (104). Huck's moral dilemma is also Twain's moral dilemma. Though neither Huck nor Twain can yet trust sentimental hands, they can trust what is handiest. What is handiest at the time, for Twain, is to interrupt the moral complexities of his text with a wreck; out of the darkness, a steamboat comes crashing through the raft. For Forrest G. Robinson, the steamboat symbolizes a psychic breakdown—a collapse from the stress of moral ambivalence.[50] But the steamboat carries more than psychological freight; the steamboat is machine technology asserting its dominance over the river. Leo Marx, in *The Machine in the Garden*, has demonstrated that a fundamental trope in American literature is the interruption of a pastoral landscape by a force of industrialization. He declares, "Much of the singular quality of this era is conveyed by the trope of the interrupted idyll. The locomotive, associated with fire, smoke, speed, iron, and noise, is the leading symbol of the new industrial power."[51] There is no railroad in *Huckleberry Finn*; Huck's description of the steamboat though, is like a train: "we could hear her pounding along" (106), "looking like a black cloud" (107), "whistling of steam" (107). Huck's anxieties about the rushing steamboat reflect Twain's anxieties about what one historian calls "the first modern, managerial enterprises"—the railroad.[52] The railroad in the 1880s, like the steamboat forty to fifty years earlier, is a symbol of relentless, destructive systematization that threatens to interrupt authentic relationships in an idyllic life. Even as he wrecks an authentic domestic space, signaling the fragility of true sentimentalism in the face of a rushing economy, Twain links the central moral dilemmas of sentimental culture to the destructive forces wrought by a new economy.

The Deep Silence

The steamboat breaks up the only authentic space of moral sensibility. When Huck leaves the raft after the accident, he forgets about Jim, and the true sentimental is lost. The feud chapters offer an extended parody of Southern gentility, beginning with the parody of a death obsession in the cult of sensibility. Emmeline Grangerford, dead at age fourteen, left an unfinished masterpiece:

> a picture of a young woman in a long white gown, standing on the
> rail of a bridge all ready to jump off, with her hair all down her
> back, and looking up to the moon, with the tears running down
> her face, and she had two arms folded across her breast, and two
> arms stretched out in front, and two more reaching up towards the
> moon. (133)

Emmeline endeavored to paint a body that would be as emotionally affecting as possible, but her blind deployment of the machinery of sentiment and her obsession with the body's potential for pathos leave a disfiguring picture.[53] Hands, once the vehicle of profound contact, have become the symbol for indulgent grotesquerie in a world that has lost its moral sense.

The Grangerford episode, like so many in Twain's text, erupts into violence. Huck's adventures, now, are no longer a playful game, nor even just an escape from physical violence, but an endeavor to stay ahead of his own psychic pain. The raft is a utopian space, but it is marred by "solid lonesomeness" (126). It is no wonder, then, that Huck eagerly helps two fleeing men onto the raft. The duke and the king are eminent hucksters; the duke's dabbling in phrenology is a major clue.[54] When the king has upstaged and outnobled the duke, jealous tension begins to rise on the raft, until the king says, "Come, give us your hand, Duke, and less all be friends" (131). Huck watches: "The duke done it, and Jim and me was pretty glad to see it. It took away all the uncomfortableness, and we felt mighty good over it, because it would a been a miserable business to have any unfriendliness on the raft; for what you want, above all things, on a raft, is for everybody to be satisfied, and feel right and kind towards the others" (131). For the duke and the king, unlike for Huck and Jim on Jackson's Island, the handshake comes quickly. The quickness of their handshake, though, is a clue to their forthcoming deception. As Roodenburg writes, hand-shakes "were matters of state" in diplomatic circles;[55] in fake diplomatic circles, handshakes are matters of deceit. Huck, as earnest as ever, still susceptible to the rote mechanics of sentimental gestures, reads the handshake as deeply meaningful. Indeed, for Huck, the touch of hands makes everybody "feel right." We know though, as Jim knows, that the duke and the king are interruptions on a utopian space. The sentimental gesture has not been earned.

The sentimental space becomes increasingly fragile. Only when the duke and the king are asleep can Twain reassert an earnest sentimentality. The progress of Huck's moral education becomes a function of closeness with Jim. Soon, Jim's body becomes fully legible to Huck:

> When I waked up, just at day-break, he was setting there with his head down betwixt his knees, moaning and mourning to himself. I didn't take notice, nor let on. I knowed what it was about. He was thinking about his wife and his children, away up yonder, and he was low and homesick; because he hadn't ever been away from home before in his life; and I do believe he cared just as much for his people as white folks does for their'n. It don't seem natural, but I reckon it's so. (155)

Huck seems to learn the central lesson of *Uncle Tom's Cabin*—that blacks are not *"things"* but "human beings, with beating hearts and living affections" (Stowe 51). We should remember, though, that Huck's moral lesson is not about blacks and high ideals, but about Jim. Still, Huck learns as Stowe would want to teach—the sight of a virtuous body in pain moves the virtuous person to recognize a common humanity. The moral center of *Adventures of Huckleberry Finn*, like the moral center of *Uncle Tom's Cabin*, ultimately relies on the legibility of the body and the adherence to a sentimental code of corporeal recognition.

As the bond between Huck and Jim tightens on the raft, Huck's moral education progresses. Their relationship becomes more and more like a parent and child, and Jim speaks about fatherhood. He remembers hitting his daughter when she ignored him, a slap that "sont her a-sprawlin'," and left her with "de tears runnin' down" (156). But when the wind slams the door shut behind her, she doesn't move. Jim declares, "My breff mos' hop outer me; en I feel so—so—I doan' know *how* I feel" (156). Jim reaches the limits of his own language.

For the realist author, nothing is unrepresentable; for the sentimental character, however, there are moments when language will not suffice. Jim continues, "Oh, Huck, I bust out a-cryin' en grab her up in my arms, en say, 'Oh, de po-little thing! De Lord G-d Amighty fogive po-ole Jim, kaze he never gwyne to fogive hisself as long's he live!' Oh, she was plumb deef en dumb, Huck, plumb deef en dumb—en I'd ben a-treat'n her so!" (156). The passage contains some of the hallmarks of sentimentalism—an emotional confession, a frail daughter who epitomizes vulnerability, tears that reveal sincerity, and a touch that endeavors to redeem. But here, when Twain deploys sentimental tropes, Jim surpasses a sentimental stereotype. Unlike Uncle Tom, Jim is not a saintly figure with messianic patience. He is, instead, an imperfect father who has made terrible mistakes and lives with deep regrets. Jim straddles sentimentalism and realism: when he is most emotionally vulnerable he is also most fully realized as a character with a psychological depth beyond a stereotype. Jim's voice leads us, with Huck, to a fuller sympathy, but it is important that the episode he narrates is one in which language does not function. It is the "deef en dumb" daughter—most crucially, it is her "mournin'," stunned, silent body—that makes Jim a more sympathetic father, and makes us more sympathetic readers.[56]

Jim's exclamation ends the conversation. As Toni Morrison points out, "Huck has nothing to say. The chapter does not close; it simply stops. Blanketed by eye dialect, placed auspiciously at chapter's end, held up, framed, as it were, for display by Huck's refusal to comment, it is one of the most moving remembrances in American literature."[57] The silence resonates. We do not get Huck searching for words, saying he does not know how to respond or can't quite explain his feelings; the text itself is silent. Now it is Twain, in a conspicuous void, who maintains the inadequacy of language. Suddenly, the text asserts a sentimental doctrine: words mean, but silent bodies mean most.

Feeling Wrong and Feeling Right

Huck, for the first time in his life, is close to a thoughtful, compassionate father. The silence that follows Jim's confession marks the height of Twain's sentimentalism. But the duke and the king continue to interrupt the idyllic raft; with their expertise in manipulating emotional language, they plunge the text away from earnest sentimentalism. In the boldest and most heinous hucksterism, the duke plays a "deaf and dumb" heir ready to claim the huge Wilks inheritance. The double of Jim's "deef en dumb" daughter is a fraud, but he is able to evoke deep emotion from an audience eager to feel. The duke and the king know the easiest way to manipulate an audience—cry. The actors almost replay a scene from *Uncle Tom's Cabin*, as they convey emotion to manipulate their audience: "they bust out a crying so you could a heard them to Orleans, most . . . I never seen two men leak the way they done. . . . Well, when it come to that, it worked the crowd like you never see anything like it, and so everybody broke down and went to sobbing right out loud—the poor girls, too" (162). Crying begets crying. Huck, at least, is appalled, claiming, "I never see anything so disgusting" (162). But the duke and king have mastered the rhetoric of sentimentalism and use it to great effect. For the king, as Huck explains, "it's a trial that's sweetened and sanctified to us by this dear sympathy and these holy tears, and so he thanks them out of his heart and out of his brother's heart, because out of their mouths they can't, words being too weak and cold" (162). The king articulates the tenets of sentimentalism. Sentimentalism no longer signifies sincerity, but the height of manipulative artifice. The duke and the king expose the mechanical qualities at the heart of sentimentalism, which has always relied on its formulaic, coded figurations. When hucksters use sentimentalism, they cleave it from the moral sense and expose the ease with which those who manage a culture of profit can manipulate crowds whose feeling is no longer grounded in a common social morality.

But if sentimentalism manipulates, it also saves. As if displaying his ambivalence, Twain oscillates quickly between huckster emotion and earnest sentimentalism. Huck's sentimental feelings for the Wilks daughters convince him that he must keep the money from the duke and the king. He develops a true sentimental bond with Mary Jane. When Huck confides in her, their bond is secured by a touch: "laying her silky hand on mine in that kind of a way that I said I would die first" (181). Mary Jane's sentimental touch coexists with her sentimental body; Huck tells her, "You ain't one of these leather-face people. I don't want no better book than what your face is. A body can set down and read it off like coarse print" (183). Even in a society where phrenology is the realm of hucksters, the earnest, truly sentimental body is still legible.

Mary Jane, though, is more complex than a stereotypical sentimental heroine. Nancy A. Walker claims that "it is precisely for her *lack* of sentimentality that Huck admires Mary Jane Wilks."[58] Walker points out that Mary Jane is responsible, intelligent, and courageous—not merely an innocent, young damsel. With Mary Jane, Twain endeavors to move beyond the typical sentimental portrayal of women. Yet her interaction with Huck has the textual hallmarks of a sentimental relationship. Both are on the verge of tears, Huck explains, when Mary Jane "shook me by the hand" and said, "I sha'n't ever forget you" (184). Huck is suddenly at his most nostalgic, "I hain't ever seen her since, but I reckon I've thought of her a many and a many a million times" (184). Even if Mary Jane is an attempt to portray a female character more complex than a heroine of domestic sensibility, Twain asserts the literary power of sentimentalism and nostalgia. Even as he self-consciously moves forward into realism, Twain acknowledges that sentimentalism is powerful not only for Huck, but for his own postbellum readers as well.[59]

Huck's decision to fully invest himself in Jim's escape comes only after a fierce internal struggle. Huck must reconcile his desire to help Jim with what he has learned from the Puritans to be a mortal sin. Crucially, he remembers that Jim "would always call me honey, and pet me, and do everything he could think of for me, and how good he always was" (202). The recognition of a physical contact that cannot lie outweighs Puritanical dogma. Huck rejects what he sees as his inherited morality and says to himself, "All right, then, I'll *go* to hell" (202). Huck's famous words are an assertion of his moral sense; he trusts his own judgment—a judgment based, above all, on feeling.

Managing the End

Huck's moral victory, though, does not close the book. Instead, we are left with the exhaustingly elaborate plans of Tom Sawyer. The evasion chapters are the most critically fraught section of the book. Lionel Trilling, in 1948, explains the ending as a device "needed to permit Huck to return to his anonymity, to give up the role of hero, to fall into the background which he prefers."[60] Leo Marx, in his 1953 "Mr. Eliot, Mr. Trilling, and *Huckleberry Finn*," famously attacks the ending as a moral lapse. For Marx, the last chapters give up on the social critique, make a burlesque out of Jim's quest for freedom, fail to take into account Huck's moral development, and turn Jim into a "submissive stage-Negro."[61] Marx declares that the critic should be concerned, first and foremost, with politics and morality: "but he cannot perform that function if he substitutes considerations of technique for considerations of truth."[62]

In his widely influential essay, Marx separates aesthetics from politics. We should remember, though, that in the sentimental worldview, aesthetics cannot be separated from politics. For Stowe, artful text should stir benevolent feelings and lead to political action. Much of the criticism of Twain's text, though, pits aesthetics against politics. For Eliot, a defender of the ending, symmetry is key: "it is right that the mood of the end of the book should bring us back to that of the beginning."[63] For Julius Lester, on the other hand, Twain's failure is moral: "Twain did not take slavery, and therefore black people, seriously."[64] The continued debate between the text's aesthetic value and its potentially pernicious political consequences points to the central ambivalence of the text itself. The terms of the critical conversation—aesthetics versus politics—mark the breakdown of moral sense philosophy, which asserted that aesthetics and politics were coextensive. We see this breakdown of moral sense philosophy most clearly in the ending, the site of Twain's most scathing attack on his sentimental and romantic cultural inheritance.

The ending serves simultaneously as a final critique of unquestioning adherence to a textual inheritance and a final strike against managerialism. No wonder that critics have seen the ending as a lapse in Twain; indeed, the text experiences a literal lapse, as Huck Finn himself becomes known as Tom Sawyer. Huck tells us that "Being Tom Sawyer was easy and comfortable" (210); ease and comfort should signal a warning, though, for the raft "felt mighty free and easy and comfortable" (125), even as it drifted south toward trouble. Tom, playing his brother Sid, quickly takes over the escape plans for Jim. Tom becomes the complicating factor as he begins to manage the escape, declaring that Huck's plan is "too blame' simple" (217). When Jim and Huck haul a grindstone back to Jim's hut for Jim to carve "mournful inscriptions" (239), Huck explains, "Tom superintended. He could out-superintend any boy I ever see" (240). As the leader who manipulates but does not actually add his own labor to the work process, Tom is a parody of the middle manager of Twain's America.

Once again Twain ties literary manipulation to economic manipulation, as Tom becomes the yoke between coercive text and coercive capitalism. Tom's plans become more and more ridiculous as he insists on the absurd artifice of a romance novel escape for Jim. Tom adheres to what Harry Braverman would define as the third principle of scientific management: the use of a "monopoly over knowledge to control each step of the labor process and its mode of execution."[65] Tom, the manager who is removed from physical work, cultivates ignorance in his workers just as he asserts the infallibility of his own knowledge. Twain distinguishes the cheap melodrama on the shore from the true sentimental drama on the raft—the idealized, premanagerial space. Huck, though, is not in on the joke, and, most important, neither is Jim. Jim can do nothing but put his trust in the boys. When Huck explains that "Jim only had time to grab us by the hand and squeeze" (221), we know that Jim is earnest. Bodily contact, for Jim, remains the most meaningful form of expression. Critics have long argued that Jim's sincerity and submissiveness in the midst of Tom's burlesque is an unexplainable collapse of Jim's character. But as Leslie Fiedler explains:

> In the first place, the essential virtue of Huck and Jim is to endure whatever befalls them; and to them, moreover, there is nothing any more ridiculous about what Tom does than there is about what society inflicts on them every day. After all, what can a man, who all his life has known *he can be sold*, find more absurd than that? To Huck as well as Jim, all heroism and all suffering are equally "unreal," equally asinine.[66]

Jim's acceptance of his absurd conditions, like Huck's early acceptance of genies, is a critique of a society in which workers do not question their labor because social conditions leave them no other choice, and in which inexplicable cruelty is normal. Twain offers a portrait of an ugly culture whose members accept the most vicious institutions.

Jim's unwillingness to object forcefully to Tom's cruel whims, his virtual silence in the face of white power, becomes a literal silence after he is caught. Huck explains, "They cussed Jim considerable, though, and give him a cuff or two, side the head, once in a while, but Jim never said nothing, and he never let on to know me" (258). Jim's silence now is strategic.[67] Indeed, silence is an effective technique for Jim; the doctor who captures Jim declares, "the nigger never made the least row nor said a word, from the start. He ain't no bad nigger, gentlemen" (259). Jim plays the role of Uncle Tom, submissive and quietly resolute in the face of oppression. But Jim's silence, unlike Uncle Tom's quietude, is inscrutable for characters and readers alike. Here, silence is not just a literary technique for Twain, but a survival technique for Jim. Jim is the opposite of the voluble Tom Sawyer, who reveals everything. It turns out, of course, that Tom's transgression of the law was make-believe, that Jim was free the whole time. The institution of slavery remains undisturbed; in fact, Jim should be thankful to his former owner. The quest is rendered irrelevant.

When Jim finally does break his silence, his first words are, "*Dah*, now, Huck, what I tell you?—what I tell you up dah on Jackon islan'? I *tole* you I got a hairy breas', en what's de sign un it; en I *tole* you I ben rich wunst, en gwineter to be rich *agin*" (264). Jim speaks to assert the authority of his body. In this way Jim is a throwback to sentimentalism—the body is the ultimate source of meaning. But significantly, at the moment Jim proclaims the power of his body he asserts the power of his voice. Jim's repetition and Twain's stress of "tell" and "tole" shift authority from the body to the word. It is important that Jim has a hairy breast, but it is more important that he *told* Huck that he had a hairy breast. Just as Jim asserts a sentimental conception of materiality—that the body contains the truth—he asserts a realist doctrine, that words mean most of all.

Jim embodies the vexed relationship Twain has with his literary predecessors. Jim is at once the victim of an abusive, coercive literature and the living proof of a deep moral sense. He is also the victim of Tom's managerial scheme and so becomes the embodiment of Twain's anxiety concerning the social changes brought forth with a new economy. Huck is eager to escape this civilization, ready to "light out for the Territory." But readers know it is only a matter of time before railroads crosshatch the West. Huck, too, knows; he only wants to light out "ahead of the rest" (265). As for the boy-rebel Tom—the manager of this story—he is once again the civilizing force. Our last view of him is with his watch: "Tom's most well, now, and got his bullet around his neck on a watch-guard for a watch, and is always seeing what time it is" (265). As long as Tom is in the story (which he promises to be), we will always be reminded of the link to a larger, systematized world.

Tom's bullet-watch contains the same tensions that we find within Tom himself. The bullet-watch is a prop—a nostalgic trophy that brings pleasure. But the bullet-watch is also an explosive weapon—an object of true violence, the thing that can kill. Tom likes to think of himself as a clever, imaginative robber outlaw, but his actions have had real and devastating consequences. The dialectic that Tom and his bullet-watch embody is the same one that governs Twain's relationship with sentimentalism. On the one hand, sentimentalism is an absurd, even hilarious fantasy—a throwback to the age of legible bodies, grand gestures, and ever-present feeling. On the other hand, sentimentalism signals deep involvement with high-stakes politics—offering proof of the way that language itself and the emotions it unleashes can determine issues of slavery and freedom, death and life. Since Tom is the champion of both cheap sentimentalism and abusive managerialism, the book suggests that we can laugh at both just as it insists that we should take both seriously.

The bullet and the watch—symbols for violence and time-manipulation—seem to be the material inspiration for Twain's next novel. In *A Connecticut Yankee in King Arthur's Court*, as I suggested in the opening of this chapter, to be managerial is to be coercive and violent. The Yankee is a managerial-class dictator who commands mass violence but also invites and indulges in melodramatic scenes of weeping. As Chadwick Hansen writes, the Yankee's feelings "are not really a matter of sympathy for others, but an emotional bath for himself."[68] In the Yankee's world, mechanical industry rules all, including feeling—which proves easily susceptible to mechanical reproduction. The Yankee is Tom professionalized, grown up, and unleashed. The implicit and episodic violence of *Huckleberry Finn* is made explicit and spectacular in *A Connecticut Yankee*. As he did with Tom in *Huckleberry Finn*, Twain aligns the cruelty of managerialism with the coercive qualities of false sentimentalism. While Tom's boss-fantasies were limited by his adolescence, the Yankee's managerial fantasies are unchecked. Near the end of *A Connecticut Yankee*, the Yankee declares in triumph: "The campaign was ended, we fifty-four were masters of England! Twenty-five thousand men lay dead around us" (405). Tom's bullet-watch turns out to be a compressed warning about what is to come.

A Connecticut Yankee offers a dystopic vision of a world with a grown-up Tom Sawyer in charge, but the end of *Adventures of Huckleberry Finn* is happy. Twain has been widely criticized for succumbing to the form of a happy ending. Indeed, the silliness of the final romance plot does not fit with the seriousness of the quest. But Twain's ultimate invocation of a formal ending—the text ends "Yours truly, Huck Finn"—shows the author's keen awareness of the absurdities of form. A narrative that has continually warned us about the difficulty of gleaning truth from texts ends "truly." Since Huck offers the ending of a letter in what is not an epistolary novel, Huck's final words invite us to question his sincerity. He uses a literary convention when it does not fit, just as Twain has both attacked and deployed sentimental conventions. Our struggle to assess the truth of Huck's "truly" mirrors Twain's struggle to realize the truth of sentimental bodies. Under a managerial regime, the sentimental touch has lasted (in fact, it has been Taylorized), but the moral sense has been lost—given up by hucksters and managers and a population eager to feel right without acting right. Sentimental gestures once signaled the deep communal bonds that held society together, bonds powerful enough to threaten the institution of slavery, but now testify to a culture that has lost its moral intuition. The sentimental touch, like "Yours truly," is a literary convention that jars when it does not seem to fit, but that also suggests a lurking authenticity and a latent moral force that can emerge even in the face of an antagonistic culture.

3 / Holding On to the Sentimental in *Winesburg, Ohio*

Winesburg, Ohio, fittingly subtitled *A Group of Tales of Ohio Small Town Life*, does not offer a sustained, conventional plot; there is no single unifying narrative. The sudden shifts and starts that mark the movement from one tale to the next show how Anderson self-consciously sets his text against the novel form.[1] But even as the form of Anderson's text suggests something new, *Winesburg, Ohio* still acts like a novel by offering a deep psychological portrait of individuals at a certain place in a certain time. To use the language of Ian Watt, the action is "acted out by particular people in particular circumstances."[2]

While Anderson seeks to avoid the formal qualifications of the novel, so, too, does he seek to elude the sentimental trappings of the novel. As he wrote to Arthur Barton, "What I think we want to do is to get away from the idea of making the small town ridiculous or too dreary or sentimental."[3] Indeed, Anderson's portrayal of "Ohio Small Town Life" is not idyllic; where we might expect to find a nostalgic depiction of uncorrupted pastoral life we instead find unfulfilled dreams, outbursts of violence, and characters racked by guilt and jealousy. Even in a town not fully corrupted by the ravages of modernity, loneliness is enveloping, and neuroses are overwhelming.

However, just as the text acts like a novel even when it declares itself antinovelistic, so does the text persist in using sentimental tropes even as it sets out to be unsentimental. We readers, along with Alice Hindman, the clerk in Winney's dry goods store, must force ourselves "to face bravely the fact that many people must live and die alone, even in

Winesburg."[4] The text is centrally concerned with touching the reader, and like the sentimental novels of the nineteenth century, we readers are touched when characters are touched, and finally, when characters touch.

While we are moved by characters as we trace their emotional sensitivities, we are also moved by the narrator as we follow the text from one story to the next; the characters move our emotion, the narrator moves our attention. Both movements are jarring—we are surprised by the abrupt wrenchings of tough characters suddenly become tender, or of tender characters suddenly become tough; and we are surprised by the severe demands made on us by the narrator, as we move quickly from "Mother" to "The Philosopher," or from "The Untold Lie" to "Drink."[5] The emotional drive in the story, as we will see, is a reaction to a certain mode of alienation and loneliness that comes with the growth of managerial capitalism. Anderson shows how the cultural changes that came with the expansive bureaucratization of American business threaten the personal relationships that once promised to sustain American life.

The narrative drive of the story, like the emotional drive, is also a reaction to an economy that has grown increasingly impersonal. Indeed, the narrator subjects us to a managerial style of narration. While in *Adventures of Huckleberry Finn* characters manipulated one another in a stream of managerial schemes, in *Winesburg, Ohio* readers are manipulated by a narrator-manager. If the ambition of realist literature was to present an objective account of the world—in other words, to have no style—the modernist ambition is to make literary style reflect a specific worldview.[6] Anderson's managerial aesthetic suggests that the literary world responds to the economic world: when the visible hand of the manager replaces the invisible hand of market forces, the visible hand of the modernist writer replaces the invisible hand of the realist narrator. The figure of the manager will loom large in *Winesburg, Ohio*, not just invoked by the figures in the text, but by the structure of the narrative itself.

Surface Tension

Anderson's relationship with his literary inheritance is simultaneously one of self-conscious rupture and unconscious connection. Like many of the modernists, Anderson set out to forge a new literary path during the upheaval of the early twentieth century. Anderson was born in 1876, and by 1919 had lived through many of the vast cultural changes that marked the era around the turn of the century. In "Godliness," the sixth tale of *Winesburg, Ohio*, Anderson writes:

> A revolution has in fact taken place. The coming of industrialism, attended by all the roar and rattle of affairs, the shrill cries of millions of new voices that have come among us from overseas, the going and coming of trains, the growth of cities, the building of the interurban car lines that weave in and out of towns and past farmhouses, and now in these later days the coming of the automobiles has worked a tremendous change in the lives and in the habits of thought of our people of Mid-America. Books, badly imagined and written though they may be in the hurry of our times, are in every household, magazines circulate by the millions of copies, newspapers are everywhere. (52–53)

For Anderson, the revolution is a cultural sea change by way of new technologies, massive immigration, urbanization, and transformations in communication and transportation. The revolution has changed not only the behavior of Americans but also "the habits of thought of our people."

Anderson traces the change in the interior lives of mid-Americans by charting the spread of books, magazines, and newspapers.[7] Anderson continues:

> In our day a farmer standing by the stove in the store in his village has his mind filled to overflowing with the words of other men. The newspapers and the magazines have pumped him full. Much of the old brutal ignorance that had in it also a kind of beautiful childlike innocence is gone forever. The farmer by the stove is brother to the men of the cities, and if you listen you will find him talking as glibly and as senselessly as the best city man of us all. (53)

Changing literary developments match the changing culture, as big business media replaces face-to-face interactions and down-home knowledge. Anderson's description of the growing role of the printed word in America, like much of *Winesburg, Ohio*, simultaneously spurns "the old brutal ignorance" and yearns for the "beautiful childlike innocence" that was lost alongside. The new age brings a new national brotherhood but also a new national senselessness. Crucially, Anderson asserts and demonstrates that a changing culture has a literary response; the narrator cites practices of writing and reading to draw conclusions about society. Just as Anderson traces the cultural changes of America through books, so, too, can we track the cultural change that his own book suggests by examining the text's relationship to changes in literature.

Anderson introduces his list of revolutionary changes with "the coming of industrialism," yet the anxieties that rack Winesburg are not primarily driven by industrialization; industrialism has not yet come to Winesburg. Nor can urbanization be the central concern of the residents; Winesburg, after all, is a "Small Town." Anderson does not explicitly mention the new prevalence of managerial capitalism, but the depersonalization of the economy penetrated sectors of American life far away from cities and factories.[8] Managerial culture is a unifying factor in "the going and coming of trains, the growth of cities, the building of the interurban car lines." Indeed, managerialism first emerged in the railroads, where the demands of a collectively owned industry that spanned thousands of miles required a new class of managers to oversee daily operations. Managerial culture spread as quickly as tracks were laid across the country. In the 1870s and 1880s, fully operating railroad and telegraph networks hastened company mergers, and thus hastened the growth of large companies that needed managers. By the second decade of the twentieth century, the managerial innovations of the railroad industry penetrated almost every sector of the large-scale American economy.[9] There had been a true revolution in the business world; as Alfred D. Chandler writes in 1977, a "businessman of today would find himself at home in the business world of 1910, but the business world of 1840 would be a strange, archaic, and arcane place."[10] Managerial culture lurks underneath Anderson's explicit invocations of the Industrial Revolution; the social anxieties of managerial culture lurk, too, beneath the narrative of *Winesburg, Ohio*.

Anderson himself controlled a paint factory before he abruptly quit to devote himself to literature.[11] He writes of this time in *A Story Teller's Story*: "What were the other men thinking about? What was I thinking about? Suppose it were possible to know something of the men and women, to know something of oneself, too. The devil!"[12] As a businessman, Anderson was baffled by his fellows and baffled by himself.[13] Critics have long recognized the overwhelming cultural alienation that hangs over the characters in Winesburg. Irving Howe articulates the critical consensus of the mid-twentieth century when he writes that "the book's major characters are alienated from the basic sources of emotional sustenance . . . and, most catastrophic of all, from each other, the very extremity of their need for love having itself become a barrier to its realization."[14] Howe describes a society without community; townspeople are connected not through deep mutual understandings grounded by a sense of place, but only, ironically, by their mutual senses of isolation and desperation. "The feeling of loneliness and isolation," as Anderson writes, comes even "in the crowded streets" of town (224). The world of Winesburg is one of abstract connections, of passive relationships with life, of joyless work, and of unknowing individuals who do not realize the depth of their malaise.

Many critics have pointed to Anderson's treatment of a culture moving toward mechanization and industrialization. As John H. Ferres writes, *Winesburg, Ohio* is "our most sensitive literary record of the human effects of the transition from an agrarian to an industrial-technological age in the American small town."[15] Critics have not, though, linked Anderson's work to managerial capitalism. The concept of managerialism is both more expansive and more specific than a term like "industrialization." Managerial capitalism underlies massive societal changes, industrial or otherwise. Managerialism, too, refers specifically to relationships between and among people in a mystifying, swiftly changing environment.[16] By thinking about *Winesburg, Ohio* in terms of managerial culture, we link the text to changes in modernity's social structure—an implicit subject of the text—and to the problem of human contact, the explicit subject of most of Anderson's tales. Most important, a concern with managerial capitalism links the subject matter of *Winesburg, Ohio* to its form.

Anderson was obsessed with creating a literature that reflected the new realities of American society. As he wrote to Van Wyck Brooks in 1919, "the novel form does not fit an American writer. It is a form which has been brought in. What is wanted is a new looseness; and in *Winesburg* I made my own form."[17] Anderson endeavors to form a more perfect union between literature and society; the task is urgent, for the institutions that might have sustained the Winesburg psyche are collapsing. For Anderson, middle America, once thought to be the robust center of a thriving United States, is in crisis.

Likewise for the modernist, the institutions that have sustained Western culture are crumbling. The modernist mind yearns for a coherence and unity that is absent in early twentieth-century life—where religious, artistic, social, and political structures cannot be relied upon—and so seeks wholeness in aesthetics and language. T. S. Eliot proclaimed in 1923 that "the novel is a form which will no longer serve."[18] For Eliot, the modernist writer should not fade into obsolescence with the novel, which "ended with Flaubert and with James," but should venture to give "a shape and significance to the immense panorama of futility and anarchy which is contemporary history."[19] Anderson's concern with form seems to have anticipated Eliot's declaration of a new literature for a new time; the writer can offer structure to what seems shapeless. Indeed, characters in *Winesburg* are drawn to the young writer George Willard precisely because his writing promises to offer "a shape and significance" to the "futility and anarchy" of their lives. The narrator, meanwhile, manages the futility and anarchy of the entire town by controlling a narrative that is at once ordered and random. Reading *Winesburg, Ohio* is navigating through a network of characters whose links only crystallize when we take a wide-angle view of the entire story. Stepping back from the text, we can see how the narratives intertwine, how stories are linked by common characters, and how characters are linked by a common place. The town, though, is never fully revealed—relationships remain hidden and unexplained, and the rationale behind the order of the stories is never made clear. It is significant that the narrator engages in the very arbitrariness of modern life that his text seeks to control; the manager, after all, is himself a part of the giant network he runs. The narrator shapes a culture of management, but the culture of management also shapes the narrator.

Anderson, most critics agree, is a modernist. Michael Bell offers a concise explanation of modernist philosophy as a metaphysics of hermeneutics: "It is not just that external appearances, and the commonsensical or rational means of understanding them, are limited and fallible. It is that such appearances and reasoning may be actively disguising contrary truths to which, by definition, there is no other access."[20] The modernist mind must look beyond surfaces to find the truth; only after interpretation might we find a buried revelation. Modernist thought, then, is the epistemological opposite of the sentimental worldview.[21] For the sentimentalist, we can access truth immediately from our reactions to surfaces; we know a virtuous body when we see one. For the modernist, the body can mislead, for below its surfaces are the elaborate workings of mysterious, mystified structures. Critics were quick to point out not only Anderson's formal experimentation but also his apparently Freudian interest in the sexual lives of his characters.[22] The book's dedication is to the author's mother, Anderson writes, "whose keen observation on the life about her first awoke in me the hunger to see beneath the surface of lives." Like Marx, Freud, and Nietzsche—the three thinkers most often cited as the progenitors of modernist sensibility—Anderson distrusts the surface.[23] Beneath Anderson's modernist aesthetics, though, lies the thoughtful portrayal of a maturing young man. As Rita Barnard observes, "the experimental interest of Sherwood Anderson's story cycle *Winesburg, Ohio* derives from a generic oscillation between the traditional *Bildungsroman* and a form of serial composition that owes much to Stein."[24] *Winesburg, Ohio* simultaneously offers the fractured consciousness of the modern mind and the earnest, novelistic development of George Willard.

Anderson's seemingly conflicted sensibility is in fact typical of the American mind in the early decades of the twentieth century. According to the historian Lawrence W. Levine:

> The central paradox of American history, then, has been a belief in a progress coupled with a dread of change; an urge towards the inevitable future combined with a longing for the irretrievable past; a deeply ingrained belief in America's unfolding destiny and a haunting conviction that the nation was in a state of decline. This duality has been marked throughout most of America's history but seldom has it been more central than during the decade after the First World War.[25]

Anderson's use of sentimental tropes is his reach for "the irretrievable past" in a world looking toward the future. The fading of sentimentality is a sign of both literary progress and irredeemable loss.

Anderson's careful deployment of sentimental contact, as we will see, is both symptomatic and diagnostic of modernity. At first, *Winesburg, Ohio* manifests a distrust of surfaces and bodies. Even the most basic communication is a fierce struggle in the modern world, and characters who rely on their bodies and instinctive reactions are utterly lost. Characters who most display the traits of sentimentality—Wing Biddlebaum and Wash Williams—are misunderstood in catastrophic ways. In Winesburg, trust in others is a sign of calamitous naïveté.[26] The forms of the nineteenth century, for the characters and the author alike, should be cast off in the new age.

Wing Biddlebaum and Wash Williams are lost in the world of the manager, but it is precisely their overwhelming sense of alienation that marks them as characters in a modern text. As Michael Levenson argues in *Modernism and the Fate of Individuality*, "the struggle between character and form often takes the aspect of a conflict between tradition and modernity. . . . One way to understand this moment of transition in the history of the novel is in terms of nineteenth-century characters seeking to find a place in twentieth-century forms."[27] Levenson's analysis is especially apt for *Winesburg, Ohio*, where the drama between sentimental character and modernist form is heightened by a narrator who seems to pluck characters from a lost time and drop them into a crucible of detached stories in an unsympathetic world. Levenson continues: "The pressures of social structure stand in close and provocative analogy to the pressures of literary structure. The dislocation of the self within society is recapitulated, reenacted, reconsidered, in the dislocation of character within modernist forms."[28] The pressures of social structure and literary structure combine to crush the likes of Wing Biddlebaum and Wash Williams. Anderson will not even follow their struggles after their stories are quickly and efficiently related; the text flies from Wing and cleanses itself of Wash. Wing and Wash, victims of both managerial social structure and managerial literary structure, disappear into the machinery of the text, obscure and lonely figures in a giant network.

As managerial networks harden, as the prescribed relationships solidify between individuals in a capitalist society, new ways of communication are necessary. For characters in the text, this means that sentimental understanding will no longer do; for the author, this means that the traditional novel will not suffice. Indeed, Edwin Fussell, among other critics, celebrates "Anderson's remarkable vision of humanity, a vision tender without sentimentality."[29] But with the hardening of managerial networks also comes the hardening of cultural forms. Anderson, even as he sets out to cast aside the literary devices of the past age, cannot entirely escape his literary inheritance. The only truly successful mode of communication in *Winesburg, Ohio*, ultimately, is the sentimental touch.

Grotesque Communication

The mysterious prologue of *Winesburg, Ohio*, called "The Book of the Grotesque," contains two unnamed characters—a writer and a carpenter. The two old men move from discussing plans for fixing the writer's bed to discussing the legacy of the Civil War. The foundation of Anderson's text simultaneously invokes construction and Reconstruction; *Winesburg, Ohio* begins with building, writing, and moving on from the trauma of the Civil War. The two old men look alike, both with white mustaches, as if to suggest that writing, like carpentry, is a self-conscious craft, and that artificial, thoughtful forms of creation are how best to deal with the plight of history. Here is Anderson as a modernist; the artist must redeem human life from the pain of society's failures. James Schevill notes that the writer in "The Book of the Grotesque" is "a symbolic, Mark Twain–like figure with his white mustache, cigars, and Joan of Arc fantasies hovering in his memories."[30] Twain is a suitable icon for a book that endeavors to plumb the national spirit in a portrayal of middle America.[31] But if Twain is an inspiration for Anderson, he is also a specter whose influence must be overcome.

After the main character and the very title of "The Book of the Grotesque" invoke writing, the narrator describes the futility of writing. The writer's plan for raising the bed is "forgotten" (3), and soon the writer is lying still, calmly, paradoxically ready to "some time die unexpectedly" (4). The narrator explains that the thought of impending death "did not alarm" the writer, that the "effect in fact was quite a special thing and not easily explained" (4). The narrator seems baffled and declares that the writer "was like a pregnant woman, only that the thing inside him was not a baby but a youth. No, it wasn't a youth, it was a woman, young, and wearing a coat of mail like a knight. It is absurd, you see, to try to tell what was inside the old writer as he lay on his high bed and listened to the fluttering of his heart" (4). The narrator, suddenly, cannot narrate. More precisely, the narrator cannot describe. We cannot tell if the breakdown in description is a failure of the writer to understand his own interior, a failure of the narrator to access the interior of the "Mark Twain–like figure," or a failure of language to articulate an unspoken thought. Undoubtedly, though, a failure of communication haunts the beginning of Anderson's text.

The failure of literary communication, in combination with the "Mark Twain–like figure" waiting to die, signals the imminent death of realism. If the artist using his craft to redeem humanity represented modernism, the artist as a dying writer represents realism. Indeed, as the realist writer ends his domination of American letters, the craftsman with whom he is aligned—here a carpenter—ends his reign in the American economy. As David Montgomery writes, "new methods of industrial management undermined the very foundation of craftsmen's functional autonomy. Job analysis through time and motion study allowed management to learn, then to systematize the way the work itself was done."[32] The craftsman, like the realist writer, symbolizes an old way of conducting business.

The writer, as authorial archetype and dying specter, as redemptive artist and fading craftsman, embodies the tensions that we find in Anderson himself. Anderson is an experimental writer eager to create his "own form," yet he is a throwback to the sentimental novelist. Anderson viewed himself as an author of another age. The very title of *A*

Story Teller's Story—one of Anderson's several autobiographical works—shows that Anderson conceived himself as a prenovelistic writer. As Walter Benjamin tells us, storytelling is an old form of communication that depends on the personal presence we find only in tight communities. When a community of listeners disappears, so fades the storyteller. In his 1936 essay "The Storyteller: Reflections on the Work of Nikolai Leskov," Benjamin writes:

> That old co-ordination of the soul, the eye, and the hand which emerges in Valery's words is that of the artisan which we encounter wherever the art of storytelling is at home. In fact, one can go on and ask oneself whether the relationship of the storyteller to his material, human life, is not in itself a craftsman's relationship, whether it is not his very task to fashion the raw material of experience, his own and that of others, in a solid, useful, and unique way.[33]

The storyteller is to the novelist what the craftsman is to the managed laborer; when society becomes a collection of isolated individuals, when artisans turn into workers (to use the historian Bruce Laurie's resonant language),[34] storytelling vanishes. Anderson aspires to be both artisan and storyteller.[35] Yet, as he repeatedly acknowledges, he is stuck in an age absent of deep community, where the craftsman may have lost his place, where the body is not always a coherent whole. The old writer and the carpenter teeter on the edge of obsolescence, but the narrator will not let them die.

As the narrator continues, the gap between writing and the mind grows wider: the writer has "a dream that was not a dream," then imagines that a "young, indescribable thing within himself was driving a long procession of figures before his eyes" (4). The "indescribable thing" suggests that any attempt to name the interior drive of the writer will be an inaccurate linguistic imposition, a gross violation of the truth. No wonder, then, that the procession of figures inspires the writer to write "The Book of the Grotesque." Huck Finn warned us that his creator was a liar, but "The Book of the Grotesque" suggests a falseness that is not a function of lying or misleading. The narrator explains the writer's theory of the grotesque: people make themselves grotesques when they grasp on to a single truth and become blind to the rest of the world. The writer's notion is that "the moment one of the people took one of the truths to himself, called it his truth, and tried to live his life by it, he became a grotesque and the truth he embraced became a falsehood" (6). The grotesque has a simplified, obscured vision of the universe—as if gazing through a fish-eye lens, the grotesque focuses on a single point as the periphery remains always askew.[36]

Anderson's self-referential title, "The Book of the Grotesque" (originally the title of the entire work), suggests first that the characters are grotesques, but also that the writer and narrator might be grotesques (it is their book), and that we are grotesques while we read and possess the book. Anderson alerts us to the impossibility of transparent communication. Because we cannot navigate precisely between ideas and words, we must grasp on to the words we have, knowing full well that most of what might be worth saying is "indescribable." The gap between the text and the world does not distinguish *Winesburg, Ohio* from the other texts in this study. Indeed, *Uncle Tom's Cabin* is a text that posits that feeling is truer than text; *Adventures of Huckleberry Finn* is a text that declares that its creator is not trustworthy. *Winesburg, Ohio*, like the works of Stowe and Twain, warns us of the elusiveness of textual truth. What separates Anderson's work from his predecessors, and what makes Anderson especially modernist, is the foregrounding of the problem of language in the face of deep, inaccessible truths.[37] *Winesburg, Ohio*, both a "Group of Tales" and a "Book of the Grotesque," is obsessed with its own medium.

With "The Book of the Grotesque"—a meditation on the problems of writing and the writer—the narrator brings attention to himself as a manager of the text. His hand in shaping the story is immediately visible. Indeed, the narrator's admission that the words he chooses may not adequately match his nebulous thoughts does not undermine his narratorial power, but serves to strengthen his presence. The managerial hand may be inept or even random, but as our only access to the text, it reminds us that our experience of life in *Winesburg, Ohio* is a function of human manipulations. We will never forget that writing, first and foremost, is the work of hands.[38]

Anderson's invocation of the old writer in the guise of Mark Twain is an acknowledgment of the literature of an earlier generation and also a signal that the writings of a previous age may not suffice. The old writer brings with him a parade of grotesques, ready to give testimony to an age of disintegrating truths. As Geoffrey Harpham declares in "The Grotesque: First Principles," "The plain assumption of the grotesque is that the rules of order have collapsed; for this reason it is strongest in eras of upheaval or crisis, when old beliefs in old orders are threatened or crumbling."[39] *Winesburg, Ohio* is about the crumbling of "old beliefs in old orders." However,

Anderson follows the old orders more than he may realize. Anderson yearns to break free from an earlier generation, but we will see that he has inherited the literary codings of the past age. The old writer may be feeble and mostly bedridden, but he still looms over the text.

"The Book of the Grotesque," finally, is about the struggle to access the truth. Truth, in the sentimental tradition, lies in the realm of the body; we can trust the materiality of our bodies, for there is a direct relation between interiority and physicality. Grotesques problematize the relation of the body to the world. The radical distortion of the grotesque may suggest a misshapen soul, or it may suggest a body that is untrustworthy, from which we cannot draw moral conclusions. We should remember, too, that the grotesque figure is defined by the figure's society. As Harpham explains, "the grotesque depends not only on physical conditions the deformity of which most people would recognize, but also on our conventions, our prejudices, our commonplaces, our banalities, our mediocrities. . . . Each age redefines the grotesque in terms of what threatens its sense of essential humanity."[40] If, for Anderson, fixing on a single truth at the expense of the rest of the world threatens his "sense of essential humanity," we must conclude that Anderson's world—the modernist world—is one where truth is not easily grasped, where trying to hold on to a single truth is an act of those who are deformed.

In such a world, the sentimental touch should not work. An act where two characters share a single truth through their bodies seems doubly impossible: there are no reliable bodies, and truths lurk far below the surface. The sentimental bodies in Anderson's work are utterly lost in the modernist age. The grotesques struggle through life but cannot articulate their struggle. They look to George, the writer, to give them a voice when they cannot speak. As Doctor Parcival pleads, "You must pay attention to me. . . . If something happens perhaps you will be able to write the book that I may never get written" (38–39). The doctor pleads for attention not to fulfill an immediate need, but so that his book may be written. In a world of grotesques—where the most basic modes of communication are threatened—the fundamental problem is how to write. Conveying struggle, documenting emotion—as Harriet Beecher Stowe would surely agree—remains the central task of the writer.

Fallen Wing

The first tale in *Winesburg, Ohio* is called "Hands."[41] Touch is central, even before the story begins. The narrator tells us that the "story of Wing

Biddlebaum is a story of hands" (9). We begin in a world where it seems, once again, that we can access the character through the body, where the sentimental touch will be possible. But the story continues: "The hands alarmed their owner. He wanted to keep them hidden away and looked with amazement at the quiet inexpressive hands of other men who worked beside him in the fields, or passed, driving sleepy teams on country roads" (10). Anderson's use of "owner" to describe Wing's relationship to his own hands is alarming, since it signifies a split between body and subjectivity. The word reminds us that ownership carries a new connotation in the managerial age, since owners no longer ran the businesses they possessed.[42] Wing's alienation from his own body, dramatizing the break between ownership and management, signals a new cultural disembodiment.[43]

At first glance, we see a fracture between physicality and character, separating Wing's consciousness and his hands. But Wing's hands are not merely objects; indeed, he is jealous of the "inexpressive hands of other men." The narrator insists that an investigation into the hands will reveal a deep truth, telling us, "The story of Wing Biddlebaum's hands is worth a book in itself" (10). Anderson's use of "book" to denote "worth" emphasizes his modernist belief in the value of aesthetic objects in the face of elusive truths. The narrator foregrounds his own hand in the creation of textual worth and will not let us forget his managerial role.[44]

The hands become an overdetermined signifier; hands signify the character, even when there is no longer a direct link between the character and the hands. The human is hidden behind entities that falsely stand for the human. The narrator continues, "in Winesburg the hands had attracted attention merely because of their activity. . . . They became his distinguishing feature, the source of his fame" (10). The importance of the hands has eclipsed the importance of the man. Indeed, when hands exist outside the realm of subjectivity, when fingers lack a human imprint, we are alienated beyond, even, the realm of Marx's fetishized commodities. Marx writes, "the products of the human brain appear as autonomous figures endowed with a life of their own, which enter into relations both with each other and with the human race. So it is in the world of commodities with the products of men's hands."[45] In Anderson's text, the hands themselves replace "the products of men's hands." The world of commodities has turned upon the worker. The hands take on "a life of their own," as if there is a true social relation between the hands and Wing, between the hands and the world.

Wing's hands fascinate George Willard. Anderson writes, "As for George Willard, he had many times wanted to ask about the hands. At times an almost overwhelming curiosity had taken hold of him" (10). George walks with Wing in an effort to get close to Wing's hands. Wing begins to open up to George, until:

> Pausing in his speech, Wing Biddlebaum looked long and earnestly at George Willard. His eyes glowed. Again he raised the hands to caress the boy and then a look of horror swept over his face.
>
> With a convulsive movement of his body, Wing Biddlebaum sprang to his feet and thrust his hands deep into his trousers pockets. Tears came to his eyes. "I must be getting along home. I can talk no more with you," he said nervously. (11–12)

Wing's long and earnest look, his glowing eyes, reveals the deep connection between Wing and George. As in *Uncle Tom's Cabin* and *Adventures of Huckleberry Finn*, the touch will verify and secure the relationship. There is no touch, though; instead, there is "horror" and mysterious shame. Tears, the ultimate somatic reaction, no longer signify a sentimental moment in which bodies share a deep understanding. Rather, tears signify the separation of bodies, and a body alienated from itself.

We soon learn the traumatic background of the hands' mystery. Wing Biddlebaum was formerly Adolph Myers, a teacher who would fit well in the world of the sentimental novel. Biddlebaum's past mirrors the literary past. He was a loving teacher who touched his boys:

> Here and there went his hands, caressing the shoulders of the boys, playing about the tousled heads. As he talked his voice became soft and musical. . . . In a way the voice and the hands, the stroking of the shoulders and the touching of the hair were a part of the schoolmaster's effort to carry a dream into the young minds. By the caress that was in his fingers he expressed himself. . . . Under the caress of his hands doubt and disbelief went out of the minds of the boys and they began also to dream. (13)

The interaction between bodies provided the most direct connection between minds. The teacher was a master of the sentimental touch; his caressing hands were an extension of his "soft and musical" voice, itself an extension of his sensitive character. Adolph's hands were the passageway of dreams, the physical proof of a caring mind, the most profound connection between a teacher and his students.

Tragedy strikes, though, when a "half-witted boy . . . imagined unspeakable things and in the morning went forth to tell his dreams as facts. Strange, hideous accusations" (13). The wrath of vengeful parents soon drives the schoolmaster to change his name and move to Winesburg, Ohio. Critics have debated whether Wing is homosexual. The important point is not to realize the deep truth of Wing's sexuality, but to acknowledge that the sentimental touch has become a sign of perversion. The school where an adult can physically bond with his students becomes a relic of a past age. The sentimental world is dead. Biddlebaum is baffled: "Although he did not understand what had happened he felt that the hands must be to blame" (14). Biddlebaum locates his trauma at the site of his sentimental interaction with the world. Even outside of the sentimental world, the hands still retain the mark of a fallen power.

The sentimental touch once held the promise of perfect unambiguous communication. The literary representation of the touch has always been a paradox—sentimental texts taught us that words can never represent the truth of feeling. As we saw in *Uncle Tom's Cabin*, the sentimental author is a teacher—instructing us in the proper emotional response to a representation of touching bodies. Anderson's lesson, though, is that sentimental teaching is a failure. Not only does Adolph Myers fail in teaching boys as a man of sensibility, but the narrator instructs us that an emotional response to hands is defunct.

The opening story of *Winesburg, Ohio* signals that the sentimental universe belongs to the past. Physical presence no longer signifies unquestionable truth. The historian Martin Sklar notes that the impersonality of markets under corporate capitalism dissolved the once-important status of physical presence in the business world: "Handshakes counted for little and even contracts could often be disregarded or broken with impunity."[46] In Winesburg, bodies cannot touch one another without arousing suspicion. Minds do not even know their own bodies. Anderson's world is a new world; the text is a new text. As Rebecca West declares, Anderson's work

> will not follow logic and find connections and trace "plots," but stands in front of things that are of no importance, infatuated with their quality, and hymns them with obstinate ecstasy; it seems persuaded there is beauty in anything, in absolutely anything. In such a spirit Mr. Anderson moves about his ugly little town and watches his dull ugly people. It lives, it glows, they exist as immortal souls. If we have listened truly to the sanctified old tunes we must know that this difficult new tune also is music.[47]

For Anderson, truth is still beauty, but beauty is ugly. The "new tune," as West points out, does not follow the formal logic of the sentimental novel, nor should it believe in the truth of the sentimental body. Indeed, "Hands" is touching precisely because, tragically, hands cannot touch. As Hart Crane said in 1921, Anderson "is without sentimentality."[48] Anderson's unsentimental "new tune," though, retains some of the "sanctified old" melodies. Indeed, the vestiges of the sentimental, like Biddlebaum's hands, are bewildering in their new context, as they carry a truth that seems out of mode.

Dirty Wash

In Wash Williams we get a character who is truly out of mode, marked as a specimen of a past age. Wash is a relic of sentimentality, doomed to failure in a new era. His story, "Respectability," begins with the narrator at his most disrespectful: "Wash Williams, the telegraph operator of Winesburg, was the ugliest thing in town. His girth was immense, his neck thin, his legs feeble. He was dirty. Everything about him was unclean. Even the whites of his eyes looked soiled" (104). The physical description of Wash becomes moral judgment. Just as we can assess Simon Legree from his hands, "immensely large, hairy, sun-burned, freckled, and very dirty, and garnished with long nails, in a very foul condition" (Stowe 477), we know that Wash's overwhelming dirtiness signifies an unclean soul. He of "soiled" eyeballs needs a moral wash. But the narrator shifts suddenly, declaring,

> I go too fast. Not everything about Wash was unclean. He took care of his hands. His fingers were fat, but there was something sensitive and shapely in the hand that lay on the table by the instrument in the telegraph office. In his youth Wash Williams had been called the best telegraph operator in the state, and in spite of his degradement to the obscure office at Winesburg, he was still proud of his ability. (104–5)

The narrator makes his presence felt, bringing our attention to his management of time. Though the narrator complains of a narrative out of control, the very declaration "I go too fast" is a reassertion of control. The narrator reminds us that he is faulty, but more crucially, that he is present. The looming narratorial presence resonates with the practices of Frederick Taylor's scientific management. Managers had always controlled workers, but with Taylor, the control "assumed unprecedented dimensions."[49] Under Taylorism, managers dictated not only the place, hours, and general rules of working but also the precise manner in which each task was to be performed, down to the "simplest individual acts," as Taylor himself puts it.[50] Harry Braverman writes that "the pivot upon which all modern management turns" is "the control over work through the control over the *decisions that are made in the course of work*."[51] Narrators, clearly, have always controlled our acts of reading. Anderson's narratorial style, though, reminds us of the extent of the narrative control, and, like modern management, will consciously intrude and assert control in even the tiniest circumstance. But while the narrative seems to adhere to a Taylorist style of control within the chapter, we must remember that the looseness and unpredictability of the entire text—the almost haphazard order of the chapters—opposes Taylorism. The narrator continues to embody the central tension of the text: *Winesburg, Ohio* both exemplifies and renounces a culture of management.

Like Stowe's narrator, Anderson's narrator is not content to fade into the background. The sentimental narrator appears just as sentimental language emerges. The phrase "sensitive and shapely," like "unclean" and "soiled," is a moral judgment in the guise of a physical description. Indeed, "sensitive" as a physical descriptor literally hearkens back to the moral sense, the notion that interior value can be gleaned immediately (can be sensed) from a cursory glance. For Wash, there is a direct link between character and physicality.

We know, then, that he of complete ugliness but sensitive hands is a character torn. Wash is a silent, brooding misanthrope, ignored by the people in town. He is, though, a fine telegraph operator, and was at one point "a comely youth" (106). Wash's ugliness is a mystery fit for a fairy tale; the prince has become a monster, and no one in the town knows why. Wash tells his story only once, and only to George Willard. Wash was once "madly in love" (108); he remembers of his unnamed wife, "when the hem of her garment touched my face I trembled" (109). The telegraph operator is especially sensitive to touch. Wash continues, "When after two years of that life I found she had managed to acquire three other lovers who came regularly to our house when I was away at work, I didn't want to touch them or her" (109). The worker who transmits messages with his touch believes that touch can contaminate. Wash's somatic response to his wife's infidelity reminds us that he is a sentimental body; indeed, he admits, "When she had gone I cried like a silly boy" (109). Tears, as sentimental literature shows us, signify the direct connection between interior feeling and the material body. Sentiment overflows from Wash.

Wash explains that after he sent his wife back to her mother, the mother invited Wash to the house. Wash's voice rises as he remembers waiting in the parlor:

> I was trembling all over. I hated the men I thought had wronged her. I was sick of living alone and wanted her back. The longer I waited the more raw and tender I became. I thought that if she came in and just touched me with her hand I would perhaps faint away. I ached to forgive and forget. (110)

For the sentimentalist, feeling will conquer, the touch will redeem. But instead of the sentimental hand Wash receives a fully naked body. The mother had coaxed her daughter's clothes off and sent her, ashamed, as an offering to Wash. Wash calmly explains to the "ill and weak" George Willard how he attacked the mother, "I struck her once with a chair and then the neighbors came in and took it away. She screamed so loud you see. I won't ever have a chance to kill her now. She died of a fever a month after that happened" (110). Wash speaks calmly of his rage, as if his actions were rational, something other than a visceral reaction to emotional pain, as if part of the sentimentalist within him has died. Indeed, the moment of the naked offering seems to have stripped Wash of his illusions of sentimentality.

Wash wanted the sentimental touch, not the stripped body. By offering the naked body, the mother forced Wash's desire to be one of power and lust. In other words, the mother forced Wash to interpret his own longing for touch as a synecdochic hunt for the sexual consumption of the whole body. The mother forced an interpretation where an interpretation will not do; the sentimental touch, after all, is a direct transmission between surfaces, an immediate bodily response. The sentimental touch, as it resists interpretation, opposes modernism, which posits that interpretation yields a hidden truth.[52] Wash's entire worldview is shaken, and he turns from love of a single woman to hatred of all women, declaring to George, "they are creeping, crawling, squirming things, they with their soft hands and their blue eyes" (107). For the sentimentalist, "soft hands" and "blue eyes" should signify purity of body and spirit. For Wash, what were once markers of beauty now point to wormlike vileness; in Wash's eyes, women signify the illegibility of the modern world.

"Respectability" is a parable of the dangers of sentimental reading in the age of modernism. Desire for unmediated love will be misinterpreted—the most respectable will be taken as the basest. Wash, as a telegrapher, is an expert in communication, but only in the long-distance encoded transmissions of telegraphy. His hands can send and receive messages easily, but only through the mediation of a mystifying technology. The messages are not his own, for the telegrapher is himself a mediator between two bodies that have no contact.[53] The irony of Wash's situation grows when we realize that the telegraph system, like the railroad, was one of the earliest industries to require teams of salaried managers to run the business. Anderson himself links the telegraph and the railroad—Wash tells his story to George first sitting "on the railroad ties" (108) and then walking "along the tracks" (109).[54] Wash's work quickens the growth of a culture connected by wires and networks but little else. Wash was oblivious to the early lovers his wife took and seems equally oblivious to his participation in an industry that quickens the spread of a culture that destroyed him.[55]

The Sentimental Writer

George's family exemplifies the unsentimentalized Ohio family. George's mother, Elizabeth Willard, is a quietly desperate middle-aged woman of middle America who wanders around the family hotel "doing the work of a chambermaid among beds soiled by the slumbers of fat traveling men" (21). George is a bright spot in her life; she whispers to herself, "Within him there is a secret something that is striving to grow. It is the thing I let be killed in myself" (25). The thing is unspeakable and unknowable but is the foundation of the mother-son bond. Some "thing" haunts most of the lives in Winesburg; as John Updike says, "the vagueness of 'the thing' is chronic."[56] There are moments, though, when the thing comes close to being revealed. In her promiscuous youth, Elizabeth was drawn to men precisely because of the promise of a revelatory touch: "On the side streets of the village, in the darkness under the trees, they took hold of her hand and she thought that something unexpressed in herself came forth and became a part of an unexpressed something in them" (28). Elizabeth sought the inexpressible feeling, the emotion so profound that it lay beyond the realm of language. Elizabeth, though, may be deluded; she only "thought" that the touch contained the inarticulable "something." Like Huck's narration during his escape from Pap's cabin, Elizabeth's inability to articulate "something" is her own failing, not the inadequacy of language. Certainly, her disappointing life after these anonymous touches does not point to the epiphany of human contact. Perhaps the sentimental world has truly left Winesburg, Ohio.

We would expect "Sophistication," the penultimate story of the text, to be barren of sentimental devices. Characters who have clung to the sentimental have met with disaster. The story of George and Helen looking ahead in their lives, overcoming their small-town isolation, should be a story that looks toward the literary future. The narrator describes George:

> All that day, amid the jam of people at the Fair, he had gone about feeling lonely. He was about to leave Winesburg to go away to some city where he hoped to get work on a city newspaper and he felt grown up. The mood that had taken possession of him was a thing known to men and unknown to boys. (218)

George, in a lonely crowd, is at a turning point in his life. He is about to move from a small town to the city, but, more important, from boyhood to manhood. Progress, though, is not always peering into the future. Indeed, the narrator declares, "There is a time in the life of every boy when he for the first time takes the backward view of life. Perhaps that is the moment when he crosses the line into manhood" (218). Growth, here, is marked not by looking forward, but by staring backward.

If boyhood is longing to be a man, manhood is remembering, achingly, the life of the boy. As Lawrence Levine writes of this moment in American history, "the compulsion to peer forward was paralleled by an urge to look backward to a more pristine, more comfortable, more familiar time."[57] Development for Anderson's boy, like development in the United States after World War I, is the "sadness of sophistication" (218), the lonely realization that time has passed suddenly, that "he must live and die in uncertainty" (219). Death looms for the boy suddenly turned man. Anderson writes, "With all his heart he wants to come close to some other human, touch someone with his hands, be touched by the hand of another" (219). "He" does not describe just George, but "every boy" (218). And not just every boy; as the narrator describes, "As for Helen White, she also had come to a period of change. What George felt, she in her young woman's way felt also. She was no longer a girl and hungered to reach into the grace and beauty of womanhood" (219). The universal desire is for the sentimental touch.

Just as George looks backward at the moment of his maturity, so, too, does Anderson look to the literary past at the height of "Sophistication." We get a scene from a sentimental novel. When George and Helen come together, language falters. George's "voice failed and in silence the two came back into town. . . . At the gate he tried to say something impressive. Speeches he had thought out came into his head, but they seemed utterly pointless" (221). George and Helen separate, and both are agonized, "lonely and dejected" (222). Helen thinks that "the world was full of meaningless people saying words" (223). She calls for George, and he arrives out of the darkness and takes "hold of her hand" (223). Finally, the young man and the young woman are together at the top of the hill, but the scene is not a sex scene. Their union is not one of mere physical pleasure; instead, they share what Wash Williams wanted but never found. Anderson writes:

> There was no way of knowing what woman's thoughts went through her mind but, when the bottom of the hill was reached and she came up to the boy, she took his arm and walked beside him in dignified silence. For some reason they could not have explained they had both got from their silent evening together the thing needed. Man or boy, woman or girl, they had for a moment taken hold of the thing that makes the mature life of men and women in the modern world possible. (227)

George and Helen, suddenly, become like Eliza and Mrs. Bird, St. Clare and Uncle Tom, Huck and Jim. Through a gentle, silent touch, George and Helen reach an inexpressible understanding of "the thing," of themselves, and of their larger place in the world.[58] Indeed, they have an epiphany about the "modern world." Interpretation is futile, even unnecessary: "there was no way of knowing . . . they could not have explained," but it does not matter. In a modern text, to make a true discovery about the modern world, Anderson uses the sentimental touch. Like Wing Biddlebaum's hands, Anderson's touch cannot escape the textually inherited past. Modern sophistication does not escape the touching signifier.

Even in the midst of a fully emergent managerial capitalism, the sentimental touch remains the hallmark of the epiphanic moment in the American novel. Anderson is not alone as an American modernist who retains vestiges of the sentimental in the midst of a modern text. Willa Cather, for instance, writes in a modern spare style, even as she deploys the sentimental touch to signify the most earnest moments in her texts. In *My Ántonia* (1918), when Jim returns to Black Hawk after two years in Boston, Cather writes: "We met like the people in the old song, in silence, if not in tears. Her warm hand clasped mine."[59] The "old song" is a sentimental tune but still resonates in the new age. Perhaps it is not that surprising to find sentimentality in Cather, especially in her nostalgic depiction of Nebraska. But we also find the sentimental trope in Sinclair

Lewis's 1922 *Babbitt*. George Babbitt, the middle-aged real estate agent, lives in an alienated world of consumerism and middle-management. After carrying on an affair, Babbitt goes back to his ailing wife's bedside. Lewis writes, "As she drowsed away in the tropic languor of morphia, he sat on the edge of her bed, holding her hand, and for the first time in many weeks her hand abode trustfully in his."[60] The silent, meaningful touch seems out of place in a text written in a modernist style. But just as Babbitt embraces consumer culture even after he realizes its artificiality, so, too, does Lewis use the sentimental touch even when his text shows modernism's mistrust in sentimental structure and the legible body. American modernism is never a clean break from the past; the sentimental touch is a fault line where we can discover the modernist's reliance on the very structures that, in the modernist mind, should be overthrown.

The rarity of Anderson's touch, though, and its incoherence with the rest of the unsentimental text mark the moment as especially riddled with anxiety. "Sophistication" is not sophisticated but is a throwback to a style that relies on cultural assumptions (bodies are legible, touch is meaningful) that no longer exist. The reemergence of discredited and discarded figurations signals a cultural anxiety. Even as the visible hand replaces the invisible hand, as managers replace market forces, the power of individual managers—indeed, of any individual—is rendered miniscule by vast managerial networks.[61] As a writer in *Atlantic* bemoaned in 1909, "Individuality, in the sense of a man's distinct personality, in the material domain is becoming an increasingly rare phenomenon. . . . As a whole, we have lost the inclination and capacity for separate selfhood."[62] A widespread crisis of lost personhood occurs when economic networks become ossified—hardened into permanent skeletal structures whose existence no longer corresponds to human life. Literature responds to the social anxiety of a permanent, inhuman managerial power, but literature also exhibits the symptoms of structural reification. Indeed, the persistence of the sentimental touch in depictions of an unsentimental world signals the hardening of a literary structure under the edifying power of capitalism.

The hardened literary structure, though, is one of promise and transcendence. The sentimental touch promises immediate understanding in a baffling world, symbolizes intimacy in an anonymous universe, and shows that bodies remain meaningful even when they are disfigured. After "Sophistication" comes "Departure," the final story in *Winesburg, Ohio*. The transition between the two stories is not jarring; in fact, it is the only time in the book when adjacent stories deal centrally with the same character. If the jarring transitions between stories reminded us of the narrator's intrusive hand, the smooth transition is a sudden rendering of the narrative hand as invisible. The conflicts in the text do not resolve entirely; there is still the strain of a highly managed narration in combination with a loose literary structure, and there is still a pull between the nostalgia of craftsmanship and the progress of artistry. But the tension relaxes, as if the narrator realizes that a modernist text can bear the weight of atavistic tropes. Just after the successful sentimental touch of "Sophistication," the visible hand of the text's manager withdraws slightly. The narrator has guided us through a sentimental ending, but then departs. The departure of the intrusive narrator at the end of *Winesburg, Ohio* lies in stark contrast with the final intrusions of the narrator in *Uncle Tom's Cabin*. If Stowe, in her ending, wanted to remind us of our place in the world outside of the narrative—our political position in a historical world—Anderson wants us to hold on to the world inside of his fictional universe. The withdrawal of the intrusive narrator also marks the emergence of George Willard asserting himself in the world. One writer replaces another. But while we have known the narrator through his writing, we know George not for writing, finally, but for touching. George, in the final chapter, leaves Winesburg after "everyone shook the young man's hand" (229). The young writer will make his way in the world by thinking "of little things" (231). As he leaves, he remembers

> Turk Smollet wheeling boards through the main street of his town in the morning, a tall woman, beautifully gowned, who had once stayed overnight at his father's hotel, Butch Wheeler the lamp lighter of Winesburg hurrying through the streets on a summer evening and holding a torch in his hand, Helen White standing by a window in the Winesburg post office and putting a stamp on an envelope. (231)

George remembers the particular details of particular people. Thoughts of intimacy will support the writer as he ventures into the city. When the world threatens to get darker, when American modernism dives deeper into the world of human degradation, the writer may be sustained by remembering the human touch.

4 /   A Touch of Miss Lonelyhearts

If sentimental language in small-town Ohio was a marked anachronism in an age of looming managerial dominance, then the sentimental touch in a fully bureaucratic New York City seems impossible. In capitalist society, as Marx wrote, workers do not control the means of production. In managerial capitalism, workers do not even control their own bodies and the manner of their labor.[1] Workers no longer have special knowledge and training, but carry out specific, detailed tasks as determined by a manager who is not working beside them. Managers demand that the labor force do no intellectual work, that workers perform systematically preplanned and precalculated manual labor.[2] In his 1933 *Miss Lonelyhearts*, Nathanael West offers an extreme version of the depersonalization that plagued lives in Winesburg. Miss Lonelyhearts is the male advice columnist who is bombarded with anonymous letters detailing everyday traumas of psychological and physical pain; the letters testify to the moral waste of an entire city. To find sentimental language in West's work is surprising, not only because of the unrelenting darkness of *Miss Lonelyhearts* but also because of the text's alignment with a managerial regime that has cast off its moral sense.

In *Labor and Monopoly Capital*, Harry Braverman writes that "the separation of hand and brain is the most decisive single step in the division of labor taken by the capitalist mode of production."[3] A world that demands "the separation of hand and brain"—the disunity of body and mind—is the opposite of the sentimental world. According to the moral sense philosophy underlying sentimentalism, the continuity between body and mind is vital to the social bonds that maintain society. When bodies can experience right and wrong as feelings, when they can make moral judgments with the quickness of their senses, society can count on bodies to act in morally reliable ways. Harriet Beecher Stowe, therefore, could appeal to the feelings of her readers to inspire them to political action. Utopian moments in *Uncle Tom's Cabin* do not rely on speech, but on the silent touch: "When Tom ceased to speak, St. Clare reached out and took his hand, looking earnestly at him, but saying nothing. He closed his eyes, but still retained his hold; for, in the gates of eternity, the black hand and the white hold each other with an equal clasp" (456). The black slave and the white slaveholder are silent, but their touch confirms their shared humanity, their common moral sense. What cannot be spoken can be felt; the body confirms what the mind intuits. But when minds are separated from bodies—when most of society is encouraged not to think or understand but only to perform rote work—the moral sense is absent, and social bonds threaten to dissolve. *Miss Lonelyhearts* is in many ways the opposite of *Uncle Tom's Cabin*. The domestic family ideal at the center of Stowe's text disappears in West's work, where there are no families; a steady, saving Christian belief in *Uncle Tom's Cabin* becomes a pathological obsession with Christ in *Miss Lonelyhearts*. Most important, while the most powerful force in *Uncle Tom's Cabin* is sentiment, *Miss Lonelyhearts* seems to be devoid of authentic feeling; where Stowe's text depends on our ability to "feel right," Miss Lonelyhearts endeavors not to feel at all.

Miss Lonelyhearts aspires to unfeeling in an attempt to shield himself from the flood of daily catastrophes submitted by his letter writers. In other words, Miss Lonelyhearts willfully separates his mind and body to withstand the cultural consequences of a world where minds are separated from bodies. A body that has been separated from its mind, though, cannot communicate with other minds or bodies. A culture of separated minds and bodies is, as West shows us, a culture in crisis.[4] West's narrative style underscores the thematic separation; as in *Winesburg, Ohio*, the narrator controls the narrative in a managerial style, dividing the text into small, discrete episodes. In Anderson's text, the narrator showed his authorial hand by intruding on the story and contemplating the difficulty of using words to do justice to troubled lives. In West's text, the narrator still intrudes (silently, breaking up the narrative), but it is the writer within the text—Miss Lonelyhearts himself—who struggles with the impossibility of using words to help troubled lives. For this advice columnist, language may not redeem, and sincere communication may not exist.

Yet the sentimental touch persists: to express earnest feeling, West uses language that seems more fitting to the domestic literature of the previous century. In *Miss Lonelyhearts*, sentimental language offers readers an easily overlooked glimpse of humanity in the world of an all-pervasive managerial capitalism. When human relationships have been reduced to abstract and mechanical processes, the sentimental touch hints that the hand can heal, suggests that words can lead directly to feeling, and appears to create a utopian space in the gloomiest of settings. But the success of this humanizing trope depends upon its coglike qualities. We realize the emotional resonance of the sentimental touch to the extent that it adheres to the recognizable discourse of the sentimental literary tradition. Put another way, the trope is powerful because it is reproducible and exchangeable: West inserts the sentimental trope like a moveable part into the narrative machinery of his modernist text. If the sentimental touch redeems humans from a mechanical world, it also exposes the mechanical quality of the very thing that makes us feel most human—our emotion. When *Miss Lonelyhearts* offers a heartfelt moment in the midst of a heartless world, the text demonstrates the machinery of culture at the very instant that it infuses an impersonal society with deep human purpose.

Letters and Distance

The alienation in *Miss Lonelyhearts* is not just a function of the urban environment; the plight of lost, lonely characters in West's city runs structurally deeper than a national demographic shift to the city.[5] The city does offer a literalization of the vertically integrated bodies that make up a business network and a hyperrealization of anonymity in the midst of a crowd. But to blame the city for mass alienation is to concentrate on a symptom of capitalism and miss the structural cause. Indeed, escaping the city does not cure Miss Lonelyhearts of his distress—he is as miserable in Connecticut as he was in Manhattan. In both the city and its rural outskirts, a larger cultural force is at work: managerial systems have restructured every dimension of modern life.

In the *Report of the President's Research Committee on Social Trends*, a collection written in 1932 at the request of Herbert Hoover, economists Edwin F. Gay and Leo Wolman write that "the study of improved methods of management has progressed far beyond the scope envisaged before the war by F. W. Taylor and is now directed with new emphasis to personnel and to marketing."[6] Alfred Chandler draws a similar conclusion about the final stages of the rise of managerialism: "As the large enterprises grew and dominated major sectors of the economy, they altered the basic structure of these sectors and of the economy as a whole."[7] Management culture, in other words, extends its reach beyond workers in a factory, beyond even the business world, and into society at large. A massive structural change of the whole economy becomes a fundamental change in the culture.[8] The structure of capitalism shapes lives during the labor process and beyond.[9] As Lewis Mumford writes in 1934: "mechanization and regimentation are not new phenomena in history: what is new is the fact that these functions have been projected and embodied in organized forms which dominate every aspect of our existence."[10] The separation of minds and bodies at work—a crucial step in the increasingly divided labor tasks of capitalism—becomes the separation of minds and bodies outside of work. West, like Sherwood Anderson, was himself a manager and deeply familiar with the impersonality of business structures.[11] In *Miss Lonelyhearts*, West dramatizes personal dislocation in a society where minds are separated from bodies, and bodies are separated from each other, even while they touch.

West opens his text in an office, where Taylorism has moved from the factory into a bureaucratic setting:

> The Miss Lonelyhearts of the New York *Post-Dispatch* (Are you in trouble?—Do-you-need-advice?—Write-to-Miss-Lonelyhearts-and-she-will-help-you) sat at his desk and stared at a piece of white cardboard. On it a prayer had been printed by Shrike, the feature editor.
>
> > "Soul of Miss L, glorify me.
> > Body of Miss L, nourish me.
> > Blood of Miss L, intoxicate me.
> > Tears of Miss L, wash me.
> > Oh good Miss L, excuse my plea,
> > And hide me in your heart,
> > And defend me from mine enemies.
> > Help me, Miss L, help me, help me.
> > In saecula saeculorum. Amen."[12]

In this prayer, all of the ingredients for modernist desolation are present: a solitary writer, an absent manager, a false religion, and a plea for help that promises to go unanswered forever and ever. Miss Lonelyhearts has writer's block, but we quickly see that his struggles are not merely a columnist's brief panic as the deadline approaches and his boss looms over him. As Shrike's dark humor intimates, there is a crisis in Miss L's body, blood, and soul. Shrike's obsession with physicality parodies the Christian belief that physical suffering leads to redemption; the prayer sardonically begs for the impossible bodily sacrifice that will alleviate all worldly suffering.

Shrike's prayer, while it mocks Christianity, also ridicules the sentimental philosophy that truth resides in the body. For the sentimentalist, as for the Christian, the body is the ultimate authority. Tears, as any reader of *Uncle Tom's Cabin* knows, signify the most earnest bodily response and testify to the direct connection between the material body and interior character. Shrike's mockery of bodily authority is underscored by his own bodily absence. Shrike is not on the scene, but the specter of his power hovers over Miss Lonelyhearts. Power, after sentimentalism, is not a function of bodily presence; the office is structured such that the writer always feels the editor, even when the editor is not there. The manager dominates the worker not with his body, but with the managerial structure within which both are inscribed.

The newspaper, after all, is a business. In 1932, Malcolm M. Willey and Stuart Rice wrote that "modern newspapers are profit enterprises. With them, more than in other industries, retrenchment is difficult, for a paper must be issued regularly and attempts to cut content are quickly reflected in circulation losses. Consolidation and multiple ownership arise to meet the need for adjustment in the face of mounting costs."[13] The newspaper, besides being a managerial business ("consolidation and multiple ownership" are two of the hallmarks of managerial capitalism), spreads the culture of commodified communication among its readers. As W. Clark Hendley writes of the mass media:

> An interconnecting, interconnected web of communication lines
> has been woven about the individual. It has transformed his behav-
> ior and his attitudes no less than it has transformed social organi-
> zation itself. The web has developed largely without plan or aim.
> The integration has been in consequence of competitive forces, not
> social desirability. In this competition the destruction of old and
> established agencies is threatened.[14]

The abstract network of positions that define a bureaucracy extends, through the newspaper, to the public. The newspaper, as Althusser would say, has become an ideological state apparatus, spreading cultural dislocation even as it purports to be simply reporting cultural developments.[15] The subject matter of the newspaper does not matter; the newspaper's very structure proliferates a culture of impersonal interaction.

West himself cites the layout and subject matter of the newspaper as proof of American decay. In "Some Notes on Violence," he writes:

> In America violence is idiomatic. Read our newspapers. To make the front page a murderer has to use his imagination, he also has to use a particularly hideous instrument. Take this morning's paper: FATHER CUTS SON'S THROAT IN BASEBALL ARGUMENT. It appears on an inside page. To make the first page, he should have killed three sons and with a baseball bat instead of a knife. Only liberality and symmetry could have made this daily occurrence interesting.[16]

The modern newspaper, like the sensationalist yellow journalism of an earlier generation, benefits from the most heinous crimes; the greater the violence, the greater the profit. The result is not only a culture that aestheticizes and encourages violence, but one that spreads moral decline and abstract anonymity to all its readers. The machinery of the factory extends to become the machinery of the mass media, where it extends again to become the machinery of social relations.

Most insidiously, the newspaper expands the dominion of depersonalization while it pretends to maintain an actual community. As if compensating for the alienation that the newspaper promotes, regular advice columns offer to provide a sense of social affinity.[17] Shrike's new doxology ends "in saecula saeculorum"—from generation to generation—suggesting that the Miss Lonelyhearts community shares an actual bloodlined kinship. The Latin words are the traditional closing of a prayer but are also etymologically related to "secular." Shrike not only vulgarizes a Christian prayer, he foregrounds the secularity that has always already resided within the religious words. Shrike is a cynical modernist, informing us that we cannot rely on religion, for it has always carried the seeds of its own destruction. As a newspaper editor and purveyor of mock prayer, Shrike stands at the nexus of mass culture and false spirituality.

The religiosity that pulses through the text shows how mass culture cloaks its coercive power in spirituality. Hendley speculates, "Perhaps the profound secularization of the modern world can be said truly to have begun in the 17th century when the traditional roles of advisor and confessor were taken from the church and transplanted to that most secular of modern institutions, the newspaper."[18] Shrike knows the newspaper's new place as community center and spiritual guide. At his first glimpse of Miss Lonelyhearts, "Shrike had smiled and said, 'The

Susan Chesters, the Beatrice Fairfaxes and the Miss Lonelyhearts are the priests of twentieth-century America'" (4).[19] The priests of twentieth-century America, though, lead a deeply troubled and fractured congregation. Shrike's distorted religiosity testifies to the newspaper's perversion of sentimentalism. In the office of Miss Lonelyhearts, intimacy is pretend, and the exchange of open-hearted letters is nothing more than a formula for profit.

West echoes his character Shrike. In "Some Notes on Miss L.," written in 1933 after the publication of his novel, he writes that "Miss Lonelyhearts became the portrait of a priest of our time who has a religious experience. His case is classical and is built on all the cases in James' *Varieties of Religious Experience* and Starbuck's *Psychology of Religion.*"[20] In the 1902 work that West cites, William James writes that "there is no doubt that healthy-mindedness is inadequate as a philosophical doctrine, because the evil facts which it refuses positively to account for are a genuine portion of reality; and they may after all be the best key to life's significance, and possibly the only openers of our eyes to the deepest levels of truth."[21] Evil, even as it is inscrutable, has an explanatory force for James. Indeed, a rigorous philosophy, in this view, must be grounded in "evil facts"; the true world, perhaps, is best revealed in darkness.

For many years, literary critics have read West as if informed by William James.[22] The criticism on *Miss Lonelyhearts* abounds with readings that actively deny that capitalism is a cause of the text's despair. Daniel Aaron writes of West's work, "the real culprit is not capitalism but humanity."[23] In a 1933 review of *Miss Lonelyhearts*, William Troy writes that "the conflicts are psychological, not social or economic."[24] As recently as 2004, Theodore Dalrymple writes that "*Miss Lonelyhearts* was published at the lowest point of the Depression, but its pessimism is existential rather than economic or political."[25] Theories of existential negativity and the philosophy of pervasive evil, taken together, do not leave much room for a cultural critique. If the darkness in West's world is not a function of culture but is inherent in humanity, then nothing can be done. Religious truths may be absurd, indeed evil, but we must accept them; in our recognition of "the deepest levels of truth," so the religious critic believes, we will be able to see more clearly.[26]

The social critic, though, will be wary of purely religious interpretation. Recently critics have questioned the wave of Westian criticism that discounted social forces. Jonathan Veitch writes, "in West's fiction the real culprit is not humanity, but capitalism. In fact, one might say that his fiction offers one of the most insightful critiques of the inhumanity of capitalism during the thirties (an era known for some biting critiques)."[27] Rita Barnard writes that West's novels "can be read in light of Marx's dialectical insight that religion, though the pinnacle of illusion, is also the bearer of a diagnostic truth, an accurate index of intolerable conditions."[28] A text in which the protagonist turns obsessively (and failingly) to religion and which has inspired decades of religious criticism points us not away from capitalism but directly toward it. Cultural productions register capitalist structure. In the case of *Miss Lonelyhearts*, textual and critical fixations on religion—concerns with forces of good and evil in a modern city—reveal a culture that has mystified normal relationships between people.

The "priests of twentieth-century America" preach sympathy and change but cultivate a culture of alienation. The newspaper column began as a joke for the staff of the paper, but the letters of earnest suffering are no longer funny for Miss Lonelyhearts. "Sick-of-it-all" writes, "I cry all the time it hurts so much and I dont know what to do" (2); "Desperate" writes, "I was born without a nose. . . . Ought I commit suicide?" (2–3). The Depression-era sufferers get a public voice when they might otherwise be silent.[29] Their voices, though, can never be truly authentic; their problems must be fitted to the form of the advice letter—a letter that always anticipates and invites a certain therapeutic, comforting response. Veitch writes that the advice column relies on the Mind Cure, which "begins by transforming social problems into individual ones and then insists that there is no personal problem that the mind cannot cure given the appropriate maxim and sufficient resolve."[30] Advice columns, in other words, purport to solve a culture's deepest, most personal problems but in fact obscure the social problems that are at the root of a culture of self-pathologizing individuals.[31]

The Miss Lonelyhearts letter writers embody fractured lives. The letters are all written pseudonymically and metonymically, with names that attempt to characterize the writer in a word or phrase. The writers have interpellated themselves as figures reducible to a single attribute. The names do not contain multitudes but cling to a single, defining pathology. The pseudonyms preserve anonymity, but they also foster anonymity, creating a false community whose members identify themselves only as functions of a debilitating trait. The names suggest a transparency of language—"Desperate" is desperate; "Sick-of-it-all" is sick of it all. But the tightened gap between signifiers and signifieds does not actually signal transparent language. Even Miss Lonelyhearts's own name reveals the gendered deception at the heart of the advice column. Rather, the pseudonyms—carefully chosen to fit the stylistic prescription of the advice column—alert us to the psychological effects of a reified form. In other words, writers who sign their names with a descriptive phrase begin to think of themselves in terms of their pseudonym, even though their chosen name was first and foremost a requirement of the advice column's form. Not only do subscribers ask Miss Lonelyhearts to manage their troubled lives, but the very form of their letters signals obedience to the depersonalized structure that Miss Lonelyhearts embodies.

The longest letter that we see, describing a frighteningly abusive marriage, is signed "Broad Shoulders." The writer adds a postscript: "*P.S. Dear Miss Lonelyhearts dont think I am broad shouldered but that is the way I feel about life and me I mean*" (43). With her pseudonym, Broad Shoulders inadvertently offers a meditation on the reification of form. She adheres to the form of the column, choosing a name that describes her feeling; "Broad Shoulders" is a bodily description that refers not to her body, but to her interior character. She has ascribed herself not only a name but also an identity. For the nineteenth-century sentimentalist, as we have seen, body corresponds to mind in an unproblematic way. For the anonymous twentieth-century individual, however, bodies have been separated from minds, and there is no longer a direct link between physicality and interiority. As the letter writer insists in her postscript, "broad shouldered" is a feeling. But it is not a clear feeling. She is burdened by the world, but we do not know (and it seems that she does not know) if broad shoulders are sturdy—ready to carry the weight of her circumstances and any advice—or if broad shoulders signify a misshapen body on the verge of collapse.

Using a sentimental figuration in a modernist world, Broad Shoulders points to the risk and confusion of using a trope that no longer makes cultural sense. Broad Shoulders is the butt of her own joke and feels obliged to explain what once would have been transparent; she has to translate her metaphor, for body and mind are unified only in a commodified, artificial way—to meet the form of a newspaper. The trope, though, is still useful for the writer. For Broad Shoulders, as for West, sentimental language is powerful in an unsentimental world, even if just to foreground the loss of a sympathetic worldview. Broad Shoulders still ventures to convey the way she feels "about life" and herself; and, most important, her name points to the gap between mind and body—the cultural gap that may be the social cause at the root of her personal problem. The letters that so deeply endeavor to make order out of chaotic lives—by participating in a community, by insisting on the transparency of language—merely underscore the distance between individuals. There is no true community; language is never clear. The invocations of sentimental philosophy—the insistence that a community can rally to solve a cultural problem, and that bodies correspond to minds—signal the absence of sentimentalism.

The mechanical qualities of the sentimental letter make for a democratic form: even Broad Shoulders—as abused and inarticulate as she is—can use sentimental language. Yet it is precisely when she shares her own humanity and involves herself in a communal structure that she accepts the constraints of culture and mechanizes her own identity. The conventions of the sentimental form mean that anyone can access the sentimental, but the conventions also mean that those who submit to the form are forever anonymous.

The Failed Touch

The mechanization that defines and governs Miss Lonelyhearts's professional life also rules his personal life. Sitting exhausted on a city bench, Miss Lonelyhearts notices that "the gray sky looked as if it had been rubbed with a soiled eraser" (5). The act of writing guides the metaphor. More accurately, the failed act of correcting writing, of dirty erasure, is the metaphorical vehicle. The atmosphere itself becomes symbolic of Miss Lonelyhearts's inability to escape the doom of his letters and of West's inability to escape the literary codes of an earlier generation. The sky tells us that neither writer can get a fresh start. Indeed, in a text full of writers, no writer will have a clean slate. The letters document the ubiquitous alienation of the city's residents, and the letters themselves have an alienating effect. Writing mediates: to communicate through letters is to bypass the voice and the body. Even in a crowded city, there are no touching bodies.

The world of Miss Lonelyhearts is a world of anonymous desolation, a world of private suffering and no meaningful contact. The failure of contact follows Miss Lonelyhearts even to his apartment. West writes:

[W]hen he touched something, it spilled or rolled to the floor. The collar buttons disappeared under the bed, the point of the pencil broke, the handle of the razor fell off, the window shade refused to stay down. He fought back, but with too much violence, and was decisively defeated by the spring of the alarm clock. (11)

Miss Lonelyhearts cannot control his own touch; his hands leave only a household trail of mild destruction.[32] To escape this increasingly violent cycle of frustration, Miss Lonelyhearts looks to Betty, a woman in love with him. Perhaps the touch of another body will relieve. Miss Lonelyhearts reaches for her naked body, but "[s]he made no sign to show that she was aware of his hand. He would have welcomed a slap, but even when he caught at her nipple, she remained silent" (12). The body is unresponsive; the touch has failed. For Miss Lonelyhearts, the touch has lost passion and has become devoid of all expression. Betty's silence is not the quiet of sentimental profundity but is the sign of vacated meaning.

Miss Lonelyhearts admits to Betty that he has "a Christ complex" (13). Indeed, like Christ, he is being destroyed by those he tries to aid. And he longs for the power of the healing touch. The admission of a Christ complex, though, does not come peacefully. Miss Lonelyhearts is in a rage, shouting and making huge gestures "that were too appropriate, like those of an old-fashioned actor" (12). His body, even in a fury, is not natural. Instead, the gestures are self-conscious and highly stylized, a performance that attempts to convey a specific meaning but is not a direct function of character. When Betty cries in response to the outburst, there is at least the relief of a somatic reaction; the body can still respond. Laughing and crying are soon so ubiquitous in the text, though, that they become meaningless. The old man in the bar "looked as if he were going to cry, but suddenly laughed instead" (16). In a later mercurial interaction between Miss Lonelyhearts and Betty, "he noticed that something had gone wrong with her laugh. She was crying" (55). A dehumanized culture has interrupted the relationship between individuals and their own bodies. The compulsive somatic responses that signal the deep truth of an emerging character become unnatural, mechanistic responses. Laughing becomes a mystery, crying is illegible.

The deep ontological hurt of Miss Lonelyhearts and Betty, indeed of all the characters in West's world, points to a thoroughly modern crisis. A 1935 business primer written by MIT professors in the Department of Business and Engineering Administration shows that academics were becoming aware of the increasing dehumanization of American businesses. The team of authors writes that:

> the growth in the organization lengthened the avenue of approach between the employer and employee when it did not for all practical purposes close it entirely. Both in the formation and in the performance of the contract of employment the two principals directly involved became widely separated. The sense of mutual obligation was lost. The personal touch was lacking.[33]

The crisis, here, is one of "touch." The authors use the language of sentimentalism to signal the loss of humanity that comes with the rise of organizational structures. Braverman will pick up on the crisis of the "hand" in *Labor and Monopoly Capital: The Degradation of Work in the Twentieth Century*. He writes, "The unity of thought and action, conception and execution, hand and mind, which capitalism threatened from its beginnings, is now attacked by a systematic dissolution employing all the resources of science and the various engineering disciplines upon it."[34] The moral sense philosophers would surely agree with Braverman's assessment: "the unity of thought and action, . . . hand and mind" lies at the root of a healthy social structure. When thought and action are willfully separated, individuals are no better than mechanical, industrial tools, and social bonds dissolve.

The sick heart of Miss Lonelyhearts symbolizes the diseased heart of society. West writes: "He undressed slowly and took a bath. The hot water made his body feel good, but his heart remained a congealed lump of icy fat. After drying himself, he found a little whisky in the medicine chest and drank it. The alcohol warmed only the lining of his stomach" (18). West, like Broad Shoulders, reveals the tension between metaphorical and literal meanings in a world where there is no longer a direct relationship between physicality and interiority. "Heart" is a metaphor referring to a capacity for feeling, not the body part that pumps blood; yet the metaphor is made clear only with a bodily description—"a congealed lump of icy fat." Miss Lonelyhearts experiences not just the separation of body and mind but also the disintegration of his body. The alcohol—apparently the only medicine available to Miss Lonelyhearts—affects only "the lining of his stomach." The strain on language indicates a strain on identity; Miss Lonelyhearts exists apart from his heart and stomach. Heart and stomach are no longer the sites of love and hunger, of desire and yearning, but are the machinery of an unfeeling body. If, for sentimentalism, the outside corresponded neatly to the inside, West's problematic use of a bodily metaphor alerts us both to the modernist body's vexed relationship with its interior and to the modernist writer's vexed relationship with his predecessors. West, after all, clings to a thread of sentimentalism—the heart is still a metaphor, however stretched and exhausted. Like Miss Lonelyhearts, West still clutches for the sentimental hope that language can change lives and that words can do justice.

Clinging to sentimentality, though, seems doomed to failure in the world of Miss Lonelyhearts. Betty, who adheres to the beliefs of an earlier age, is repeatedly devastated. She will not let go of a sentimental sensibility, however, and desperately holds on to the belief that the physical should correspond to the psychological, even after her own body does not respond to touch. She tries to shift Miss Lonelyhearts's attention from the gloom of his letters and his obsession with Christ. West writes, "She seemed to think that if he never talked about these things, his body would get well, that if his body got well everything would be well" (36). In the sentimental world, after all, a healthy body would indicate a healthy mind.

Betty thinks that the source of Miss Lonelyhearts's sickness is the city. Her "plan" is to take Miss Lonelyhearts to "the farm in Connecticut on which she had been born and they could go there and camp in the house" (36). Connecticut, home of Harriet Beecher Stowe, signifies an escape from modernity and the city, and an entry into domesticity and sentimentalism. The roots of alienation, though, are not in the city. Nature in Connecticut is not the site of rejuvenation: "Although spring was well advanced, in the deep shade there was nothing but death— rotten leaves, gray and white fungi, and over everything a funereal hush" (38). In a different time and place, "rotten leaves, gray and white fungi," might be read as the sources of life—the signs of cyclical growth and renewal. But there are no signs of life in West's decay. Indeed, the farm soil, as if a perverse simulacrum, is an echo of the city soil, where "there were no signs of spring. The decay that covered the surface of the mottled ground was not the kind in which life generates" (4). The rotten, sterile "surface of the mottled ground" covers all the earth in *Miss Lonelyhearts*. On their way back from the farm, even before they return, "Miss Lonelyhearts knew that Betty had failed to cure him" (38). This is the world of deep alienation. The cure is hard to find because the cause lies so deep. Miss Lonelyhearts and Betty cannot escape; their effort to relocate merely exposes their consistent functionality—they are moveable parts.

Form and Managerial Culture

The human equivalent to interchangeable parts is the "labor of standardized motion."[35] Workers are tools—unthinking, eminently replaceable parts of the labor process. Interchangeable parts have been a feature of capitalism since the eighteenth century, but it was the manager who extended interchangeable parts to the realm of labor.[36] West extends interchangeable parts to the realm of literature; each chapter in *Miss Lonelyhearts* works like a cog in the machinery of the text.

The original subtitle of *Miss Lonelyhearts* was to be "A Novel in the Form of a Comic Strip." West abandoned this idea but retained some of the techniques associated with the comic. As he wrote in "Some Notes on Miss L.," "Each chapter instead of going forward in time, also goes backward, forward, up and down in space like a picture. Violent images are used to illustrate commonplace events. Violent acts are left almost bald."[37] The violence does not point in a single direction, does not lead to anything; the violence is formally meaningless. The order of the episodic stories does not much matter, as West says, for the formal paradigm is spatial, not temporal. West's creation, "like a picture," depends on the image created by the entire narrative, not on the unfolding of scenes. It is important, certainly, that "Miss Lonelyhearts Has a Religious Experience" is the final episode—this religious experience, the ultimate religious experience, is death. But the series of episodes at the beginning of the text could be interchanged and the "picture" would remain the same. Indeed, the very names of the chapters convey their episodic nature: "Miss Lonelyhearts and the Dead Pan," "Miss Lonelyhearts and the Lamb," "Miss Lonelyhearts and the Fat Thumb," to name a few.

Miss Lonelyhearts has a violently unstable character; yet paradoxically, his character does not change much over the course of the text—only he becomes more violent and more unstable. We gain little insight into his soul.[38] West, it seems, has cast off the traditional novelistic goal of portraying a deep psychology. As he writes in "Some Notes on Violence":

> What is melodramatic in European writing is not necessarily so in American writing. For a European writer to make violence real, he has to do a great deal of careful psychology and sociology. He often needs three hundred pages to motivate one little murder. But not so the American writer. His audience has been prepared and is neither surprised nor shocked if he omits artistic excuses for familiar events.[39]

West offers a matter-of-fact condemnation of a society in which atrocity needs no explanation. More crucially, West links his writing directly to the social conditions of his country. The lack of a deep psychology in *Miss Lonelyhearts* points to an American culture where deep interiority has been replaced by commodified psyches. West's dismissal of human passion, alongside Miss Lonelyhearts's aspiration never to feel emotion, resonates with Max Weber's description of "fully developed bureaucracy":

> Its peculiar character and with it its appropriateness for capital-
> ism is the more fully actualized the more bureaucracy "deperson-
> alizes" itself, i.e., the more completely it succeeds in achieving that
> condition which is acclaimed as its peculiar virtue, viz., the exclu-
> sion of love, hatred, and every purely personal, especially irrational
> and incalculable, feeling from the execution of official tasks. In the
> place of the old-type ruler who is moved by sympathy, favor, grace,
> and gratitude, modern culture requires for its sustaining external
> apparatus the emotionally detached, and hence rigorously "profes-
> sional," expert; and the more complicated and the more specialized
> it is, the more it needs him. All these elements are provided by the
> bureaucratic structure.[40]

Dispassion and depersonalization are the virtues of bureaucracy. Instead
of the vicissitudes of emotion we find the stability of rationality, calculation, and organization. However, when the organizational structure that
suits the needs of capitalism becomes widespread—when mechanical
rationality informs every human interaction—we see dehumanization
seep into all aspects of life. Indeed, *Miss Lonelyhearts* represents the
bureaucratization of narrative itself.

The structure of *Miss Lonelyhearts* is a dialectic of order and disor-
der. The narrative is organized neatly—confined to specific episodes. But
the episodes themselves are not ordered by a specific logic, and chaos
courses through them as they document widespread, haphazard American violence.[41] The narrator, like the manager-narrator of *Winesburg,
Ohio*, controls lives—but only in a mystified way; the narrator dispenses
chapters with the mechanized regularity of an assembly line, even as the
content of each chapter is unpredictable. Unlike the narrator of *Winesburg, Ohio*, the narrator of *Miss Lonelyhearts* remains hidden. Instead,
we receive a thoroughly managerial narration: the pieces of the narrative
come in tight, discrete packets, and the characters regard one another as
objects rather than humans.

In "Miss Lonelyhearts Attends a Party," Miss Lonelyhearts dreams that
"he was a reclining statue holding a stopped clock" (51). He is not only a
human turned statue, but one that lies down and carries a representation
of stopped time; his character is bound not to change. As is made explicit
in the next chapter, "Miss Lonelyhearts and the Party Dress," individuals are objects, not characters—"the Party Dress" refers metonymically to
Betty. To say that characters are objects is not to say that they are inert and
are incapable of relationships. After all, Miss Lonelyhearts and Betty have
a relationship, however volatile. Their relationship, though, is plagued by

misunderstanding, as communication between objects is never transparent. Indeed, the obtuseness of their interactions—the opacity of their intricate social relationship—brings to mind Marx's description of commodity objects. Marx writes: "A commodity appears at first sight an extremely obvious, trivial thing. But its analysis brings out that it is a very strange thing, abounding in metaphysical subtleties and theological niceties."[42] The commodity is insidious precisely because of its hidden intricacies; complex social relations remain obscured behind an object that appears in isolation from the forces that produced it. When characters interact like objects, then, it is not that they display none of the passions of humankind, but that their human characteristics and their relationships with one another are fully mystified.

Miss Lonelyhearts himself is a commodity—we know him only by his professional function name, and he comes to view himself not as a subject teeming with deep, conflicting psychological drives, but as a "rock" (51). Jonathan Raban argues that a narrative obsessed with object relations rather than character relations "deadens our expectations of human sympathy or change."[43] Raban implicitly links sympathy to change. As we saw in *Uncle Tom's Cabin* and *Adventures of Huckleberry Finn*, sentimentalism depends on the link between sympathy and change—between feeling and acting. A world without sympathy is not merely a world devoid of feeling, but is a world with no political potential. Characters turned objects can never hope to influence the structure that has stolen their humanity. Miss Lonelyhearts is "a very strange thing, abounding in metaphysical subtleties and theological niceties," but he is an utter failure at changing the world.

The Touch

The place that seems to mark the void of sentimentality is Delehanty's bar, "in the cellar of a brownstone house that differed from its more respectable neighbors by having an armored door" (5). This depraved, untrusting underworld is the site of "Miss Lonelyhearts and the Cripple," the episode in which Miss Lonelyhearts meets the enfeebled husband of Fay Doyle, with whom Miss Lonelyhearts has had an affair. Peter Doyle is a meter reader—a middle manager of sorts, a dealer in numbers. Peter Doyle, too, is a physiological disaster and an emotional mess; he is, as Thomas H. Jackson says, "a Miss Lonelyhearts letter in the flesh."[44] Miss Lonelyhearts and Doyle, both drunk, "sat staring at each other until the strain of wordless communication began to excite them both. Doyle made vague, needless adjustments to his clothing. Miss Lonelyhearts found it very difficult to keep his smile steady" (45). This is not a sentimental silence—there is nonverbal communication, but it is a "strain" and results in awkwardness rather than profound understanding. "The cripple" breaks the silence with gibberish, "groups of words that lived inside of him as things, a jumble of the retorts he had meant to make when insulted and the private curses against fate that experience had taught him to swallow" (45–46). Doyle's linguistic failure, even more so than Huck Finn's inability to articulate and Elizabeth Willard's expressive ineptitude, is a function of the speaker's shallowness rather than an unreachable depth of meaning. The "jumble" is alive, living inside of him, but it is also dead, a group of "things." The inability to speak located at the boundary between life and death could describe the sentimental deathbed scenes in *Uncle Tom's Cabin*. Here, though, instead of silence, there is glossolalia. Instead of a peaceful passing from life to death, there is a confusion of the very categories of life and death.

Doyle wants to break out of his cluttered mind, to escape his unfathomable, literally unspeakable life. He struggles to communicate with Miss Lonelyhearts; still unable to talk, he pulls out a letter he has written. The letter, like all the letters to Miss Lonelyhearts, details the misery and dread of the writer's existence. By resorting to a letter, the cripple is capitulating to the impossibility of physical presence in the modern world. Even alone at a bar, touching is impossible. The letter begs, *"Please write me an answer not in the paper because my wife reads your stuff and I dont want her to no"* (47). Doyle requests a private response that is, crucially, a written response. Doyle, it seems, can only imagine a distant conversation, even when he is close by. The most basic communication needs mediation.

Suddenly, though, there is a moment of earnest sentimentalism:

> While Miss Lonelyhearts was puzzling out the crabbed writing, Doyle's damp hand accidentally touched his under the table. He jerked away, but then drove his hand back and forced it to clasp the cripple's. After finishing the letter, he did not let go, but pressed it firmly with all the love he could manage. At first the cripple covered his embarrassment by disguising the meaning of the clasp with a handshake, but he soon gave in to it and they sat silently hand in hand. (47)

Doyle's "crabbed writing" is a puzzle that needs solving, but the "meaning of the clasp" is immediately apparent to Miss Lonelyhearts and

Doyle. Writing needs interpretation, but feeling offers instant under-standing. The touch is silent, beyond the realm of language, and conveys a "love" for the first time in the text. West's use of the verb "manage" to refer to love, especially in a text filled with silent management and devoid of love, underscores the usual antipathy between management and love. The "meaning of the clasp," though, is not immediately appar-ent to readers. Unlike Stowe in *Uncle Tom's Cabin*, West has not trained us to respond to sentimental moments in a sentimental fashion. Stan-ley Edgar Hyman argues that the scene of hand-holding suggests Miss Lonelyhearts's latent homosexuality.[45] Thomas H. Jackson, on the other hand, writes, "that he and Miss Lonelyhearts twice end up holding hands is suggestive not of homosexuality, as Hyman says, but of identity—or is it the hero succumbing to one aspect of flux as he has already been engulfed by the other?"[46] Jackson's response—firmly countering Hyman but then literally questioning itself—indicates a critical moment fraught with uncertainty and confusion. Readers are not prepared for a senti-mental moment in a text previously devoid of earnestness.

Even if readers and West himself have lost touch with the codes of sentimentality, the touch between Miss Lonelyhearts and Peter Doyle has the hallmarks of the sentimental touch. The two characters hold hands in silence to convey a depth of emotion that words can never reach. Like chapter 23 in *Huckleberry Finn*—when Huck is silent after hearing Jim's tearful memories of his "deef en dumb" daughter—"Miss Lonelyhearts and the Cripple" ends in silence. West seems to have learned the senti-mental lesson: the written word means, but the silent body means most. Miss Lonelyhearts and Peter Doyle will soon reenter the world of degra-dation and violence, but not before this epiphanic moment of sentimen-tal touch that ends the chapter.

It is comforting to think that the deep and complex emotional life that literature reveals can resist the managerial regime in which we live. As John Crowe Ransom wrote in 1938, "Sentiments, those irrational psychic formations, do not consist very well with the indifference, machine-like, with which some modern social workers would have men fitting into the perfect economic organization. It is not as good animals that we are complicated with sentimental weakness."[47] Indeed, emotions enliven humans in the face of organized networks that deaden feeling. "Hand in hand," perhaps Miss Lonelyhearts and Doyle are like Milton's Adam and Eve—expelled from the garden, condemned to a life of toil, but redeemed by the deepest sympathy, the unutterable promise, of a hand in another hand. But we must remember that emotional formations themselves are "machine-like." The sentimental trope, if it is powerful at all, is effective because it comports with established, systematic literary convention. The sentimental touch offers a moment of personal contact and shared humanity in a mechanical society, but it is itself one more mechanized cog in the largely automatic apparatus of feeling.

The sentimental moment in *Miss Lonelyhearts* does not save, but it is a brief, utopian reprieve from the turmoil of the world. In a world in which all relationships are mediated by writing, in which the body is not natural, a moment of sentimental touch seems impossible. When the physical self has no authority and when emotional life has been forsaken, touch that conveys feeling is bound to fail. The touch between Miss Lonelyhearts and Peter Doyle, then, even as it retains the conventional, formal, and mechanical markings of the sentimental touch, does not function like the touch in *Uncle Tom's Cabin*. The moment is utopian in the etymological sense of the word; redemptive personal contact glimmers briefly below ground, but it does not sustain individuals in their daily lives.

After the Touch

The sentimental moment in *Miss Lonelyhearts*, when it takes place in the literal underworld of the city, is incongruent with the rest of the text. The moment is riddled with anxiety, not only for the characters but also for the text itself. Sympathy is surprising for the figures in a world dominated by an alienating bureaucratic culture, and a sentimental moment is surprising for the reader in a text narrated in a modernist, mechanistic style. After the touch, in "Miss Lonelyhearts Pays a Visit," Miss Lonelyhearts and Peter Doyle leave the speakeasy for dinner at the Doyles' house. As if struggling to resume a dream from which he has been startled awake, Miss Lonelyhearts "was trying desperately to feel again what he had felt while holding hands with the cripple in the speakeasy" (48). West suggests the reproducibility of the sentimental touch, as Miss Lonelyhearts and Doyle try to re-create the moment:

> Miss Lonelyhearts went over to the cripple and smiled at him with the same smile he had used in the speakeasy. The cripple returned the smile and stuck out his hand. Miss Lonelyhearts clasped it, and they stood this way, smiling and holding hands, until Mrs. Doyle re-entered the room.
> "What a sweet pair of fairies you guys are," she said.

The cripple pulled his hand away and made as though to strike his wife. (49)

Instead of reproducing the trope, West offers a critique of the mechanization of sentiment. Like Stanley Edgar Hyman, and like the parents who drove Adolph Myers out of town in *Winesburg, Ohio*, Mrs. Doyle does not read the touch as sentimental, but as a sign of perversion. Mrs. Doyle plunges us back into the darkness of a thoroughly unsentimental world: humility quickly turns into humiliation. Doyle promptly follows his wife into the unsentimental realm—his hand moving from what might have been authentic sympathy to a pretend strike, an acted violence. In a warning against convention, West exposes the limits of a systematized trope; when forced into repetition, what is supposed to constitute a meaningful moment becomes embarrassing and maudlin.

Like Doyle, Miss Lonelyhearts also succumbs to Mrs. Doyle's corrupting presence. The advice columnist tries to offer a life-changing speech to the Doyles, but his loud voice is fake—only a "stage scream" (49). West writes, "This time he had failed still more miserably. He had substituted the rhetoric of Shrike for that of Miss Lonelyhearts. He felt like an empty bottle, shiny and sterile" (50). Miss Lonelyhearts, the lone sentimentalist, inadvertently turns himself into Shrike, the eminent modernist. Put another way, the worker becomes his manager (in this case, the writer becomes his editor). Miss Lonelyhearts has succumbed to his immersion in a management structure, embodying and recapitulating the repressive structure even when he endeavors to be changing the world. When Mrs. Doyle sends her husband to buy liquor, she tries to seduce Miss Lonelyhearts: "She tried to pull him down on top of her. He struck out blindly and hit her in the face. She screamed and he hit her again and again. He kept hitting her until she stopped trying to hold him, then he ran out of the house" (50). "Miss Lonelyhearts and the Cripple" ended with a sentimental touch and bodies together; "Miss Lonelyhearts Pays a Visit" ends in violence and bodies separating. The narrator shows his abrupt style: in the course of a single episode, the visible hand has changed from a purveyor of sympathy to a fist.

Miss Lonelyhearts continues to harden himself, and soon becomes a rock, stolid against the waves of Shrike's cynical attacks during a party. Robert Edenbaum writes, "In the calm just previous to his complete 'apotheosis,' Miss Lonelyhearts *becomes* a rock as West, using one of his favorite devices, starts with a simile, then allows it to take over literally."[48] West's commitment to materiality and the literal word resonates with Stowe's commitment to the authority of physical reality and the tactile body. West writes, "What goes on in the sea is of no interest to the rock" (53). Soon after Miss Lonelyhearts becomes the rock, Betty becomes "the party dress," as the characters have fully metamorphosed into objects. Miss Lonelyhearts realizes that "she dressed for things" (54), as if he never before knew that Betty was capable of intention and thought. West writes, "Even the rock was touched by this realization. No; it was not the rock that was touched. The rock was still perfect. It was his mind that was touched, the instrument with which he knew the rock" (54). The narrator's sudden correction of himself echoes *Winesburg, Ohio*, when Anderson's narrator declares that the writer "was like a pregnant woman, only that the thing inside him was not a baby but a youth. No, it wasn't a youth, it was a woman, young, and wearing a coat of mail like a knight" (4). However, the "No; it was not" in *Miss Lonelyhearts* does not foreground the narrator's presence as it does in *Winesburg, Ohio*. Rather, the words are free indirect discourse; Miss Lonelyhearts is not immune to feeling but is in fact overwhelmed. As Caren Irr writes, Miss Lonelyhearts "cannot entirely bear the evidence of mass suffering that his job requires him to confront."[49] The battle for unfeeling that occurs in the head of Miss Lonelyhearts affirms the rupture in his character; the mind knows the rock, but only from a critical distance. West's narrator-manager remains hidden, even in the narrative's self-conscious failures, and is only revealed in the structure of the text.

The solidity of the episodic structure—the narrative's interchangeable parts keep arriving at the same pace, even as the chaos rises to violent levels—combined with the solidity of Miss Lonelyhearts as the rock, reveals a text steeped in opacity. Both the narrator and Miss Lonelyhearts aspire to impenetrability; the source of our knowledge, to use Adorno's words, "is not only kept remote, but is also treated as impersonal and thinglike."[50] In "The Stars Down to Earth," a 1952 essay on *the Los Angeles Times* astrology column, Adorno writes:

> The Source remains entirely abstract, unapproachable and anonymous. This reflects the type of irrationality in which the total order of our life presents itself to most individuals: opaqueness and inscrutability. Naïve persons fail to look through the complexities of a highly organized and institutionalized society, but even the sophisticated ones cannot understand it in plain terms of consistency and reason.[51]

In an impenetrable society, we cannot help but look toward impenetrable sources. In a culture governed by managerial laws, ruled by "the complexities of highly organized and institutionalized society," even our oracles of illumination—our advice columnists and our authors—are implicated in the bureaucratic structure. The opacity of the "total order of our life" is the antithesis of the transparency of bodies that sentimentalism offers. This is a culture beyond intervention, for the interveners themselves—those we trust to offer examples of how to act, to reveal order in an inscrutable society—are most exemplary of an unsympathetic, static world.

An impenetrable, unchangeable world is an unsentimental world. If asserting sentimentality—the coincidence of thought and feeling—is asserting a moral order, then removing sentimentality removes the moral order. As the opacity of *Miss Lonelyhearts* becomes more concrete, the rock moves ever distant from sentimentalism, and the moral order turns to amoral chaos. West writes that "neither laughter nor tears could affect the rock" (55). Miss Lonelyhearts, even as he imagines himself as most Christ-like, is most antisentimental. He is immune, even, to the somatic discourse of the body. West foregrounds a false sentimentality: Miss Lonelyhearts and Betty agree to get married and have a child, as if fulfilling Stowe's notion that domesticity can save a nation in crisis. But after the plans, West writes, Miss Lonelyhearts "did not feel guilty. He did not feel" (56). Before the final episode, Miss Lonelyhearts has emptied himself of all sentiment. In the absence of feeling, the "religious experience" can only be meaningless.

The narrator-manager, though, continues to assert his power, and we submit to the inexorable progression of episodes even when the moral order is gone. In "Miss Lonelyhearts Has a Religious Experience," the final episode, a series of delusions and misunderstandings brings Miss Lonelyhearts and an armed Peter Doyle locked in a struggle on a stairwell above Betty. Doyle's gun, fittingly, is wrapped in a newspaper. The text ends:

> She called to them to stop and started up the stairs. The cripple saw her cutting off his escape and tried to get rid of the package. He pulled his hand out. The gun inside the package exploded and Miss Lonelyhearts fell, dragging the cripple with him. They both rolled part of the way down the stairs. (58)

The visible hand, finally, is one of inadvertent destruction. Like death scenes in *Uncle Tom's Cabin*, West's depiction of death is marked by the touching of two bodies. But instead of the gentle ascension into heaven we get an explosion and a tumble downward. Physical contact survives, but only in earthbound death. The matter-of-fact narration does not leave us at the emotional height of a final sentimental touch. Here, rather, is the unfeeling that Miss Lonelyhearts desired. Crucially, the intermingled bodies of Doyle, the manager of numbers, and Miss Lonelyhearts, the manager of letters, do not roll completely down the stairs. The manager of the narration takes over, stops gravity, and ceases the production of interchangeable episodic parts. The narrative machinery grinds to a halt.

Our final vision of *Miss Lonelyhearts* is one of utter social failure. Even the fall is incomplete. Critics have struggled to find a redemptive message in the text. Rita Barnard writes, "West's 'positive moment,' then, is as uncomfortable as that gloomy vision of revolution which Theodor Adorno (in a very Benjaminian moment) offers us at the end of his essay on Spengler: 'that which stands against the decline of the West,' he observes, 'is not the surviving culture but the Utopia that is silently embodied in the image of decline.'"[52] For Barnard, as for Harold Bloom, West's vision is entirely dark, a modernist cathartic tragedy. We should remember, though, that there was a moment that tempered any pure negativity, when Miss Lonelyhearts and Peter Doyle touched. The sentimental touch took place hidden from view, underground, under a table, almost obscured from the readers. The text moved quickly forward—the episodic machinery would not pause for a moment of sensibility.

The Machinery of Sentiment

The trajectory of the sentimental touch in the age of the manager has been one of both endurance and loss. For all his darkness, West insists that the sentimental touch survives, even if as residue from a culture almost entirely displaced by a dominant modernism. Raymond Williams tells us that in dominant culture there is a "reaching back to those meanings and values which were created in actual societies and actual situations of the past, and which still seem to have significance because they represent areas of human experience, aspiration, and achievement which the dominant culture neglects, undervalues, opposes, represses, or even cannot recognize."[53] In West, the sentimental touch reaches back to the meaning and value granted it by the moral sense philosophy of the eighteenth century and the sentimental culture of the nineteenth century. The touch offers the promise of perfect communication, of a deep mutual recognition and understanding in the face of a mystifying world. But as Williams suggests, a massive change in cultural conditions allows the touch to slip by unnoticed, even as it retains its utopian core. Indeed, the sentimental touch in American modernism is neglected, repressed, and almost rendered invisible.

The sentimental touch in West is powerful precisely because the moment is so easily overlooked. A thoroughly alienated managerial culture does not warrant a positive ending or even a widely recognized positive vision. Indeed, a sparkling moment of a triumphant sentimentality in the midst of a cold, dislocating modernist culture could blind us to the realities of modern existence. A climactic affirmation of endless human resilience would be a complicit trope, encouraging us to forget the gloom of the world, even if the gloom of the world is what drives us to seek escape.

West's literary moment is marked by a darkness in American literature. In works such as Ernest Hemingway's *A Farewell to Arms* (1929) and Carson McCullers's *The Heart Is a Lonely Hunter* (1940), dismal visions of Western culture overpower the thrill of formal experimentation that buoyed earlier works of American modernism. By the end of *A Farewell to Arms* there is no heroism, no patriotism, no final peace, no religion, no salvation, no futurity, only rain. In *The Heart Is a Lonely Hunter,* loneliness is unrelenting and terrifying while love is inscrutable and absent; Peter Singer's funeral signals the end of meaningful relationships. Yet even as their titles suggest the disappearance of the meaningful body, both texts deploy the sentimental touch. We know, when Lieutenant Henry says, "She put out her hand and took mine," that he and Catherine Barkley share a profound love.[54] When McCullers writes that "a quick, swollen rush of love caused him to grasp the black, bony hand on the counterpane and hold it fast," we know that Jake and Doctor Copeland share a deep understanding.[55] West's sentimental touch, like the touch in Hemingway and McCullers, is not an instance of irrational escapism. Indeed, the sentimental touch is successful only for a brief moment, broken up quickly by a relentlessly managed narrative.

Tracing sentimental language through the darkness of early twentieth-century America tells us not just about the crisis of contemporary relationships and identity but reveals the structure of sentimentality and emotion itself. Sentimental language counters the systematic rule of managerialism, but sentimental language survives precisely because it is systematic itself as well. Adam Smith warns against becoming the "man of system," who is arrogant and dogmatic in following his own plan such that "he cannot suffer the smallest deviation from any part of it."[56] Smith would not approve of Frederick Winslow Taylor, nor would he approve of the twentieth-century corporate middle manager who adheres unthinkingly to an inherited bureaucratic plan. But his objection to the "man of system" is not an objection to order. Smith writes, triumphantly, that "human society, when we contemplate it in a certain abstract and philosophical light, appears like a great, an immense machine, whose regular and harmonious movements produce a thousand agreeable effects."[57] For Smith, a society's moral sense brings order and predictability to the world. Moral sensibility does not work against the machine, but makes society run as smoothly as a machine.

Sentimentality, in other words, is not inherently opposed to machine society. But when the soul-killing aspects of mechanical society emerge, when a bureaucratized, networked culture loses sight of moral sensibility, sentimentality can reinfuse an impersonal world with a sense of humanity. I examine the long-standing gestures of sentimentalism not to show their eternality, but to confront directly their mechanical qualities. By focusing on the "machine-like" iterations of the sentimental touch, I hope not to have shown the tragedy of emotion succumbing to machinery. Rather, the very "machine-like" aspects of emotion enable sentimental figurations to endure in a mechanical environment that appears to be unassailably hostile. The Taylorism of sentiment not only allows the emotional gesture to survive but also ensures that systems of management and bureaucracy are never quite as closed, rigid, and depersonalized as they are structured to be.

Epilogue

The sentimental touch, once a ubiquitous trope, seems scarce at the end of the twentieth century. Human contact, once the antidote to an alienating culture, has itself become appropriated and commodified. In a mid-1980s address to over 100,000 Wal-Mart associates via a television satellite linkup, Sam Walton declared,

> Now, I want you to raise your right hand—and remember what we say at Wal-Mart, that a promise we make is a promise we keep— and I want you to repeat after me: From this day forward, I solemnly promise and declare that every time a customer comes within ten feet of me, I will smile, look him in the eye, and greet him, so help me Sam.[1]

Sam, on a first-name basis with over 100,000 employees, feigns the same earnest communication toward his workers that he demands his workers display toward customers. Sam asks for the raised right hand of a legal oath; the body verifies words, even when Sam's own body, to the employees, is nothing but a mass of pixels. When workers are discouraged from recognizing that they are part of a giant bureaucracy, when a sense of community is manufactured to increase profit, when corporate power lies hidden behind corporeal closeness, and when God has been replaced by Sam Walton ("so help me Sam"), we must ask whether sentimental contact has become, in the end, cynical and exploitative. Certainly Sam Walton recognizes the value of a sentimental gesture, even if he deploys a sentimental worldview only to increase profit and further the ends of his own managerial structure.

While sentimental and managerial forces usually reveal themselves in different realms of culture, both act primarily on the body. The sentimental author works to control the reader's body, writing to invoke a somatic reaction in the reader. The manager seeks to control the worker's body, providing strict guidelines for the worker's precise role within a system. No wonder, then, that the hand, as the site of the body's tactile engagement with the world, is a powerful symbol both in the realms of literature and economics. The visible hand in literature—in the form of the sentimental touch—manifests the cultural assumption that physical interactions between bodies are the most profound source of meaning; the visible hand in economics—as a metaphor coined by Alfred Chandler to describe managerial power—emblematizes the way that managers control economic forces once thought to lie beyond the reach of individuals. The body becomes a contested site; at their manipulative heights both sentimental power and managerial power ensure that the reader and the worker never feel outside coercion, only inner compulsion. The ideal sentimental reader does not question the feeling that rises from within; the ideal worker in a managerial system does not question the social conditions that seem to have determined the labor structure.

Sam Walton, through the magic of television, has conflated workers and readers. Walton has turned his underlings into a sentimental audience—a communal "we" eager for instruction, ready to participate in an earnest endeavor (one full of kept promises and personal contact), and willing to labor toward a utopian future "from this day forward." As the Walmart website declares, "A career at Walmart is more than a job."[2] For the anonymous authors of the website, working at Walmart is not an act but an identity; the ideal corporate worker views his or her job not as a series of individual choices but as a vital component of his or her character.[3] For individuals at any level of the vast managerial network, working should not feel like an imposition but rather a natural extension of a deep and true subjectivity. Roland Barthes's oblique critique of sentimentalism seems fitting here. Writing about a photography exhibition that celebrates the universality of humanity, Barthes writes that "we are held back at the surface of an identity, prevented precisely by sentimentality from penetrating into this ulterior zone of human behaviour where historical alienation introduces some 'differences,' which we shall here quite simply call 'injustices.'"[4] Barthes's use of the word "sentimentality" offers a damning charge: the evocation of deep emotion is merely an anodyne—a soothing instrument that consoles and pacifies just as it hides the cultural formations at the heart of social injustice. For Barthes—and for most literary and cultural critics who cast a skeptical eye toward sentimentalism—Walton's use of sentimental figurations would not be the liberal, democratizing gesture that it claims to be, but would in fact be an insidious deployment of emotional language that ultimately makes an unjust labor system seem natural.

The takeover of sentimentality by big business is not a new phenomenon. As Roland Marchand points out, since early in the twentieth century corporations have been engaging in public relations techniques that rely on sentimental tropes. Marchand offers a number of examples of big business managers realizing that their corporations need to cultivate a sentimental image "to address the disproportions in size and power that the giant corporation still signified."[5] He writes, for example, "In the early 1920s an AT&T public relations executive frankly aspired 'to make the people understand and love the company. Not merely be consciously dependent upon it—not merely regard it as a necessity—not merely to take it for granted—but to love it—to hold real affection for it.'"[6] The very largest corporations and the most impersonal businesses seem to deploy sentimental figurations most vigorously. AT&T—whose business depends on the distance between individuals—urges us to "reach out and touch someone." Allstate Insurance—whose actuarial calculations reduce policy owners to statistics—declares "you're in good hands." The political world, too, has used sentimental figurations to make those who sit atop massive political systems seem personally invested in individuals. Bill Clinton famously declared, "I feel your pain." George W. Bush practiced what he called "compassionate conservatism." According to Jacob Weisberg, Bush picked up the phrase "compassionate conservative" from Doug Wead, "who had been using it since at least 1979, when he gave a speech with that title at a charity meeting."[7] In 1977, Wead wrote a book called *The Compassionate Touch*.[8] In the corporate and political realms, sentimental language suggests and even offers bodily immediacy and personal investment while obscuring a hierarchical system that denies intimate connections between individuals. What is missing from corporate and political deployments of sentimentalism is not just closeness, but the moral sense that undergirded sentimental philosophy at its origins.[9]

It might seem that individuals under this regime live in what Max Weber described as a "cage." Toward the end of *The Protestant Ethic and the Spirit of Capitalism*, Weber wonders what will happen in a society where capitalist pursuit has been stripped of any religious or ethical meaning. He writes:

> No one knows who will live in this cage in the future, or whether at the end of this tremendous development entirely new prophets will arise, or there will be a great rebirth of old ideas and ideals, or, if neither, mechanized petrification, embellished with a sort of convulsive self-importance. For of the last stage of this cultural development, it might well be truly said: "Specialists without spirit, sensualists without heart; this nullity imagines that it has attained a level of civilization never before achieved."[10]

Sam Walton presents himself as a "new prophet," and his sentimental conception of the body may be "a great rebirth of old ideas and ideals." But more likely, given the absence of any moral sense and the digitized grandiosity with which he endows himself, his recycling of sentimental gestures is a "mechanized petrification, embellished with a sort of convulsive self-importance." "Mechanized petrification," in fact, is a good metaphor to describe the potential fate of the sentimental touch. The language of emotion in American literature has hardened into a set of codified gestures just as the economic and social systems have hardened into a set of networks that appear to be impenetrable.

I want to suggest that this dark view of sentimentalism—while warranted—does not fully capture the complexity of sentimentalism's legacy. Indeed, the Barthes critique, though persuasive for corporate appropriations of sentimentality, cannot account for the persistence of sentimental tropes in avowedly unsentimental authors who share Barthes's ethical concerns. For Twain, Anderson, and West, all of whom are fierce critics of sentimentality, the sentimental touch is a site of authentic and earnest connection between humans, even if the moment becomes more and more vexed as the settings become more and more alienated. The modernists, particularly, use the sentimental touch—a trope that demands that bodies have a stable, transmittable meaning—even when their texts suggest that we should never trust bodies and that exterior qualities do not correspond to interior value.

"Mechanized petrification," then, may not be an entirely negative metaphor. Indeed, Weber's phrase foregrounds what has always been both problematic and powerful about sentimental language: it is systematic and therefore mechanically reproducible. Harriet Beecher Stowe knew this, of course, which is why, even though she did not know personally all her readers, she could trust that they "feel right" (624). Mark Twain knew this as well, which is why *Adventures of Huckleberry Finn* offers a stern warning against being seduced by huckster sentimentalism before it offers the authentic, transparent sentimentalism of Jim and Huck. The recognizability and reproducibility (that is, the "mechanized petrification") of the sentimental touch open the touch up to potential exploitation, but also provide access for individuals to relate to one another across massive cultural barriers. Because of the conventionality of the sentimental touch, readers of *Uncle Tom's Cabin*, just like Huck in Twain's novel, can recognize deep emotion in humans across racial divides and can consider blacks not as "*things*" but as "human beings, with beating hearts and living affections" (Stowe 51).

The sentimental moments in Anderson and West become more fragile and anxious than the moments in Stowe and even in Twain. Writing in an age where managerialism is a dominant social force, Anderson makes clear that instances of human touch are no longer always moments of sentimental compulsion, but are fraught with the uncertainties of a culture in which bodies have become increasingly abstract and mysterious. Characters in *Winesburg, Ohio* can no longer trust each other's bodies, yet Anderson trusts that readers will understand the sentimental touch between George and Helen. Readers know that this moment of transcendence is earnest because Anderson's sentimental figuration adheres to the rules of sentimentality; Anderson relies on the mechanical nature of the structure that he wants to overthrow. Nathanael West offers an even starker example of an author using a trope that is fully at odds with the ruptured, alienated culture that he represents. The sentimental trope is powerful in *Miss Lonelyhearts* precisely because it is such a radical departure from the rest of the text. When we see the sentimental touch out of context, as in *Miss Lonelyhearts*, the trope's mechanical nature reveals itself fully. Because the moment gives us pause, because we cannot simply read past it, the sentimental touch becomes all the more powerful.

To see a sentimental touch in an unsentimental novel is in some ways to see the skeletal framework of literary structure. Because the sentimental touch is unexpected, because it does not fit with the articulated assumptions of the unsentimental text, and because therefore it captures a moment of literary anxiety, the trope is revealed for what it is: a mechanical literary convention that relies on specific conceptions of the human body to manipulate emotion. When characters touch hands in a moment of silence and narrative stillness, readers recognize the moment as utopian: legible bodies can experience unmediated emotion. To expose the roots of sentiment by revealing its literary scaffolding, to face the fact that our most deeply felt sensations may be programmed and conventional responses, is not to belittle feeling, but rather to recognize a crucial element of emotion.[11] As the sentimental touch reveals, even the most mechanical of bodies in the most mechanical of ages can feel.

The sentimentalist Stowe reminds us, like the realist Twain, and like the modernists Anderson and West, that to be anonymous and interchangeable is not to be unfeeling. The age of the manager, even as it is defined above all by anonymity and interchangeability, still contains sentiment. Indeed, the sharpest critiques of sentimentalism—that it indulges and naturalizes bodies in a way that obscures the workings of history, that its mechanical reproducibility empties it of all meaning—do not sufficiently speak to the persistent power and moral weight that sentimental tropes continue to carry. The fate of the sentimental touch—passing from the sentimentalists through the realists and the modernists—leads not just to the profit-mindedness of Sam Walton, whose coercive use of sentimentalism forces us to acknowledge the most insidious aspects of mechanized tropes, but also to the ethical concerns of someone like David Foster Wallace.

Wallace's *Infinite Jest* (1996) is in some ways the end-of-the-century analog to Nathanael West's *Miss Lonelyhearts* (1933). While West's efficient prose and episodic narration suited the mechanized, bureaucratic capitalism of the early century, Wallace's webbed narrative and diffuse plotlines fit the computer-driven economy of the late century. While personal interactions were subsumed to the demands of business in *Miss Lonelyhearts*, time itself is commodified in *Infinite Jest*. Loneliness consumes both texts.[12] Moments of sympathy in Wallace's text seem restricted to scripted addict support-group meetings. Characters touch hands, but only "to say the our Father in a big circle."[13]

Yet, at a crucial moment in the novel, we get a scene that adheres to the long and surprising legacy of sentimentalism. While *Infinite Jest* offers an encyclopedic vision of the many interlocking systems that make up a not-so-futuristic United States, the moral lens of the novel comes to focus on Don Gately, a former thief and addict who helps manage "The Ennet House Drug and Alcohol Recovery House (sic)" (176). He experiences "managerial headaches" (604), asks for "managerial assistance" (606), and suffers "managerial stress" (607) before he is shot. When Tiny Ewell, a fellow Ennet House resident, visits Don

Gately in a trauma hospital, there is almost a sentimental touch. Ewell comes to Gately's bedside:

> "I'm scared," from what seemed somewhere overhead and rising, was the last thing Gately heard Ewell whisper as the ceiling bulged down toward them. Gately wanted to tell Tiny Ewell that he could totally fucking I.D. with Ewell's feelings, and that if he, Tiny, could just hang in and tote that bale and put one little well-shined shoe in front of the other everything would end up all right, that the God of Ewell's understanding would find some way for Ewell to make things right, and then he could let the despicable feelings go instead of keeping them down with Dewars, but Gately couldn't connect the impulse to speak with actual speech, still. He settled for try-ing to reach his left hand across and pat Ewell's hand on the railing. But his own breadth was too far to reach across. And then the white ceiling came all the way down and made everything white. (816–17)

Through a haze of drugs and pain, Gately yearns to communicate with Ewell. As in the sentimental novels of the nineteenth century, the accep-tance of God allows a sincere communion. Here, though, God is quali-fied and personalized—adhering to steps two and three of Alcoholics Anonymous.[14] The unspoken phrase "totally fucking I.D." is a sympa-thetic offering, but its colloquial vulgarity suggests discomfort. "Fuck-ing" brings both closeness and detachment. The phrase illustrates a contemporary alienation from sentimental tropes: we cannot imagine Stowe writing "totally fucking I.D.," but more to the point, we cannot imagine Wallace writing "for, in the gates of eternity, the black hand and the white hold each other with an equal clasp" (Stowe 456). Yet "totally fucking I.D." embodies the deepest utopian ambition of sentimentalism: for an individual to experience full, unmediated sympathy with another individual. Wallace's leap back to what appears to be the ethical concerns of the nineteenth century in fact marks the continuation of what has been a hidden legacy—the way that American realists and modernists have smuggled sentimental figurations deep into the twentieth century.

Wallace is wary of the sentimental moment, but he is not cynical, and the text is certainly not a repudiation of sentimentalism. In the world of the sentimental, silences are vital: bodies can express true feeling, words cannot. Language at the moment of a fully invested sympathetic com-munion would only seem hollow, fatuous, even vulgar. For Wallace, the words at such a moment are in fact vulgar. Crucially, though, Wallace's words are unspoken; Gately remains silent. The touch of hands might be able to express what Gately cannot say. But Gately's own sick body blocks his attempt at physical communication. Instead of being a passageway for deep sympathy, the body's very physicality obstructs the sentimental touch. The sentimental touch has become a battered trope. The moment of the sentimental touch continues to follow its modern trajectory, becoming rarer, increasingly fragile, more and more incongruous, more and more vexed, as culture becomes less and less responsive to individual humans. In *Infinite Jest*, finally, only the vestige of the sentimental touch remains. Wallace calls on the laws of sentimental reading, even to show the failure of sentimental communion. The utopianism of the trope, then, is not lost.[15] Though the sentimental touch is never quite fulfilled, Wallace, like Gately, imagines the utopian possibility of unmediated communication. The literary and ethical concerns of David Foster Wallace hearken back to those of the nineteenth-century sentimentalists; but, more important, they embody the way that American authors have both struggled with and held on to sentimental tropes long after sentimentalism itself lost its cultural power and appeal.

Wallace, like the modernists in this study, writes about being human in an age when it is difficult to be human. Or, as he puts it, "Fiction's about what it is to be a fucking *human being*."[16] After David Foster Wallace's suicide, Jonathan Franzen wrote that he and Wallace agreed that fiction was for that "neutral middle ground on which to make a deep connection with another human being."[17] "To be a fucking *human being*," then, is to "totally fucking I.D." with another human being. While the phrase "totally fucking I.D." articulates a sentimental desire, it also resonates with the penetrating effects of managerial culture. "I.D." is administrative jargon. The phrase reminds us that under a managerial regime, individuals are often reduced to their I.D.—an imposed, literally and metaphorically abbreviated identity that suits, first and foremost, the needs of the managerial network. Gately's words, in fact, are marked above all by their adherence to the vocabulary of Alcoholics Anonymous. Adhering to a system—whether it be a twelve-step program or the laws of sentimental literature—is not to disavow emotion. Support-group clichés are by definition prefabricated, reproducible packets of language; but, as Wallace shows, it is precisely their prefabrication and reproducibility that make them meaningful. When Wallace writes about the world of Alcoholics Anonymous, he writes about a world where anonymity and interchangeability are virtues of a system that saves lives.

In this way, Wallace foregrounds the power of convention and linguistic interchangeability. To be sentimental is to be vulnerable not just to other humans but also to institutions and organizations. Sentimentality in the age of the manager requires submission to the "mechanized petrification" of sentimental tropes. As Barthes warned, the language of sentimentalism can offer seemingly natural bodies that mystify our relationship to reality and history. But the conventionality of sentimental language allows humans to connect to other humans in an otherwise mystifying world. When we are awake to the history of sentimentalism—that is, when we realize and utilize its mechanical conventions—it becomes clear that the language of sentimentalism can offer the promise of physical presence in a world that otherwise seems abstract and inscrutable. Because of its reliance on the body, sentimentalism does not avoid history, but rather pushes toward a full bodily investment in the world. The sentimental touch shows us not just the ethical value of bodies and feeling, but also the ethical value of literary convention.

NOTES

Introduction

1. Stowe, *Uncle Tom's Cabin*, 155.

2. See, for instance, Love, *Babbitt*; and Augspurger, "Sinclair Lewis' Primers." See also Warner et al., *Social Class in America*, in which the authors declare that *Babbitt* "is founded on accurate knowledge of the structure of community life" (232).

3. Lewis, *Babbitt*, 374 (hereafter cited in the text).

4. Andrew Franta explains the cultural transformation during the shift to a complex commercial society: "in the late eighteenth century manners were replacing virtues and social values were replacing political values" (Franta, "Godwin's Handshake," 708). T. J. Jackson Lears writes: "For centuries, the internal dynamic of bourgeois individualism had been undermining all the older, external forms of moral authority—the authority of king over subject, priest over communicant, master over slave.... Even as they attacked the old, external forms of moral authority, bourgeois moralists labored to create a new, internalized mode of moral authority" (Lears, *No Place of Grace*, 12–13). For an explanation of the way that "the traffic or commerce of modern life was at the same time a traffic in opinions and sentiments," see Rothschild, *Economic Sentiments*, 9.

5. I want to stress that sentimental literature was not only very popular in the early and middle nineteenth century but was also an extremely strong social and political force. As Philip Fisher notes, "from roughly 1740 to 1860 sentimentality was a crucial tactic of politically radical representation throughout western culture" (Fisher, *Hard Facts*, 92).

6. Chandler, *Visible Hand*, 7. There are a number of business historians who have written about managerialism in the United States. The most groundbreaking and influential study is Alfred Chandler's *The Visible Hand: The Managerial Revolution in American Business*. Though it was written in 1977, most economists and business historians agree that it remains an accurate assessment of economic change. Olivier Zunz writes of Chandler: "By pointing to structural changes in the economy caused

by the activities of a new managerial class, Chandler implicitly challenged social historians to move beyond their focus on the proletariat and open their studies to other
causes and consequences of large-scale economic change" (Zunz, *Making America
Corporate*, 7). There are some disagreements and reservations concerning *The Visible
Hand*, but most of these have to do with applying his model to economies beyond the
United States (see Schmitz, *Growth of Big Business*, 3). For other studies that posit the
centrality of managerialism in the development of American culture, see Braverman,
Labor and Monopoly Capital; Cochran, *American Business*; Drucker, *Practice of Man-
agement*; Montgomery, *Worker's Control*; Wiebe, *Search for Order*; and Zunz, *Making
America Corporate*.

7. Chandler himself does not speculate about the psychological effects of the rise
of vast managerial networks. He does imply, though, that his observations have far-
reaching effects, declaring, "I hope that these facts may also be useful to scholars with
other questions and concerns other than those relevant to the generalizations pre-
sented here" (Chandler, *Visible Hand*, 6). This study is in some ways a response to
Chandler's suggestion that scholarly projects should address some of the unexplored
implications of his work.

8. Weber, "Max Weber on Bureaucratization," 126–27.

9. Weber wrote about both European and American business practices. Zunz
explains that while American bureaucracies did not possess all of the Weberian traits,
American "middle-level corporate managers did follow the Weberian bureaucratic
model in that these men became specialized, adhered to formalized work rules, and
advanced in a differentiated hierarchy" (Zunz, *Making America Corporate*, 39).

10. As Martin Sklar puts it, business activity is not just economic but "presupposes, and is permeated by, a complex mode of consciousness, that is, by ideas and
ideals about deliberate calculation of ends and means with respect to other persons;
about the shape of society, its approved goals and moral standards; and about the law
and jurisprudence, party politics, and the range and limits of government authority.
Business activity presupposes, and is permeated by, expectations about one's own and
other persons' character structure, values, and normal behavior, particularly as they
relate to broader social relations in which some persons are taken to be superiors, some
equals, and some subordinates—as they relate, that is, to social hierarchy" (Sklar, *Corporate Reconstruction of American Capitalism*, 8). Business activity, in other words,
pervades culture in a broad sense.

11. Galambos, *Public Image of Big Business*, 3.

12. Louis Galambos writes that bureaucratization is formative of American culture: "Changes of this magnitude could hardly have taken place without influencing
the attitudes and values that made up the national culture. Indeed, this organizational
revolution appears to have forced Americans to adopt a new culture, one attuned to
the needs of bureaucracy in an urban setting" (ibid., 14). See also Frederick Tonnies's
conceptual scheme in *Gemeinschaft und Gesellschaft* (1887). In *Gemeinschaft* (often
translated as community), "there is a complete unity of human wills" (Tonnies, *Community and Civil Society*, 22). In *Gesellschaft* (often translated as civil society), people
"live peacefully alongside one another, but in this case without being essentially
united—indeed, on the contrary, they are here essentially detached" (52). Though
Tonnies lays out only a theoretical model (not based on empirical or historical evidence), under managerialism, *Gesellschaft* would dominate *Gemeinschaft*.

13. Drucker, *Practice of Management*, 280.

14. Chandler, *Visible Hand*, 1.

15. Eleanor Courtemanche rightly points out that use of the word "capitalism" is "open to historical debate, since the idea that capitalism is a system and not merely the actions of a group of 'capitalists' dates from the mid-nineteenth century, long after Smith's death" (Courtemanche, *"Invisible Hand" and British Fiction*, 4). As Courtemanche goes on to say, we still acknowledge Smith as the "founding father of the economic system" that we call capitalism (4).

16. Zandy, *Hands*, 1.

17. Philoponus, *On Aristotle's "On the Soul 3.1–8,"* 149.

18. For an explanation of the "Adam Smith problem—that is, to the puzzle over the compatibility of *The Theory of Moral Sentiments* with *The Wealth of Nations*," see Hirschman, *Passions and the Interests*, 109. See also Broadie, "Sympathy and the Impartial Spectator"; and Courtemanche, *"Invisible Hand" and British Fiction*. For an explanation of how both *"The Theory of Moral Sentiments* and *The Wealth of Nations* had been part of a grander plan for a Science of Man," see Phillipson, *Adam Smith*, 279.

19. Though the phrase "invisible hand" occurs only once in Adam Smith's *The Wealth of Nations*, its use as a common metaphor in economics speaks to the resonance of the phrase. Adam Smith used the "invisible hand" to illustrate the principle that an individual acting for his or her own self-interest will often promote the common good. He writes, "Every individual necessarily labours to render the annual revenue of the society as great as he can. He generally neither intends to promote the public interest, nor knows how much he is promoting it. . . . By preferring the support of domestic to that of foreign industry, he intends only his own security; and by directing that industry in such a manner as its produce may be of the greatest value, he intends only his own gain, and he is in this, as in many other cases, led by an invisible hand to promote an end which was no part of his intention. Nor is it always the worse for society that it was no part of his intention. By pursuing his own interest he frequently promotes that of the society more effectually than when he really intends to promote it. I have never known much good done by those who affected to trade for the public good" (Smith, *Wealth of Nations*, 484–85). Smith also uses the phrase "invisible hand" in two other places with two different meanings: in *The Theory of Moral Sentiments* (IV.I.9) and in *The History of Astronomy* (III.2).

The economists Kenneth Arrow and F. H. Hahn declare of the "invisible hand": "the notion that a social system moved by independent actions in pursuit of different values is consistent with a final coherent state of balance, and one in which the outcomes may be quite different from those intended by the agents, is surely the most important intellectual contribution that economic thought has made to the general understanding of social processes" (Arrow and Hahn, *General Competitive Analysis*, 1).

20. Harry Braverman writes that to "manage" "originally meant to train a horse in his paces, to cause him to do the exercises of the *manege*. As capitalism creates a society in which no one is presumed to consult anything but self-interest, and as the employment contract between parties sharing nothing but the inability to avoid each other becomes prevalent, management becomes a more perfected and subtle instrument. . . . Like a rider who uses reins, bridle, spurs, carrot, whip, and training from birth to impose his will, the capitalist strives, through management, to control" (Braverman, *Labor and Monopoly Capital*, 67–68).

21. In *No Place of Grace*, T. J. Jackson Lears describes the sense of alienation that was widely felt when economic life at the turn of the twentieth century became

increasingly rationalized. He writes: "For white collar clerks and professionals there was a further problem. Despite their relative security their work seemed strangely insubstantial. The new bureaucratic world of work often fragmented their labor and reduced their sense of autonomy: more important, it isolated them from the hard, substantial reality of things. Among the middle and upper classes, the transformation of work reinforced difficulties pervading the wider culture; the splintering sense of selfhood, the vague feelings of unreality" (Lears, *No Place of Grace*, 60).

22. Milton, *Paradise Lost*, 12.197–98. Milton critics have noted the symbolic significance of the hands of Adam and Eve in *Paradise Lost*. Roy Flannagan explains, "Their 'handedness' (see 4.739) has been an important emblem of their conjugal union, as it will continue to be after the Fall (12.468). Eve's single 'rash hand' will also play an important part in the Fall (9.780), as will Adam's 'liberal hand' (997 below); Adam's hand will become brutal after the Fall ('Her hand he seis'd' [1037 below])" (Milton, *Paradise Lost*, 596).

23. Howard, "What Is Sentimentality?" 76.

24. Barry Shank puts it well: "feeling is structured by forces beyond the heart" (Shank, *Token of My Affection*, 268).

25. In *Marxism and Literature*, Raymond Williams explains that he is interested in "structures of feeling" because they can illuminate "meanings and values as they are actively lived and felt" (Williams, *Marxism and Literature*, 132). Williams writes, "we are also defining a social experience which is still *in process*, often indeed not yet recognized as social but taken to be private, idiosyncratic, and even isolating, but which in analysis (though rarely otherwise) has its emergent, connecting, and dominant characteristics, indeed its specific hierarchies" (132). One of the ambitions of this study is to analyze the structure of sentimental feeling in order to illuminate the "specific hierarchies"—the institutions and cultural formations—that we may not even recognize as shaping the way we feel.

26. Eagleton, *Ideology of the Aesthetic*, 34.

27. Barthes, *Mythologies*, 101.

28. Gilmore, *American Romanticism*, 12–13.

29. A number of critics ponder the relationship between literature and the economy. In *New Deal Modernism: American Literature and the Invention of the Welfare State*, Michael Szalay demonstrates that authors were subject to the same organizational forces that governed the business and political worlds. Walter Benn Michaels has argued that works of literature are best examined in relation to the economic conditions and values of the age in which they were written. As he explains in *The Gold Standard and the Logic of Naturalism*, all experience is economic—life is made up of transactions, contracts, and agreements; characters and authors cannot help but reflect economic values. In his study of American naturalism, Michaels finds that literature endorses rather than rejects capitalist values. Indeed, within capitalism, one cannot judge consumer culture: "you don't like it or dislike it, you exist in it, and the things you like and dislike exist in it too" (Michaels, *Gold Standard*, 18). I use a similar presupposition that literature will necessarily be a function of the culture that produces it. I also argue, though, unlike Michaels, that literature is not merely a creation of existent social structures, but that it can respond to historical pressures.

30. Trachtenberg, *Incorporation of America*, 184.

31. Theodor Adorno writes that "the development of artistic processes, usually classed under the heading of style, corresponds to social development" (Adorno,

Aesthetic Theory, 5). He goes on to say that "the unsolved antagonisms of reality return in artworks as immanent problems of form" (6). On the relationship between form and history, Roland Barthes offers a similar view: "The more a system is specifically defined in its forms, the more amenable it is to historical criticism. To parody a well-known saying, I shall say that a little formalism turns one away from History, but that a lot brings one back to it" (Barthes, *Mythologies*, 112).

32. As Barry Shank says of the emotional language found on mass-produced greeting cards at the turn of the twentieth century, "the stereotyped images and sentimental language found on the cards do not hide the social tensions that produced the need for them" (Shank, *Token of My Affection*, 8).

33. For Leslie Fiedler, sentimentalism in the United States, though wildly popular, produced our most poorly wrought, embarrassing works of literature. As he writes in *Love and Death in the American Novel*, sentimentalism was "a universal influence which was also a universal calamity" largely because America lacked the aristocratic tradition that served as the cultural backdrop to the great sentimental novels of Britain (Fiedler, *Love and Death*, 75). In Fiedler's view, many American authors realized the inadequacy of sentimentalism and turned away from female characters to a world of men escaping "civilization" (26). He explains that "there is at the sentimental center of our novels, where we are accustomed to find in their European counterparts 'platonic' love or adultery, seduction, rape, or long-drawn-out flirtation, nothing but the love of males!" (368). The American novel cannot deal with the entanglements that women bring to mature relationships; heroes must leave the female world of domestic fiction and enter the male wilderness. But even as the American novel cannot be sentimental, there is still, as Fiedler says, a "sentimental center." While Fiedler insists that the sentimental center is the primary site of difference between the American novel and European sentimental fiction, this study aims to show the importance of examining the sentimental center as the site of strange sameness. What is most surprising, for the purposes of this study, is not that the sentimental tropes have shifted from marking a heterosexual world to marking a homosocial universe, but that the sentimental tropes persist at all.

34. Tompkins, *Sensational Designs*, xiii. I, too, want to account for the often-overlooked enormous impact of sentimentalism. While Tompkins primarily studies the influence of sentimental texts on American culture in order to show that sentimental works have been neglected by literary critics, my project aims to show the influence of a sentimental trope on texts that literary critics have not neglected. While Tompkins writes in order to reclaim the power and significance of sentimental texts in American literature, my study claims that sentimentality is central to texts already in the canon. In *Sentimental Modernism: Women Writers and the Revolution of the Word*, Suzanne Clark offers an extension of Tompkins's argument. Clark sets out to "restore the sentimental *within* modernism" (Clark, *Sentimental Modernism*, 4). For Clark, the degradation of sentimentality under modernism dismantled the literary contributions of women.

35. Berlant, *Female Complaint*, xii, 21.

36. I am inspired by Martha Nussbaum's sense that emotions have "a complicated cognitive structure that is in part narrative in form" (Nussbaum, *Upheavals of Thoughts*, 2). For Nussbaum, to understand emotion we should "turn to texts that contain a narrative dimension, thus deepening and refining our grasp of ourselves as beings with a complicated temporal history" (2–3). Since novels endeavor to portray

the deep psychological life of human beings of a particular place and time, it makes sense to turn to novels to examine the confluence of emotions and economic structure.

37. See Stowe, "Appeal to Women of the Free States of America"; and Hutcheson, *Essay on the Nature and Conduct of the Passions and Affections*. See also Cott, "Passionlessness"; and Strasser, "Hutcheson on the Higher and Lower Pleasures." For explanations of sexual ideology in American sentimental fiction, see Goshgarian, *To Kiss the Chastening Rod*; and Camfield, *Necessary Madness*.

38. Lears, "From Salvation to Self-Realization," 23.

39. Stuart Blumin writes that "the half-century following the recording of the 1840 census was a period of recurring crisis. Starting in the mid-point of a severe six-year economic depression, it included at least two shorter but sharp economic downturns (in the late 1850s and mid-1880s), a six-year depression in the 1870s noted for some of the most extensive and violent labor-capital confrontations in all of American history, and, most tragically of all, a Civil War of breathtaking destructiveness" (Blumin, "Social Implication of U.S. Economic Development," 834).

40. Dewey, *Later Works*, 66 (hereafter cited in the text).

41. As Dewey admits, "quantification, mechanization, and standardization . . . have their good side; external conditions and the standard of living are undoubtedly, improved." But, he goes on to say, "their effects are not limited to these matters" (52).

42. As Louis Galambos explains, the period between 1879 and 1892 was marked by significant growth and organization flux "in almost every sector of the economy and every part of the country" (Galambos, *Public Image of Big Business*, 47).

43. Taylor, *Principles of Scientific Management*, 7.

1 / Touching the Body, Training the Reader

1. Stowe, *Uncle Tom's Cabin*, 195 (hereafter cited in the text).

2. Philip Fisher writes of another way that the philosophy of sentimentalism counteracts the system of slavery. He explains, "Sentimentality, by its experimental extension of humanity to prisoners, slaves, madmen, children, and animals, exactly reverses the process of slavery itself which has at its core the withdrawal of human status from a part of humanity" (Fisher, *Hard Facts*, 100).

3. Eagleton, *Ideology of the Aesthetic*, 13.

4. Sanchez-Eppler, "Bodily Bonds," 100.

5. This study will return to the apparent critical loss of interest in sentimental texts during the twentieth century; sentimental figurations in novels persist but become disfigured and displaced.

6. Douglas, "Introduction," 11.

7. See Douglas, *Feminization of American Culture*; and Tompkins, *Sensational Designs*. See also Berlant, "Poor Eliza"; Brodhead, *Cultures of Letters*; and Romero, "Bio-Political Resistance."

8. Wexler, "Tender Violence," 9. See, especially, Camfield, "Moral Aesthetics of Sentimentality"; Crane, "Dangerous Sentiments"; and Merish "Sentimental Consumption."

9. Sand, "Review of *Uncle Tom's Cabin*," 459.

10. Parker, "Harriet Beecher Stowe," 318.

11. Warner, "*Uncle Tom's Cabin a Half Century Later*," 483.

12. Mullan, *Sentiment and Sociability*, 201.

13. *Hand Phrenologically Considered*, 56–58.

14. Richardson, *Clarissa*, 1362.

15. Sterne, *Tristram Shandy*, 382.

16. Ibid., 350.

17. Barry Shank explains that the construction of an "authentic, interior self" was one of the legacies of a new market-based culture. He writes, "By the end of the eighteenth century, the ability to render public an interior self had become the most important evidence that a person was capable of certain forms of classbound agency and autonomy. It was by means of displaying one's interiority that a person demonstrated the capacity for independent judgment that was both the theoretical underpinning and one of the most significant effects of the market revolution" (Shank, *Token of My Affection*, 23).

18. Klein, *Shaftesbury and the Culture of Politeness*, 20–21.

19. Ibid., 92.

20. Campbell, *Romantic Ethic*, 151.

21. Eagleton, *Ideology of the Aesthetic*, 34.

22. Stowe alludes to moral sense philosophers when she describes Dinah in the St. Clare household: "Like a certain class of modern philosophers, Dinah perfectly scorned logic and reason in every shape, and always took refuge in intuitive certainty; and here she was perfectly impregnable" (310). St. Clare, himself, has a developed moral sense: "He had one of those natures which could better and more clearly conceive of religious things from its own perceptions and instincts, than many a matter-of-fact and practical Christian. The gift to appreciate and the sense to feel the finer shades and relations of moral things, often seems an attribute of those whose whole life shows a careless disregard of them" (440).

23. Smith, *Theory of Moral Sentiments*, 373.

24. Camfield, "Moral Aesthetics of Sentimentality," 326.

25. Dillon, "Sentimental Aesthetics," 498.

26. The science of phrenology was still widely accepted in the middle of the nineteenth century. As Susan Nuernberg explains, "the 'American school of ethnology' affirmed on the basis of cranial measurements and other archaeological evidence that blacks were permanently inferior to whites" (Nuernberg, "Stowe," 38). Charles Colbert explains that phrenology's "primary concern was to identify the moral code inscribed in the human form" (Colbert, *Measure of Perfection*, 2). Colbert reminds us that "Stowe's novel relies on phrenology regularly to provide the psychological dimensions of the characters" (240).

27. Richard Brodhead explains, "Writing always takes place within some completely concrete cultural situation, a situation that surrounds it with some particular landscape of institutional structures, affiliates it with some particular group from among the array of contemporary groupings, and installs it [in] some group-based world of understandings, practices, and values" (Brodhead, *Cultures of Letters*, 8). Critics should take into account the material and cultural circumstances of textual production.

28. Alfred Chandler writes, "Although personal relations remained important in arranging specific shipments and sales and above all in the extension of credit, the importer, exporter, jobber, auctioneer, bank cashier, insurer, and broker dealt daily with buyers and sellers with whom he had little personal contact. Rarely did a merchant know both the producer and consumer at either end of the long chain of middlemen, transporters, and financiers who moved the goods through the economy"

(Chandler, *Visible Hand*, 48). In an expanding economy, the links of economic trans-action multiplied quickly.

29. See Mintz and Kellog, *Domestic Revolutions*.

30. Dillon, *Gender of Freedom*, 201.

31. Brown, *Sentimental Novel*, 190.

32. Fredrickson, "Uncle Tom and the Anglo-Saxons," 433.

33. Hedrick, *Harriet Beecher Stowe*, 208.

34. Cooper, *Last of the Mohicans*, 32.

35. Hawthorne, *Scarlet Letter*, 82.

36. This is not to say that language itself breaks down under the system of slavery; it is to say that the system of reading bodies that defines slavery quickly deconstructs itself. Winfried Fluck argues that "the fact that the public meaning of the sign 'black' misrepresents Tom as a person does not lead the novel to a deliberate foregrounding of the tyranny of signs (as would be the case in high modernism and postmodernism), but to a concerted effort to resemanticize this one sign within a cultural system and mode of literary representation which the novel wants to strengthen, not to question, in order to achieve its own cultural and political goals" (Fluck, "Power and Failure of Representation," 326). Unlike this study, Fluck does not see sentimentalism and slavery as two incompatible modes of representation. The novel certainly shows the inadequacy of the word "black," but precisely not to recover blackness, but rather to show the falsity of the entire system of signification under slavery.

37. Augustine St. Clare, arguing with his brother, will hint at the problem of the one-drop rule in a culture of violently mixed blood: "Well, there is a pretty fair infu-sion of Anglo Saxon blood among our slaves, now. . . . Sons of white fathers, with all our haughty feelings burning in their veins, will not always be bought and sold and traded. They will rise, and raise with them their mother's race" (392). While Augustine declares that bodies determine character, he reminds us, once again, that bodies are crucial to the Southern economy.

38. Although the Oxford English Dictionary states that the first use of the word "pass" to refer specifically to "a person of Negro ancestry who is held to be or regards himself as a white person," occurred in 1935, Nella Larsen's novel *Passing* was pub-lished in 1929, at which point it is likely that the word was commonly understood racial vocabulary. The OED does tell us that since Shakespeare, "pass" could mean "to be accepted as equivalent to . . . often with the implication of being something else."

39. Fredrickson, "Uncle Tom and the Anglo-Saxons," 431.

40. Ibid., 436.

41. Oxenhandler, "Changing Concept of Literary Emotion," 117.

42. Ibid.

43. Jauss, "Literary History," 72.

44. Laura Korobkin speaks to the way in which sentimentalism is effective because of its ability to inspire emotion from within a wide variety of readers. She writes that "all texts are arguably empty until 'made' by reading, but Stowe's novel, more than most, is quite literally incomplete until an involved reader constructs its potentialities. As a mother of young children, I should and do read *Uncle Tom's Cabin* differently from the unmarried college students to whom I have taught it. This is not a sign of the text's inadequacy, but of its very particular brand of openness" (Korobkin, *Criminal Conversations*, 202).

45. Eagleton, *Ideology of the Aesthetic*, 40.

46. Ibid., 43.

47. The 1850 Fugitive Slave Law caused a tremendous amount of upheaval. Previous laws had required citizens in free states to return fugitive slaves, but the 1850 law eliminated due process. There was now no denying that slavery was an American problem rather than just a Southern problem.

48. O'Farrell, *Telling Complexions*, 5.

49. Brook Thomas, in *Cross Examinations of Law and Literature: Cooper, Hawthorne, Stowe, and Melville*, argues that the episode of Senator and Mrs. Bird demonstrates the conflict between the spheres of private, feminized morality and rational, masculine business. Gregg D. Crane, on the other hand, argues convincingly in "Dangerous Sentiments: Sympathy, Rights, and Revolution in Stowe's Antislavery Novels" that the Bird conversation is not a conflict between law and emotion but instead is a conflict between head and heart that takes place within the law.

50. Crane, "Dangerous Sentiments," 183.

51. Brown, *Sentimental Novel*, 80.

52. Many critics have argued that Eliza's white skin allows white readers to sympathize with her more easily. Lori Merish writes, "The figure of the mulatta best effects, for Stowe, the sentimental regeneration of blackness, the construction of a body that is both black and white. The 'tragic mulatta' was a common figure in antebellum antislavery stories, and she served a double function: to represent the history of sexual violence under slavery and to make that violence intolerable for white readers" (Merish, "Sentimental Consumption," 20).

53. Stowe was acutely aware of the pain of child loss; she herself lost her youngest child, Charley, to cholera less than a year before she began writing *Uncle Tom's Cabin*.

54. Camfield, "Moral Aesthetics of Sentimentality," 332.

55. Sentimental and romance literature abounds with descriptions of somatic responses that are intended to cue the reader to a properly sentimental reaction. For instance, in Susan Warner's 1850 *The Wide, Wide World*, the heroine child, Ellen Montgomery, displays the proper sentimental response to a text as she reads to Mr. Van Brunt: "Once as she finished reading the tenth chapter of John, a favourite chapter, which between her own feeling of it and her strong wish for him had moved her even to tears, she cast a glance at his face to see how he took it. His head was a little turned to one side, and his eyes closed; she thought he was asleep. Ellen was very much disappointed. She sank her head upon her book and prayed that a time might come when he would know the worth of those words" (Warner, *Wide, Wide World*, 413).

56. A number of critics have written about the importance of this scene in which *Uncle Tom's Cabin* "ponders its capacity for intervention in history" (Gilmore, "*Uncle Tom's Cabin* and the American Renaissance," 60). Gregg Camfield explains, "If benevolent feelings spur beneficent action, then art in service of progress should devote itself to eliciting benevolent feelings" (Camfield, "Moral Aesthetics of Sentimentality," 340). As Stephen Railton puts it, "here shared feelings lead toward political actions" (Railton, "Black Slaves and White Readers," 107).

57. O'Connell, "Magic of the Real Presence of Distress," 17.

58. Berlant, "Poor Eliza," 640.

59. For a thorough discussion of how *Uncle Tom's Cabin* shaped the political debates over slavery, see Reynolds, *Mightier Than the Sword*. Reynolds writes that the novel's "dramatic portrait of the evils of slavery intensified the public sentiment behind the rise of Lincoln and the Republicans, while it caused a reactionary surge of

proslavery feeling in the South, exacerbating the tensions that led to the Civil War" (xii). Reynolds goes on to declare that *Uncle Tom's Cabin* "accomplished what Lincoln said was more important than making statues: it molded public opinion. And it did so with a vigor unmatched by any other American novel" (116).

60. Sundquist, "Introduction," in *New Essays on Uncle Tom's Cabin*, 18.

61. Gilmore, "*Uncle Tom's Cabin* and the American Renaissance," 60, 61.

62. Ibid., 64.

63. Warner, *Wide, Wide World*, 561.

64. Cooper, *Last of the Mohicans*, 342.

65. Hawthorne, *Scarlet Letter*, 166.

66. Melville, *Moby-Dick*, 348–49.

67. Montgomery, *Worker's Control*, 11.

68. Thomas, "Introduction," 10.

69. Roodenburg, "'Hand of Friendship,'" 176.

70. Several critics have noticed the significance of hands in the novel. Lori Merish notes that "slavery transforms the hand from an instrument of feeling and care, whose touch promotes and symbolizes interracial connection and sympathy (as in Eva's touching and embracing the slaves), into an instrument of violence and force" (Merish, "Sentimental Consumption," 23). Indeed, as Richard Brodhead asserts, "Legree's human mark is his strong (and obscenely physical) fist, the fist that he boasts 'has got as hard as iron *knocking down niggers*'" (Brodhead, *Cultures of Letters*, 36). Cindy Weinstein writes that "the appeal to Christ's hands in Stowe is meant to avert the situation in which one's hands are never one's own, but it would seem that even Christ's hands cannot completely erase the vestigial sense of the hand as (slave) labor" (Weinstein, *Literature of Labor*, 39).

The hand was also used as a metaphor for domesticity by Stowe's sister. Catharine Beecher writes, "The success of democratic institutions, as is conceded by all, depends upon the intellectual and moral character of the mass of the people. If they are intelligent and virtuous, democracy is a blessing; but if they are ignorant and wicked, it is only a curse, and as much more dreadful than any other form of civil government, as a thousand tyrants are more to be dreaded than one. It is equally conceded, that the formation of the moral and intellectual character of the young is committed mainly to the female hand" (Beecher, *Treatise on Domestic Economy*, 36–37).

71. Brodhead, *Cultures of Letters*, 39.

72. Critics have argued that Stowe betrays her project when she calls for mass emigration. Colonization seems not to be in line with Stowe's otherwise progressive politics (though, as George Fredrickson reminds us, antislavery does not mean pro-equality). More important for the purposes of this study, Stowe's solution seems unsatisfactory because it does not correspond to the sentimental system of legibility. She has shown us the falsity of slavery's binary system; she has shown us the utopian touch during which racial hierarchy is erased. Her call for emigration does not match.

73. The sentimental touch, as a trope, is emblematic of the sentimental style that has bothered many modern critics. As Winfried Fluck declares, "The aesthetic problem surrounding sentimental fiction would, in this case, not be its lack of rhetorical restraint, but its insistence on an idea of literary representation which disregards our modern awareness of the arbitrariness and inherently supplementary character of the process of signification" (Fluck, "Power and Failure of Representation," 333). The rest

of this study explores the circumstances by which the literal depiction of emotion has persisted well beyond what Fluck and other critics would seem to expect.

2 / Managing Sentimentalism in *The Adventures of Huckleberry Finn*

1. Twain, *Adventures of Huckleberry Finn*, 265 (hereafter cited in the text).

2. Twain's sentence is ambiguous: it is not quite clear if Tom's bullet is physically attached to a watch or if Tom's bullet sits in place of a watch. The important point is that Twain invokes the measurement of time. Edward W. Kemble's illustration, whose caption reads "Tom's Liberality," appeared in the original edition of the book and portrays Tom as a young businessman checking the time.

3. Twain, *Connecticut Yankee in King Arthur's Court*, 36 (hereafter cited in the text).

4. See, especially, Weinstein, *Literature of Labor*. See also Hansen, "Once and Future Boss"; Cox, "Machinery of Self-Preservation"; Smith, *Mark Twain's Fables of Progress*; and Biddle, "Veblen, Twain, and the Connecticut Yankee."

5. For a discussion about the ways that a shift in "time-sense" influenced the "inward apprehension of time" of individuals (57), see Thompson, "Time, Work-Discipline, and Industrial Capitalism." Thompson writes, "a general diffusion of clocks and watches is occurring (as one would expect) at the exact moment when the industrial revolution demanded a greater synchronization of labour" (69).

6. Zerubavel, "Standardization of Time," 20.

7. See John Fabian Witt, who writes: "In the early 1880s, a new generation of managerial engineers began to rationalize labor management theory, advocating administered, hierarchical, and rationalized modes of labor management" (Witt, *Accidental Republic*, 107). T. J. Jackson Lears notes that the 1870s and 1880s saw the growth of rigid adherence to quantified time. He writes that "the 'pace of modern life,' a staple of popular sociology, is a direct result of the bureaucratic imperative in organized capitalism—the demand for disciplined, systematic work" (Lears, *No Place of Grace*, 11).

8. Taylor, *Principles of Scientific Management*, 5.

9. Taylor writes that "to work according to scientific laws, the management must take over and perform much of the work which is now left to the men; almost every act of the workman should be preceded by one or more preparatory acts of the management which enable him to do his work better and quicker than he otherwise could" (ibid., 26). For a classic discussion of the elements of business management and a concise explanation of scientific management, see Drucker, *Practice of Management*.

Taylorism was profoundly influential in the development of American business practices. As Harry Braverman writes, "If Taylorism does not exist as a separate school today, that is because, apart from the bad odor of the name, it is no longer the property of a faction, since its fundamental teachings have become the bedrock of all work design" (Braverman, *Labor and Monopoly Capital*, 87). Even though Taylor's own efforts at scientific management did not have the success he imagined, the once-radical notion of treating workers as parts of a vast machine quickly became normal practice. For an explanation (and critique) of the way that Taylor's ideas continue to inform modern consulting and management, see Stewart, *Management Myth*.

10. Henry Ford himself was obsessed with watches. In his autobiography, he writes that one of the biggest events of his early years was "getting a watch" when he was twelve years old (Ford, *My Life and Work*, 22). The year would have been 1875. According to Robert Kanigel, after *The Principles of Scientific Management* was published, "you could hardly buy a stopwatch in Detroit, so swiftly were they snapped

up" (Kanigel, *One Best Way*, 497). In John Dos Passos's minibiography of Frederick Winslow Taylor in *U.S.A.*, Taylor is found "dead with his watch in his hand" (Dos Passos, *U.S.A.*, 787).

11. In 1890, Twain writes that James W. Paige is "the Shakespeare of mechanical invention. In all the ages he has no peer" (Twain, *Autobiography*, 102). In 1906, after having lost his fortune, he writes of "having been robbed of a hundred and seventy thousand dollars by James W. Paige" (ibid., 455).

12. Susan L. Mizruchi writes that Twain "seemed to have had his hand in every significant economic venture of the era. . . . He described himself as 'Capitalist' in his *Who's Who* entry" (Mizruchi, "Becoming Multicultural," 681). Twain invested in "a steam generator, a steam pulley, a new method of marine telegraphy, a watch company, an insurance house, a new process of engraving, . . . the Webster Publishing Company, in which Twain was chief investor and senior partner; and the Paige typesetting machine" (Cox, "Machinery of Self-Preservation," 396).

13. Doyno, "Afterword," 7.

14. See also Robert Shulman, who explains that the narrative—at once yearning for solitude and for community—is a commentary on the "rootlessness and striving" of Twain's own culture (Shulman, *Social Criticism*, 31).

15. Wiebe, *Search for Order*, 47.

16. By 1890, Southern farmers were especially wary of big business. Louis Galambos writes that "while the cotton farmer (especially if he lived east of the Mississippi) was trapped in a painful cost-price squeeze, his economic plight alone does not provide an adequate explanation of his growing animosity toward the trusts. The anxiety grounded in economic interests was, in his case, bound up with a general sense of social disorganization" (Galambos, *Public Image of Big Business*, 62). I want to stress the widespread, pervasive influence of business culture.

17. Trachtenberg, *Incorporation of America*, 201.

18. Writing was a self-conscious craft for Twain, who often wrote about authorship. See, especially, *Life on the Mississippi* (1883), "The Art of Authorship" (1890), "Fenimore Cooper's Literary Offenses" (1895), and "How to Tell a Story" (1895).

19. In *Life on the Mississippi*, Twain launches a scathing attack on Sir Walter Scott: "Sir Walter had so large a hand in making Southern character, as it existed before the war, that he is in great measure responsible for the war" (304). For Twain, it is nearly impossible to overestimate the role of the South's romantic fantasy in determining the fate and character of the country.

20. In *Uncle Tom's Cabin*, Stowe pitted a sentimental system of reading the body against the slave system, showing how sentimentalism's rendering of legible bodies revealed the vicious irrationality in slavery's understanding of the body. In other words, Stowe's sentimental understanding of the body, though not devoid of racism, showed the inherent falseness of applying a binary system of reading (white is free, black is slave) to a spectrum of bodies. Sentimental bodies do not adhere to a system divided only into black bondage and white freedom. But as Twain realizes, sentimentalism, because of its persuasiveness, can be a force of insidious coercion.

21. Budd, "American Background," 34.

22. Eric Sundquist, like Louis J. Budd, points to a postbellum culture that spawned realism out of a realization that the United States had not lived up to the promise of its founding documents. He writes, "Both the ideals and the public idealization of the founding fathers seemed at best badly shaken, and at worst impossibly irrelevant,

following the Civil War, and a corresponding pressure may be discerned in the literature that at once incorporated that loss in the tribute of muted nostalgia and in part gave way to its consequences" (Sundquist, "Country of the Blue," 5). Gregg Camfield similarly suggests that Twain "is registering not so much hypocrisy as the gap between the political ideals of his youth and the economy of his age" (Camfield, "Republican Artisan," 123). Twain sets his text when the disjuncture between the rhetoric of America's civil religion and the actuality of American life was at its most gaping—in the age of slavery.

This chapter agrees with the long-standing critical assumption that *Adventures of Huckleberry Finn* is a realist narrative. There have been compelling arguments that question Twain's realism, most notably Bell, "Mark Twain, 'Realism,' and *Huckleberry Finn*."

23. Auerbach, *Mimesis*, 491.

24. Howells, "Call for Realism," 500. We should not mistake the literary movement led by Howells for actual mimesis. As Robert H. Wiebe writes, "When William Dean Howells, who came out of Martin's Ferry, Ohio, to serve as the arbiter of literary fashions, excluded violence and casual brutality from his definition of realism because they were 'unnatural' and 'sensationalist,' he denied everyday life in the slums and shanty towns" (Wiebe, *Search for Order*, 9).

25. Twain, *Adventures of Tom Sawyer*, 276.

26. Kate Chopin's 1899 *The Awakening* has been widely praised by critics for its unsentimental rendering of a liberated, willful, powerful woman. The sentimental touch persists though, as Robert drew Edna "down upon the sofa beside him and held her hand in both of his" (Chopin, *Awakening*, 166). Edna falls in love with Robert, and, as George Spangler argues, Edna's suicide at the end of the novel is unfitting, "a conclusion for an ordinary sentimental novel, not for a subtle psychological treatment of female sexuality" (Spangler, "Ending of the Novel," 187–88). Chopin reduces the awakened woman to a conventional pathetic figure that satisfies a sentimental readership. The literary shift away from sentimentalism is not a clean break, but the sentimental gesture becomes a lapse, signaling an old-fashioned sensibility reserved for characters who cannot survive in a new age.

Frank Norris, arguably the most unsentimental of the naturalist writers, makes an ambivalent use of sentimental tropes. His 1899 *McTeague* features a hulking dentist who struggles to control his primal desires. Michael T. Gilmore has shown that McTeague becomes smarter during the course of the narrative, actually overcoming the apparent destiny of his brutish body (Gilmore, *Surface and Depth*, 126). Even as the text questions the authority of the body, though, a subplot features the sentimental, hand-touching love of Miss Baker and Old Grannis: "quietly, quietly, their hands in each other's hands, 'keeping company,' but now with nothing to separate them" (Norris, *McTeague*, 329). The touch signals a profound love, but only for an earlier generation. Sentimental contact, it seems, will die of old age with an unreproductive couple.

The silent, deep touch appears, too, in Theodore Dreiser's 1900 *Sister Carrie*. Hurstwood "took Carrie's little hand, and a current of feeling swept from one to the other" (Dresier, *Sister Carrie*, 83). Soon Carrie will fall for Hurstwood. Their relationship is doomed, though—the sentimental touch does not signal everlasting love. As Amy Kaplan argues, Dreiser's sentimentalism is not a failure that blocks his realism but "is recontextualized and given new life in Dreiser's aesthetics of consumption" (Kaplan, *Social Construction of American Realism*, 140). Indeed, sentimental tropes take on new power in the context of a realist text. The realists no longer believed that the body was eminently legible; but when physicality no longer trumps all, an invocation of the body's power to produce meaning stands out with added intensity.

27. Howells, "Call for Realism," 500.

28. Trachtenberg, *Incorporation of America*, 201.

29. Twain seems to have used reverse psychology to invite moral judgments; the NOTICE at the front of the book reads: "Persons attempting to find a motive in this narrative will be prosecuted; persons attempting to find a moral in it will be banished; persons attempting to find a plot in it will be shot" (27). The Concord Public Library tried to find a moral and could not, so banned the book, deeming it "the veriest trash" (Boston *Transcript*, 308). An 1885 review in the Springfield *Republican* declared that "the trouble with Mr. Clemens is that he has no reliable sense of propriety" (Springfield *Republican*, 308). Andrew Lang defended the book in 1891 in the *Illustrated London News*, declaring, "nothing can be more true and more humorous than the narrative of this outcast boy, with a heart naturally good, with a conscience torn between the teachings of his world about slavery and the promptings of his nature" (Lang, "Art of Mark Twain," 40). For the defenders of the novel, Huck's "naturally good" heart, in battle with society, was crucial. The book was attacked and defended on moral grounds, suggesting that sentiment lay at the core of the novel.

30. Van Wyck Brooks, in *The Ordeal of Mark Twain* (1920), thought Twain was a frustrated, unsuccessful writer, while Bernard DeVoto, in *Mark Twain's America* (1932), celebrated *Huckleberry Finn* as "American life formed into great fiction" (DeVoto, *Mark Twain's America*, 320). Lionel Trilling and T. S. Eliot hastened the canonization of *Adventures of Huckleberry Finn* in the middle of the twentieth century when they wrote glowing introductions to the text; for Trilling (1948), the text was "an almost perfect work" (Trilling, "Certain Formal Aptness," 285), for Eliot (1950), "a masterpiece" (Eliot, "Boy and the River," 286). Trilling was fundamentally concerned with the moral significance of literature, as Eliot was concerned with literature's ability to evoke emotion.

Since its canonization at the hands of Eliot and Trilling, the most contentious source of debate has surrounded the text's racial representation. In the most polarized terms: either Twain is racist, reverting to ugly stereotypes, especially in the ending; or Twain is antiracist, exposing and subverting the ugly stereotypes that plague his culture. Critics have used the text to defend opposite sides in the same argument, suggesting that Twain is caught in a conundrum common to satire: satire is a critique, but satire implicates itself in the very thing it critiques.

31. As Jonathan Arac explains, "Because of its masculinist system of characters and its deadpan narrative mode, *Huckleberry Finn* was preserved, it seemed, from the taint of sentiment (although it has recently become possible to revise that view) and so could be praised safely as a racial exemplar when that once again became a good thing to be" (Arac, "*Uncle Tom's Cabin* vs. *Huckleberry Finn*," 89).

32. Camfield, "Sentimental Liberalism," 97. Laura Skandera-Trombley, in *Mark Twain in the Company of Women*, explains that women were an important influence for Twain. For more on Twain and sentimentalism, see Stone, "Mark Twain's Joan of Arc"; Harris, "Four Ways to Inscribe a Mackerel"; Stoneley, *Mark Twain and the Feminine Aesthetic*; Fishkin, "Mark Twain and Women"; and Krauth, *Proper Mark Twain*.

33. Kete, *Sentimental Collaborations*.

34. Stacey Margolis points out that recent criticism has shifted away from the text and toward "the social consequences of its canonization" (Margolis, "Huckleberry Finn," 329). A text as widely read and critiqued as *Adventures of Huckleberry Finn* is bound to invite criticism about how the text is taught and received as a cultural keystone. But we need not move away from the text to think about critical reception; the text itself invites a critique of cultural inheritance. Steven Mailloux writes that "*Huckleberry Finn* prefigures an aspect of its own reception when it satirically thematizes the potent effect of novels on impressionable young readers" (Mailloux, "Bad-Boy Boom," 43). In other words, *Adventures of Huckleberry Finn* dramatizes the problem of cultural inheritance. The trouble may not lie merely with the texts that a culture passes down, though. As *Huckleberry Finn* shows us, authors are certainly responsible for the messages they put forth into the world, but readers need to read carefully. Walter Scott may be a pernicious writer, but Tom Sawyer, for one, is a horrible reader.

35. Here, Twain's critique of a hidden sentimental ideology resonates with Lauren Berlant's notion that sentimental texts critique patriarchal familialism but also sacralize family values and preserve the fantasy of the family. See Berlant, *Female Complaint*.

36. Taylor, *Principles of Scientific Management*, 36.

37. We should remember, of course, that scientific management is not actually science. Harry Braverman writes: "It lacks the characteristics of a true science because its assumptions reflect nothing more than the outlook of the capitalist with regard to the conditions of production.... It enters the workplace not as the representative of science, but as the representative of management masquerading in the trappings of science" (Braverman, *Labor and Monopoly Capital*, 86). The very study of scientific management (a self-named discipline) implies that choices governing the realm of labor are functions of science, subject only to the unchangeable rules of nature.

38. Hoxie, *Scientific Management and Labor*, 132.

39. Twain, *Letters from the Earth*, 239. *Letters from the Earth* is a collection of writings compiled in 1939 by the Twain scholar Bernard DeVoto. The sentences I have quoted come from the section called "The Damned Human Race," which DeVoto thinks was written by Twain between 1905 and 1909, toward the end of Twain's life.

40. Harris, "Four Ways to Inscribe a Mackerel," 150.

41. This kind of critique against sentimentalism, which Twain himself deploys before he redeems sentimental values, is the foundation of many twentieth-century arguments against the sentimental. See, especially, Lauren Berlant's *The Female Complaint: The Unfinished Business of Sentimentality in American Culture*, in which she argues that "the gender-marked texts of women's popular culture cultivate fantasies of vague belonging as an alleviation of what is hard to manage in the lived real—social antagonisms, exploitation, compromised intimacies, the attrition of life" (5). See also Jefferson, "What's Wrong with Sentimentality?"; and Tanner, "Sentimentality."

42. Here Pap taps into the mid-nineteenth-century philosophy of the body. As William Cohen writes of Victorian ideas of the hand, "Whether through its physiology, the lines that mark it, or the writing with which it is synonymous, the hand is so freighted with significance as to reveal all the vital information about the body and mind behind it" (Cohen, "Manual Conduct in Great Expectations," 222).

43. Camfield, *Sentimental Twain*, 7.

44. Tompkins, *Sensational Designs*, xvi.

45. Doyno, "Composition of *Adventures of Huckleberry Finn*," 12.

46. Roodenburg, "'Hand of Friendship,'" 179.

47. Jim explains that he speculated in the market, but "got busted out" (68). When Huck asks what kind of stock Jim invested in, Jim answers, "Why, live stock. Cattle, you know" (68). Twain's joke certainly would resonate more with his readers in the 1880s than with an audience from the 1840s. The rise of managerial capitalism brings with it the rise of modern financial structure. As the market for stocks grew, the potential for widespread economic panic grew—as evidenced in the stock market crash of 1873.

48. Twain, *Letters from the Earth*, 239.

49. Recent critics have argued that Twain has not forsaken domesticity. Michael J. Kiskis writes: "Looking especially at the portion of material that Twain published during his lifetime (principally in the *North American Review* in 1906 and 1907), we face a Mark Twain who is deeply involved in the tradition of literary domesticity. His concerns are with hearth and home. With family" (Kiskis, "Mark Twain and the Tradition of Literary Domesticity," 23).

50. Forrest G. Robinson explains, "the accident marked the end of the first stage of composition and a long creative withdrawal from the adult complications that had crept into his ostensibly juvenile fiction" (Robinson, "Silences in *Huckleberry Finn*," 63). The recent discovery of Twain's manuscript in 1991 reveals that "Twain wrote the 1876 portion beyond the steamboat/raft crash, going on to take Huck into the Grangerford home" (Doyno, "Composition of *Adventures of Huckleberry Finn*," 11). Robinson's point, though, is not lost.

51. Marx, *Machine in the Garden*, 27.

52. Christopher Schmitz writes of railroads: "Around 1870, there were virtually no other business organizations operating on such a scale, and none in which managerial hierarchies and the divorce of ownership and control had become so widespread" (Schmitz, *Growth of Big Business*, 11).

In *A Tramp Abroad* (1880), a book that Twain wrote while taking a break from composing *Huckleberry Finn*, Twain recalls a journey down the Neckar and pits the raft against the railroad: "The motion of a raft is the needful motion; it is gentle, and gliding, and smooth, and noiseless; it calms down all feverish activities, it soothes to sleep all nervous hurry and impatience; under its restful influence all the troubles and vexations and sorrows that harass the mind vanish away, and existence becomes a dream, a charm, a deep and tranquil ecstasy. How it contrasts with hot and perspiring pedestrianism, and dusty and deafening railroad rush" (80).

53. Emmeline Grangerford calls to mind William James's harsh description of the sentimentalist, who is "so constructed that 'gushing' is his or her normal mode of expression. Putting a stopper on the 'gush' will only to a limited extent cause more 'real' activities to take its place; in the main it will simply produce listlessness" (James, "What Is an Emotion?" 199).

54. Charles Colbert writes that "when Twain created the character, the halcyon days of phrenology had long passed, and the author enjoyed the advantage of hindsight in ridiculing the foibles of an earlier generation" (Colbert, *Measure of Perfection*, 38). Phrenology is indeed a foible, but the body remains the site of meaning.

55. Roodenburg, "'Hand of Friendship,'" 179.

56. In *The Melodramatic Imagination*, Peter Brooks says that a person who is mute is "the virtuoso emblem of the possibilities of meaning engendered in the absence of the word" (62). Jim's deaf daughter cannot speak herself, but we read her silence as the absence of language.

57. Morrison, "Re-Marking Twain," 378.

58. Walker, "Reformers and Young Maidens," 183.

59. Critics have often associated nostalgia as a literary weakness characteristic of sentimentalism. For Ann Douglas, sentimentalism "asserts that the values a society's activity denies are precisely the ones it cherishes; it attempts to deal with the phenomenon of cultural bifurcation by the manipulation of nostalgia. Sentimentalism provides a way to protest a power to which one has already in part capitulated" (Douglas, *Feminization of American Culture*, 12). In Douglas's view, women exerted their power in the nineteenth century through sentimental literature, but the literature was a conservative influence and helped keep women oppressed. Nostalgia has no value for Douglas because it can do no political work; indeed, she would say, the work nostalgia does is regressive, encouraging passive leisure over active political participation. Julius Lester specifically condemns Twain for his nostalgia, declaring, "Twain's notion of freedom is the simplistic one of freedom from restraint and responsibility. It is an adolescent vision of life, an exercise in nostalgia for the paradise that never was" (Lester, "Morality and *Adventures of Huckleberry Finn*," 347). Nostalgia, in fact, may be inherently false: not only is nostalgia based in memory (already unreliable), but it is based on a selective remembrance that seeks to redeem and recover. Twain recognizes the danger of nostalgia—the Grangerford and Wilks episodes both demonstrate how nostalgia can be a destructive force. But Twain's text also shows how nostalgia can be redemptive.

60. Trilling, "Certain Formal Aptness," 285.

61. Marx, "Mr. Eliot, Mr. Trilling, and *Huckleberry Finn*," 296.

62. Ibid., 305.

63. Eliot, "Boy and the River," 289.

64. Lester, "Morality and *Adventures of Huckleberry Finn*," 343.

65. Braverman, *Labor and Monopoly Capital*, 119.

66. Fiedler, *Love and Death*, 288.

67. Forrest G. Robinson, in "The Characterization of Jim in *Huckleberry Finn*" (1988), compares Jim's silences to Frederick Douglass's subversive silences in his *Narrative*.

68. Hansen, "Once and Future Boss," 71.

3 / Holding On to the Sentimental in *Winesburg, Ohio*

1. Anderson was disdainful of short stories that hinged on plot twists, such as those of O. Henry and Guy de Maupassant. In *A Story Teller's Story*, Anderson writes: "There was a notion that ran through all story telling in America, that stories must be built about a plot and that absurd Anglo-Saxon notion that they must point a moral, uplift the people, make better citizens, etc., etc. . . . What was wanted I thought was form, not plot, an altogether more elusive and difficult thing to come at" (255). Anderson's self-proclaimed focus on form over plot underlines the attention we should pay to his careful deployment of sentimental tropes.

2. Watt, *Rise of the Novel*, 15.

3. Anderson, "To Arthur Barton," 148.

4. Anderson, *Winesburg, Ohio*, 103 (hereafter cited in the text).

5. The point here is not just that the titles of these stories reveal discontinuities in the narrative of the text, but that each of these stories introduces a new character (indeed, each of these stories begins with the names of the characters we are meeting

for the first time—Elizabeth Willard, Doctor Parcival, Ray Pearson, and Tom Foster). It makes sense that "Mother" and "The Philosopher" introduce new characters; these stories, after all, are at the beginning of the book. However, by the time we get to "The Untold Lie" and "Drink" (stories at the end of the book), we realize that the sudden introduction of a new character does not serve to develop a grand, unifying narrative, but in fact serves to unravel any attempt to discover a single narrative thread that ties the book together.

6. C. Hugh Holman, in line with the critical consensus, describes realism as "committed to the doctrine of presenting truthful types of common humanity, and presenting them without the intrusion of the author and with nearly complete objectivity as they could achieve" (Holman, "Everything," 487).

7. Literacy in the United States grew from 80 percent in 1870 to 94 percent in 1920 (Snyder, *120 Years of American Education*, 21).

8. See, especially, Wiebe, *Search for Order*; and Galambos, *Public Image of Big Business*. For an early twentieth-century account of the ways that "the large business man controls the exigencies of life under which the community lives" (3), see Veblen, *Theory of Business Enterprise*.

9. For a contemporary account of the way that businesses organized themselves in an age of rapid growth, see Gowin, *Selection and Training of the Business Executive*. Writing in 1918, Gowin declares, "The large-scale producer, simply because his operations are large, can separate these operations into highly specialized duties, delegating to managers, technical experts, clerical workers, skilled mechanics, laborers and machines, tasks which unseparated in the old-time shop were all performed by a single man, the proprietor" (6).

10. Chandler, *Visible Hand*, 455.

11. For a reconstruction and documentation of Anderson's breakdown in 1912, see William A. Sutton's *Exit to Elsinore*. Sutton argues that Anderson used literature as compensation for what he lacked in his business life: "his basic approach to literature was therapeutic, to give him release from the consciousness of the world he rejected, to work out through the manipulation of imagined life the problems of his own, to find understanding for himself through probing into the lives of his imagined characters" (Sutton, *Exit to Elsinore*, 28). Some critics have argued, though, that Anderson's breakdown and subsequent move to literary work was a function more of failed business than literary desire. Bernard Duffey writes: "Anderson's actions had always a major significance for himself. It is correct to suggest that he exaggerated, that his accounts of his departure from his paint warehouse grew more dramatic and more distorted with the telling, that actually he was as much running away from a shaky business enterprise as he was projecting himself into a life of mind and imagination" (Duffey, "Chicago Renaissance," 47–48).

12. Anderson, *Story Teller's Story*, 221.

13. In his memoirs and letters, Anderson wrote much about his isolating experience in the business world. In his *Memoirs*, he confesses that he was a fake: "I had, all the time, I dare say, a kind of pride in my ability as a word slinger and most people who buy house paint are like the people who buy anything, at bottom probably yaps. I have, I say, represented myself as a good deal of a Babbitt but I wasn't one" (Anderson, *Sherwood Anderson's Memoirs*, 244). In 1919, he wrote a despairing letter to Waldo Frank: "One thing I have found out. I cannot continue to live the life I have lived as a businessman. In a sense I have been like one living in a damp, dark cellar ever since

I went back into business after my few months of freedom in New York last year" (Anderson, *Letters of Sherwood Anderson*, 50–51).

14. Howe, "Book of the Grotesque," 96.

15. Ferres, "Nostalgia of *Winesburg, Ohio*," 466.

16. In a 1911 speech, Woodrow Wilson declared, "The life of America is not the life it was twenty years ago. It is not the life it was ten years ago. We have changed our economic conditions from top to bottom, and with our economic conditions has changed also the organization of our life" (Wilson, *Public Papers*, 285). Wilson's use of the word "organization" to describe the cultural conditions that follow widespread economic change points to the influence of a new bureaucratic culture.

17. Thurston, "Technique in *Winesburg, Ohio*," 313.

18. Eliot, "*Ulysses*, Order, and Myth," 177.

19. Ibid.

20. Bell, "Metaphysics of Modernism," 10.

21. In *Sentimental Modernism: Women Writers and the Revolution of the Word*, a study of women writers that endeavors to "restore the sentimental *within* modernism," Suzanne Clark writes that "modernism inaugurated a reversal of values which emphasized erotic desire, not love; anarchic rupture and innovation rather than the conventional appeals of sentimental language" (4, 1).

22. As a 1919 review from the *New York Tribune* declared, "We can't believe that even a small town could produce such a large percentage of neurotics as Anderson unearths. We are also inclined to think that the young women of this town were more seduced than usual" (Broun, "Review," 160). For discussions of Anderson and Freud, see Hoffman, *Freudianism and the Literary Mind*; and Michaud, *American Novel To-Day*.

23. Several critics use the language of delving below the surface when describing Sherwood Anderson's writing. Alfred Kazin writes in 1942, "Anderson was fascinated by the undersurface of that [American] life and became the voice of its terrors and exultations" (Kazin, *On Native Grounds*, 210). David Stouck writes in 1996 that Anderson wants to "bring to the surface the hidden depths of thought" (Stouck, "Anderson's Expressionist Art," 211).

24. Barnard, "Modern American Fiction," 55.

25. Levine, *Unpredictable Past*, 191.

26. The townspeople of Winesburg rarely converse; as John J. Mahoney writes, "It is the fact that none of the utterances in *Winesburg* is replied to; that the book is wholly lacking in conversation" (Mahoney, "Analysis of *Winesburg, Ohio*," 248).

27. Levenson, *Modernism and the Fate of Individuality*, xii.

28. Ibid., xiii.

29. Fussell, "Art and Isolation," 110.

30. Schevill, "Notes on the Grotesque," 232.

31. Irving Howe declares, "If Turgeneiv's influence on *Winesburg* is not quite certain, there can be no doubt about Mark Twain's. Between the America of Anderson's boyhood, which is the setting of his best work, and the America of Huck Finn there are only a few intervening decades, and the nostalgia for a lost moment of American pastoral which saturates *Huckleberry Finn* is also present in *Winesburg*" (Howe, "Book of the Grotesque," 92).

32. Montgomery, *Worker's Control*, 26.

33. Benjamin, *Illuminations*, 108.

34. See Laurie, *Artisans into Workers.*

35. Anderson is clearly nostalgic for a premachine age. In his *Notebook*, he writes, "Might it not be that with the coming into general use of machinery men did lose the grip of what is perhaps the most truly important of man's functions in life—the right every man has always before held dearest of all his human possessions, the right in short to stand alone in the presence of his tools and his materials and with those tools and materials to attempt to twist, to bend, to form something that will be the expression of his inner hunger for the truth that is his own and that is beauty" (Anderson, *Sherwood Anderson's Notebook*, 153–54).

36. Geoffrey Harpham writes, "The victimized innocents of *Winesburg, Ohio*, clutching a single moment of revelation, distort the truth of that moment by taking it out of the flow of experience, just as, for example, a fixed smile when not counterbalanced or framed by other expressions will seem terrifying, mocking, or satanic" (Harpham, "Grotesque," 465). As Anderson shows us, when "the flow of experience" is forever baffling, grotesquerie threatens every Winesburg resident.

37. Michael Bell explains that "the pervasive concern with the construction of meaning helps explain the emphasis in all the modernist arts on the nature of their own medium" (Bell, "Metaphysics of Modernism," 16). Derek Attridge explains that the modernist concern with language and meaning has an ethical power. He writes, "Modernism's foregrounding of language and other discursive and generic codes through its formal strategies is not merely a self-reflexive diversion but a recognition (whatever its writers may have thought they were doing) that literature's distinctive power and potential ethical force resides in a testing and unsettling of deeply held assumptions of transparency, instrumentality, and direct referentiality, in part because this taking to the limits opens a space for the apprehension of the otherness which those assumptions had silently excluded" (Attridge, "Literary Form," 253). Attridge suggests that Anderson's obsession with newness has a moral quality, offering literary access to thoughts and figures that were previously occluded.

38. This is not to argue that it is revolutionary for an author to bring attention to the narrator; indeed, the earliest novels often drew attention to their form and their narrator's manipulation of the text. Henry Fielding's 1749 *Tom Jones*, for instance, opens by foregrounding the author's position: "An author ought to consider himself, not as a Gentleman who gives a private or eleemosynary Treat, but rather as one who keeps a public Ordinary, at which all Persons are welcome for their Money" (Fielding, *History of Tom Jones*, 31). Fielding's narrator explicitly invokes the movement from a patronage economy to the market economy; readers are consumers, now, and will support an author. The narrator is himself a character, glorying in the artifice of the literary project of which he is a part. Most crucially, Henry Fielding's narrator, like Sherwood Anderson's narrator, reminds us that the novel is a product of particular material circumstances.

39. Harpham, "Grotesque," 466.

40. Ibid., 463.

41. Several critics have written about the significance of hands in *Winesburg, Ohio*. Walter B. Rideout writes that "the possibility of physical touch between two human beings always implies, even if by negative counterpart, at least the possibility of a profounder moment of understanding between them" (Rideout, "Simplicity of *Winesburg, Ohio*," 173). Like Rideout, David Stouck writes that hands symbolize the yearning for communication: "Hands dramatize the individual's deep need for connection to others. Even minor characters are sometimes remarkable for their hands"

(Stouck, "Anderson's Expressionist Art," 223). Herbert Schneidau writes, similarly: "hands often speak more eloquently than lips, and what their gestures signify is more meaningful; in fact, they always imply the inadequacy of words" (Schneidau, *Waking Giants*, 161).

42. See Chandler, *Visible Hand*, where he explains exactly how "ownership and management . . . separated" when larger industries required stockholders rather than single owners, and stockholders were not equipped to run an industry (87).

43. In his study of Anderson's writing process, William L. Phillips writes, "In the main his deletions simply removed overworked or awkwardly used words, although in one instance he added to the universality of the story by deleting the single word 'his': 'The story of Wing Biddlebaum is a story of -his- hands'" (Phillips, "How Sherwood Anderson Wrote *Winesburg, Ohio*," 76). The deletion of "his" not only adds to the universality, but suggests a sense of split consciousness—that Wing's hands are in fact not his own.

44. In *A Story Teller's Story*, Anderson contemplates the relationship between his thoughts and his writing as a relationship between his consciousness and his hands: "My own hands had not served me very well. Nothing they had done with words had satisfied me. There was not finesse enough in my fingers. All sorts of thoughts and emotions came to me that would not creep down my arms and out through my fingers upon the paper. How much was I to blame for that? How much could fairly be blamed to the civilization in which I had lived? I presume I wanted very much to blame something other than myself if I could" (272). *Winesburg, Ohio* is an answer to Anderson's hope that the break between his subjectivity and his hands is a cultural failing rather than a personal failing.

45. Marx, *Capital*, 165.

46. Sklar, *Corporate Reconstruction of American Capitalism*, 164.

47. West, "From *New Statesman*," 235.

48. Crane, "From *The Double Dealer*," 245.

49. Braverman, *Labor and Monopoly Capital*, 90.

50. Taylor, *Principles of Scientific Management*, 7.

51. Braverman, *Labor and Monopoly Capital*, 107.

52. Mark Whalan writes that the form of the text both suggests and blocks interpretation. He states that although the text "invites interpretation, and even very obviously encodes a textual place for a modern reader to engage in interpretation, it ultimately frustrates such an exercise across the entire text through the diversity of its individual text units" (Whalan, "Dreams of Manhood," 242).

53. Even though telegraphers had unique, identifiable styles of transmitting messages, they were easily viewed as anonymous extensions of the machine.

54. For an explanation of the relationship between the rise of managerialism and new modes of transportation and communication, see Chandler, *Scale and Scope*. He writes: "The new forms of transportation and communication, in turn, permitted the rise of modern mass marketing and modern mass production. The unprecedented increase in the volume of production and in the number of transactions led the entrepreneurs who established the new mass-producing and mass-distributing enterprises—like the railroad men before them—to recruit teams of salaried managers. As these enterprises expanded their activities and moved into new markets, the shareholdings of the founding entrepreneurs and their families were dispersed and operating decisions became concentrated in the hands of the managers" (1).

55. It is significant that Wash wanted to kill not his wife, but her mother. Domesticity no longer signifies the sentimental realm as it once did. The mother in "Respectability" offers a material exchange—a body for a reestablishment of marriage—in lieu of emotional support. Commerce, it seems, has replaced the heart. The mother does not give feminine virtue but forces shameful crudity. She mediates the most fundamental relation between two bodies; in *Winesburg, Ohio*, love needs a manager. Wash's unrelenting hatred, as he declares, is directed at all women, but it is not aimed at the traditional virtues of femininity. Many critics have argued that Anderson fails his women. As Marilyn Judith Atlas declares, "by exploring the lives of the women in Winesburg we explore the biases of a period . . . and an author" (Atlas, "Sherwood Anderson and the Women of Winesburg," 264–65). Anderson's critique, though, does not attack femininity but rather laments the breakdown of femininity in an age where nineteenth-century sentimental domesticity seems to have vanished. Sally Adair Rigsbee argues that femininity is the major theme of the text, indeed, that George's "growing understanding of the meaning of the feminine" is what drives his maturing process (Rigsbee, "Feminine in *Winesburg, Ohio*," 185).

56. Updike, "Introduction," xviii.

57. Levine, *Unpredictable Past*, 190. Levine's notion of looking backward resonates with Svetlana Boym's notion that nostalgia is centrally concerned with time rather than space. She writes: "In a broader sense, nostalgia is rebellion against the modern idea of time, the time of history and progress. The nostalgic desires to obliterate history and turn it into private or collective mythology, to revisit time like space, refusing to surrender to the irreversibility of time that plagues the human condition" (Boym, *Future of Nostalgia*, xv).

58. Many critics agree that "Sophistication" contains the most important epiphany in the book. Rex Burbank writes that it is "the climax of the book" (Burbank, *Sherwood Anderson*, 71). Edwin Fussell writes that "Sophistication" "contains the true message of the text" (Fussell, "Art and Isolation," 113). Walter B. Rideout writes that the story "emphasizes the unity of all human beings in their necessary submission to death and their need for communication with another" (Rideout, "Simplicity of *Winesburg, Ohio*," 177). Glen Love writes that Anderson "presents us, finally, with an important paradox, the artist who is, at bottom, skeptical of this medium: distrustful of words, he is nevertheless driven to their use, not only to record his skepticism, but also to achieve a communication which, even at its best, cannot approach the power of non-words, the more perfect communication to be found within purposeful silence" (Love, "Rhetoric of Silence," 56). Love describes the sentimental touch much as Harriet Beecher Stowe used it.

59. Cather, *My Antonia*, 205.

60. Lewis, *Babbitt*, 374.

61. Chandler explains, "The hierarchies that came to manage the new multiunit enterprises had a permanence beyond that of any individual or group of individuals who worked in them" (Chandler, *Visible Hand*, 8).

62. Knox, "Our Lost Individuality," 820, 824.

4 / A Touch of Miss Lonelyhearts

1. Charlie Chaplin's 1936 film *Modern Times* dramatizes the way that humans are literally incorporated into the machinery of the factory. As a contemporary review describes the film, "The mechanized individualist goes mad and proceeds to turn the

factory into the madhouse that it really always had been" (Giedion, *Mechanization Takes Command*, 126). For a darker dramatization of humans becoming machines, see Fritz Lang's 1927 film *Metropolis*, whose epigraph reads: "The Mediator between head and hands must be the heart!"

2. For a 1932 account of the modern corporation's influence on the relationship between worker and manager, see Berle and Means, *Modern Corporation and Private Property*.

3. Braverman, *Labor and Monopoly Capital*, 126. Braverman's book was highly influential when it was published in 1974, reconfiguring the field of industrial sociology and infusing the study of management with Marxist politics. As Michael Buroway writes, "Braverman helped to redefine sociology by restoring structure and history" (Buroway, "Classic of Its Time," 298). Braverman's work was widely celebrated before it became the subject of much scrutiny and debate at the end of the twentieth century. For a discussion of Braverman's influence in the field of labor studies and sociology, see the helpful collection Wardell, *Rethinking the Labor Process*. Recent scholars have made efforts to revive Braverman's ideas, arguing that he is a major figure in the critique of capital. See Renton, *Dissident Marxism*; Spencer, "Braverman and the Contribution of Labour Process Analysis"; and Tinker, "Spectres of Marx and Braverman."

4. Though this project charts the degradation of human contact over eighty years of American history, we should keep in mind that history is never simply a document of increasing despair. As Thomas Bender points out, American historians, taken together, have erroneously described continuous community disintegration. He writes that American history books, if placed in serial order, "offer a picture of community breakdown repeating itself in the 1650s, 1690s, 1740s, 1820s, 1850s, 1880s, and 1920s" (Bender, *Community and Social Change*, 51). The important point, though, is that a major strand of American literature points to a dehumanized economic structure that continues to grow in scope and scale.

5. Nineteen twenty was the first census year in which a majority of people in the United States were urban dwellers.

6. Gay and Wolman, "Trends in Economic Organization," 236.

7. Chandler, *Visible Hand*, 10.

8. Chandler explains that managerial capitalism is the dominant force in the American economy: "By the middle of the twentieth century the salaried managers of a relatively small number of large mass producing, large mass retailing, and large mass transporting enterprises coordinated current flows of goods through the processes of production and distribution and allocated the resources to be used for future production and distribution in major sectors of the American economy. By then, the managerial revolution in American business had been carried out" (ibid., 11).

9. As Harry Braverman writes, the capitalist division of labor "shapes not only work, but populations as well, because over the long run it creates that mass of simple labor which is the primary feature of populations in developed capitalist countries" (Braverman, *Labor and Monopoly Capital*, 83).

10. Mumford, *Technics and Civilization*, 4. According to Jay Martin, West originally wanted to give *Miss Lonelyhearts* an epigraph from Lewis Mumford: "From the form of a city, the style of its architecture, and the economic functions and social groupings it shelters and encourages, one can derive most of the essential elements of a civilization" (Martin, *Nathanael West*, 309).

11. West was the night manager at the Kenmore Hall Hotel in 1927 and was a manager at the Sutton Club Hotel in 1930.

12. West, *Miss Lonelyhearts*, 1 (hereafter cited in the text).

13. Willey and Rice, "Agencies of Communication," 205.

14. Hendley, "Dear Abby," 217.

15. See Althusser, "From *Ideology and Ideological State Apparatuses*." Althusser writes that "the reproduction of labour power requires not only a reproduction of its skills, but also, at the same time, a reproduction of its submission to the rules of the established order, that is, a reproduction of submission to the ruling ideology for the workers, and a reproduction of the ability to manipulate the ruling ideology correctly for the agents of exploitation and repression" (1485).

16. West, "Some Notes on Violence," 50.

17. In a history of advice columns, W. Clark Hendley writes, "Though it may seem paradoxical, readers feel a certain kinship with the larger community of other readers while simultaneously experiencing an almost personal relationship with the advice-giver. This distinctive combination of intimacy-community was characteristic of this, the first example of an advice column, and remains characteristic of the genre today" (Hendley, "Dear Abby," 347).

18. Ibid., 351.

19. "Susan Chester" was an advice columnist for *the Brooklyn Eagle*; she showed West letters from readers in 1929, inspiring the letters in *Miss Lonelyhearts*. "Beatrice Fairfax" was an advice columnist for *the New York Journal* from 1898 to 1905.

20. West, "Some Notes on Miss L.," 67. Stanley Edgar Hyman warns of "Some Notes on Miss L." that "some or all of this may be Westian leg pull" (Hyman, "Nathanael West," 70).

21. James, *Varieties of Religious Experience*, 163.

22. The critics of the 1950s and 1960s—those who first established West as a major American writer—have remained especially influential. For them, *Miss Lonelyhearts* is a document of modernist dystopia. West's tale offers a vision of despair, a portrait of a spiritually barren, culturally sterile world like T. S. Eliot's *The Waste Land*. But as Edmond L. Volpe put it in his prominent 1961 reading, "in Eliot's Waste Land regeneration is possible; in West's there is no hope of salvation" (Volpe, "Waste Land of Nathanael West," 101). Victor Comerchero offers a similar reading in his 1964 *Nathanael West: The Ironic Prophet*. He writes, "From Eliot West derived some of his symbolism—particularly that of the wasteland; and his vision of the contemporary scene seems to have differed little from Eliot's, except for a suggested solution: West had none" (Comerchero, *Ironic Prophet*, 6). Even those critics who have sought a hopeful message in West's work often find promise only in a negative sense. Harold Bloom, for example, writes that *Miss Lonelyhearts* is "the perfected instance of a negative vision in modern American fiction" (Bloom, "Introduction," 1). For Bloom, West is an antinomian writer whose work offers redemption through sin: only after recognizing darkness can our lives be illuminated and ameliorated.

Indeed, the despair in *Miss Lonelyhearts* runs so deep that many critics have read the text not as evidence of a social disaster, but as indicative of an existential crisis. Norman Podhoretz, in 1957, wrote that West's "'particular kind of joking' has profoundly unpolitical implications; it is a way of saying that the universe is always rigged against us and that our efforts to contend with it invariably lead to absurdity" (Podhoretz, "Nathanael West," 155). For Podhoretz, West's America is broken beyond repair and is therefore almost "un-American" (155). Malcolm Cowley echoes Podhoretz in his 1959 introduction to the text. Cowley writes that West's works reveal "the spirit of the 1920's, with all their reckless experimentation, their effort to be outrageous, their interest in wildly personal dreams, their sympathy for the individual oppressed not by social forces but by the laws of life itself" (Cowley, "Introduction," 18). Podhoretz and Cowley, along with several other critics, cut off an interpretation of *Miss Lonelyhearts* that searches for a cause in structures of capitalism; pure grotesquerie, verging on evil, does not need a social reason to exist.

23. Aaron, "Late Thoughts on Nathanael West," 169.

24. Troy, "Four Newer Novelists," 672.

25. Dalrymple, "Lessons of 'Lonelyhearts,'" 18.

26. This brand of religious interpretation—which asks us to accept our cultural circumstances, however bleak—shields us from human responsibility and intervention. The reliance on religious truth as a universal explanatory force accounts for Marx's objection to religion. He writes, "The religious reflections of the real world can, in any case, vanish only when the practical relations of everyday life between man and man, and man and nature, generally present themselves to him in a transparent and rational form" (Marx, *Capital*, 173). For Marx, we turn to religion when the social structure has become incomprehensible and mystified. Miss Lonelyhearts's obsession with Christ, indeed, is symptomatic of his deep social alienation.

27. Veitch, *American Superrealism*, xvi.

28. Barnard, "'When You Wish Upon a Star,'" 343.

29. For a thoughtful argument about the various ways that *Miss Lonelyhearts* responds to the cultural politics of the Depression, see Dickstein, *Dancing in the Dark*.

30. Veitch, *American Superrealism*, 71.

31. Jean Baudrillard writes, "What characterizes the mass media is that they are opposed to mediation, [that they are] intransitive, that they fabricate noncommunication—if one accepts the definition of communication as an exchange, as the reciprocal space of speech and response, and thus of *responsibility*" (Baudrillard, "Masses," 577). For Baudrillard, the mass media threatens society not only because true communication is absent but also because noncommunication is couched in the terms of true communication and produces a populace that will never know true communication, never know true sympathy, and never know true political action.

32. In *The Day of the Locust*, published six years after *Miss Lonelyhearts*, West documents a similar instance of a character who has lost touch with his own hands. He writes of Homer Simpson: "Every part was awake but his hands. They still slept. He was not surprised. They demanded special attention, had always demanded it. When he had been a child, he used to stick pins into them and once had even thrust them into a fire" (West, *Day of the Locust*, 82). We know the depth of alienation in Homer because we see the extent to which his mind and body are separated: "His hands kept his thoughts busy. They trembled and jerked, as though troubled by dreams. To hold them still, he clasped them together. Their fingers twined like a tangle of thighs in miniature. He snatched them apart and sat on them" (101). Homer will later offer a sentimental touch to Tod Hacket: "He took Tod's hand." But the touch is refused: "Tod couldn't stand his trembling signals of affection. He tore free with a jerk" (162). There is no moment of sentimental redemption here, and *The Day of the Locust* continues toward an apocalyptic riot.

33. Fernstrom et al., *Organization and Management of a Business Enterprise*, 211.

34. Braverman, *Labor and Monopoly Capital*, 171.

35. Ibid., 182.

36. Ken Alder writes that French gunsmith-inventor Honoré Blanc first used interchangeable parts in 1790. See Alder, "Innovation and Amnesia."

37. West, "Some Notes on Miss L.," 66.

38. Rita Barnard writes of West's fictional characters: "It is impossible to think of most of these figures as representations of 'selves' with any depth, stability, or capacity for change" (Barnard, "'When You Wish Upon a Star,'" 329).

39. West, "Some Notes on Violence," 51. West similarly dismisses psychology in "Some Notes on Miss L." He writes, "Psychology has nothing to do with reality nor should it be used as motivation. The novelist is no longer a psychologist" (West, "Some Notes on Miss L.," 66).

40. Weber, *Max Weber on Law in Economy and Society*, 351.

41. As Robert Wexelblatt puts it, "The paradoxical fact is that works about disintegration, such as *Miss Lonelyhearts*, bring form itself into question but are themselves rigorously composed" (Wexelblatt, "Rhetoric of Disintegration," 99–100).

42. Marx, *Capital*, 163.

43. Raban, "Surfeit of Commodities," 223.

44. Jackson, "Introduction," 5.

45. Hyman writes: "The communion Miss Lonelyhearts achieves with Doyle in Delehanty's consists in their sitting silently holding hands, Miss Lonelyhearts pressing 'with all the love he could manage' to overcome the revulsion he feels at Doyle's touch. Back at the Doyles, after Doyle has ripped open Miss Lonelyhearts' fly and been kicked by his wife, they hold hands again, and when Fay comes back in the room she says 'What a sweet pair of fairies you guys are.' It is West's ultimate irony that the symbolic embrace they manage at the end is one penetrating the body of the other with a bullet" (Hyman, "Nathanael West," 76).

46. Jackson, "Introduction," 6.

47. Ransom, *World's Body*, 36.

48. Edenbaum, "To Kill God," 67.

49. Irr, *Suburb of Dissent*, 192.

50. Adorno, *Stars Down to Earth*, 42.

51. Ibid.

52. Barnard, "'When You Wish Upon a Star,'" 344.

53. Williams, *Marxism and Literature*, 123–24.

54. Hemingway, *Farewell to Arms*, 138.

55. McCullers, *Heart Is a Lonely Hunter*, 302. The touch in McCullers's novel is a prelude to an explosive scene in which Jake and Doctor Copeland hurl insults at one another. Like the touch in *Miss Lonelyhearts*, the sentimental moment lasts only for an instant.

56. Smith, *Theory of Moral Sentiments*, 275.

57. Ibid., 372–73.

Epilogue

1. Collins and Porras, *Built to Last*, 115.

2. "You Make Us Walmart," Walmart Corporation, http://walmartstores.com/careers/. As of 2011, Wal-Mart Stores is the top-ranked company in the Fortune Global

500. Next to the U.S. government, Walmart is the largest employer in the United States. I discuss Walmart not because it is exceptional, but because it is representative of U.S. corporate culture.

3. For one of the darkest articulations of the way that administrative power rules society, see Marcuse, *Eros and Civilization*. He writes in this 1955 work, "With the rationalization of the productive apparatus, with the multiplication of functions, all domination assumes the form of administration. At its peak, the concentration of economic power seems to turn into anonymity: everyone, even at the very top, appears to be powerless before the movements and laws of the apparatus itself" (98). Marcuse offers a bleak vision of a Weberian bureaucracy extended beyond all human intervention. The system is self-perpetuating and obviates any social change.

4. Barthes, *Mythologies*, 101.

5. Marchand, *Creating the Corporate Soul*, 5.

6. Ibid., 4.

7. Weisberg, *Bush Tragedy*, 92.

8. *The Compassionate Touch* is about the work of Christian missionaries who help beggars, prostitutes, and lepers on the streets of Calcutta.

9. I do not mean to argue that corporations and politicians are never moral; rather, sentimental language, when divorced from moral sense philosophy, is no longer a reliable sign of morality.

10. Weber, *Protestant Ethic*, 96.

11. As Steven Pinker points out when he argues that there is such a thing as human nature, acknowledging that humans are programmed should not suggest that humans have no agency. He writes, "It is now simply misguided to ask whether humans are flexible or programmed, whether behavior is universal or varies across cultures, whether acts are learned or innate, whether we are essentially good or essentially evil. Humans behave flexibly *because* they are programmed" (Pinker, *Blank Slate*, 40–41). Though Pinker refers to a sort of natural hard-wiring of humanity, the point I want to stress is that to be predisposed and conditioned is not to be disabled but in fact quite the opposite.

12. Wallace writes of his protagonist: "One of the really American things about Hal, probably, is the way he despises what it is he's really lonely for: this hideous internal self, incontinent of sentiment and need, that pules and writhes just under the hip empty mask, anhedonia" (Wallace, *Infinite Jest*, 695). Miss Lonelyhearts aspired to unfeeling as a reaction to his loneliness and self-hatred; Hal's loneliness and self-hatred are only magnified by an emotionlessness that he cannot overcome.

13. Wallace, *Infinite Jest*, 478 (hereafter cited in the text).

14. Here are the first three steps: "1. We admitted we were powerless over alcohol—that our lives had become unmanageable. 2. Came to believe that a Power greater than ourselves could restore us to sanity. 3. Made a decision to turn our will and our lives over to the care of God *as we understood Him*" (*Alcoholics Anonymous*, 59).

15. As Northrop Frye explains, utopian thought is imaginative—the writer is less concerned with achieving the actual state than with imagining possibilities. He writes that the genre of utopia is "a species of the constructive literary imagination, and we should expect to find that the more penetrating the utopian writer's mind is, the more clearly he understands that he is communicating a vision to his readers, not sharing a power or fantasy dream with them" (Frye, "Varieties of Literary Utopias," 32).

16. McCaffery, "Interview with David Foster Wallace," 131. In the same interview, Wallace declared that "in dark times, the definition of good art would seem to be art that locates and applies CPR to those elements of what's human and magical that still live and glow despite the times' darkness" (131).

17. Franzen, "Tribute," 16.

Bibliography

Aaron, Daniel. "Late Thoughts on Nathanael West." In *Nathanael West: A Collection of Critical Essays.* 1965. Comp. Jay Martin, 161–69. Englewood Cliffs, N.J.: Prentice-Hall, 1971.

Adorno, Theodor W. *Aesthetic Theory.* 1970. Reprint, Minneapolis: University of Minnesota Press, 1997.

———. *The Stars Down to Earth and Other Essays on the Irrational in Culture.* New York: Routledge, 1994.

Alcoholics Anonymous: The Story of How Many Thousands of Men and Women Have Recovered from Alcoholism. New York: Alcoholics Anonymous Publishing, 1955.

Alder, Ken. "Innovation and Amnesia: Engineering Rationality and the Fate of Interchangeable Parts Manufacturing in France." *Technology and Culture* 38.2 (1997): 273–311.

Althusser, Louis. "From *Ideology and Ideological State Apparatuses (Notes towards an Investigation).*" Trans. Ben Brewster. In *The Norton Anthology of Theory and Criticism,* ed. Vincent B. Leitch et al., 1483–1508. New York: Norton, 2001.

Anderson, Sherwood. *Letters of Sherwood Anderson.* Ed. Howard Mumford Jones. Boston: Little, Brown, 1953.

———. *Sherwood Anderson's Memoirs: A Critical Edition.* Ed. Ray Lewis White. 1942. Reprint, Chapel Hill: University of North Carolina Press, 1969.

———. *Sherwood Anderson's Notebook.* New York: Boni and Liveright, 1926.

———. *A Story Teller's Story.* 1924. Reprint, Cleveland: The Press of Case Western Reserve University, 1968.

———. "To Arthur Barton." In *Winesburg, Ohio: Authoritative Text, Backgrounds and Contexts, Criticism,* ed. Charles E. Modlin and Ray Lewis White, 144–48. 1932. Reprint, New York: Norton, 1996.

———. *Winesburg, Ohio.* 1919. Reprint, New York: Modern Library, 2002.

Arac, Jonathan. "*Uncle Tom's Cabin* vs. *Huckleberry Finn*: The Historians and the Critics." *Boundary 2* 24.2 (1997): 79–100.

Arrow, Kenneth J., and F. H. Hahn. *General Competitive Analysis.* San Francisco: Holden Day, 1971.

Atlas, Marilyn Judith. "Sherwood Anderson and the Women of Winesburg." In *Critical Essays on Sherwood Anderson,* ed. David D. Anderson, 250–66. Boston: Hall, 1981.

Attridge, Derek. "Literary Form and the Demands of Politics: Otherness in J. M. Coetzee's *Age of Iron*." In *Aesthetics and Ideology,* ed. George Levine, 243–263. New Brunswick, N.J.: Rutgers University Press, 1994.

Auerbach, Erich. *Mimesis: The Representation of Reality in Western Literature.* Trans. Willard R. Trask. 1946. Reprint, Princeton, N.J.: Princeton University Press, 2003.

Augspurger, Michael. "Sinclair Lewis' Primers for the Professional Managerial Class: 'Babbitt,' 'Arrowsmith,' and 'Dodsworth.'" *Journal of the Midwest Modern Language Association* 34.2 (Spring 2001): 73–97.

Baldwin, James. "Everybody's Protest Novel." In *Notes of a Native Son,* 13–23. Boston: Beacon Press, 1955.

Barnard, Rita. "Modern American Fiction." In *The Cambridge Companion to American Modernism,* ed. Walter Kalaidjian, 39–67. New York: Cambridge University Press, 2005.

———. "'When You Wish Upon a Star': Fantasy, Experience, and Mass Culture in Nathanael West." *American Literature* 66.2 (1994): 325–51.

Barthes, Roland. *Mythologies.* Trans. Annette Lavers. 1957. Reprint, New York: Hill and Wang, 2000.

Baudrillard, Jean. "The Masses: The Implosion of the Social in the Media." *New Literary History* 16.3 (1985): 577–89.

Beecher, Catharine. *Treatise on Domestic Economy, For the Use of Young Ladies at Home and at School.* New York: Harper and Brothers, 1856.

Bell, Michael. "The Metaphysics of Modernism." In *The Cambridge Companion to Modernism,* ed. Michael Levenson, 9–32. New York: Cambridge University Press, 1999.

Bell, Michael Davitt. "Mark Twain, 'Realism,' and *Huckleberry Finn*." In *New Essays on Adventures of Huckleberry Finn,* ed. Louis J. Budd, 35–59. New York: Cambridge University Press, 1985.

Bender, Thomas. *Community and Social Change in America.* New Brunswick, N.J.: Rutgers University Press, 1978.

Benjamin, Walter. *Illuminations.* Trans. Harry Zohn. 1968. Reprint, New York: Schocken Books, 1988.

Berlant, Lauren. *The Female Complaint: The Unfinished Business of Sentimentality in American Culture.* Durham, N.C.: Duke University Press, 2008.

———. "Poor Eliza." *American Literature* 70.3 (1998): 635–68.

Berle, Adolf A., and Gardiner C. Means. *The Modern Corporation and Private Property*. 1932. Reprint, New Brunswick, N.J.: Transaction Publishers, 1991.

Biddle, Jeff E. "Veblen, Twain, and the Connecticut Yankee: A Note." *History of Political Economy* 17.1 (1985): 97–107.

Bloom, Harold. "Introduction." In *Nathanael West's Miss Lonelyhearts*, ed. Harold Bloom, 1–10. Philadelphia: Chelsea House, 2005.

Blumin, Stuart M. "The Social Implication of U.S. Economic Development." In *The Long Nineteenth Century*, ed. Stanley L. Engerman and Robert E. Gallman, 813–63. New York: Cambridge University Press, 2000.

"Boston *Transcript*, March 1885." In *Adventures of Huckleberry Finn: An Authoritative Text, Contexts and Sources, Criticism*, ed. Thomas Cooley, 308. 1885. Reprint, New York: Norton, 1999.

Boym, Svetlana. *The Future of Nostalgia*. New York: Basic Books, 2001.

Braverman, Harry. *Labor and Monopoly Capital*. New York: Monthly Review Press, 1974.

Broadie, Alexander. "Sympathy and the Impartial Spectator." In *The Cambridge Companion to Adam Smith*, ed. Knud Haakonssen, 158–88. New York: Cambridge University Press, 2006.

Brodhead, Richard. *Cultures of Letters: Scenes of Reading and Writing in Nineteenth-Century America*. Chicago: University of Chicago Press, 1993.

Brooks, Peter. *The Melodramatic Imagination: Balzac, Henry James, Melodrama, and the Mode of Excess*. New Haven, Conn.: Yale University Press, 1976.

Brooks, Van Wyck. *The Ordeal of Mark Twain*. London: William Heinemann, 1922.

Broun, Heywood. "Review from the *New York Tribune*." In *Winesburg, Ohio: Authoritative Text, Backgrounds and Contexts, Criticism*, ed. Charles E. Modlin and Ray Lewis White, 160-61. 1919. Reprint, New York: Norton, 1996.

Brown, Herbert Ross. *The Sentimental Novel in America 1789–1860*. 1940. Reprint, New York: Pageant Books, 1959.

Budd, Louis J. "The American Background." In *The Cambridge Companion to American Realism and Naturalism: Howells to London*, ed. Donald Pizer, 21–46. 1995. Reprint, New York: Cambridge University Press, 1999.

Burbank, Rex. *Sherwood Anderson*. New York: Twayne, 1964.

Buroway, Michael. "A Classic of Its Time." *Contemporary Sociology* 25.3 (1996): 296–99.

Camfield, Gregg. "The Moral Aesthetics of Sentimentality: A Missing Key to *Uncle Tom's Cabin*." *Nineteenth-Century Literature* 43.3 (1988): 319–45.

———. *Necessary Madness: The Humor of Domesticity in Nineteenth-Century American Literature*. New York: Oxford University Press, 1997.

———. "A Republican Artisan in the Court of King Capital." In *A Historical Guide to Mark Twain*, ed. Shelley Fisher Fishkin, 95–126. New York: Oxford University Press, 2002.

———. "Sentimental Liberalism and the Problem of Race in *Huckleberry Finn*." *Nineteenth-Century Literature* 46.1 (1991): 96–113.

———. *Sentimental Twain: Samuel Clemens in the Maze of Moral Philosophy.* Philadelphia: University of Pennsylvania Press, 1994.

Campbell, Colin. *The Romantic Ethic and the Spirit of Modern Consumerism.* New York: Basil Blackwell, 1987.

Cather, Willa. *My Antonia.* 1918. Reprint, New York: Houghton Mifflin, 1995.

Chandler, Alfred D. *Scale and Scope: The Dynamics of Industrial Capitalism.* 1990. Reprint, Cambridge, Mass.: Harvard University Press, 2001.

———. *The Visible Hand: The Managerial Revolution in American Business.* 1977. Reprint, Cambridge, Mass.: Belknap Press, 1999.

Chopin, Kate. *The Awakening.* 1899. Reprint, New York: Penguin Classics, 1986.

Clark, Suzanne. *Sentimental Modernism: Women Writers and the Revolution of the Word.* Bloomington: Indiana University Press, 1991.

Cochran, Thomas. *American Business in the Twentieth Century.* Cambridge, Mass.: Harvard University Press, 1972.

Cohen, William. "Manual Conduct in Great Expectations." *ELH* 60.1 (1993): 217–59.

Colbert, Charles. *A Measure of Perfection: Phrenology and the Fine Arts in America.* Cultural Studies of the United States. Ed. Alan Trachtenberg. Chapel Hill: University of North Carolina Press, 1997.

Collins, James C., and Jerry I. Porras. *Built to Last: Successful Habits of Visionary Companies.* New York: HarperBusiness, 1994.

Comerchero, Victor. *Nathanael West: The Ironic Prophet.* Syracuse, N.Y.: Syracuse University Press, 1964.

Cooper, James Fenimore. *The Last of the Mohicans.* 1826. Reprint, New York: Modern Library, 2001.

Cott, Nancy F. "Passionlessness: An Interpretation of Victorian Sexual Ideology, 1790–1850." *Signs* 4.2 (1978): 219–36.

Courtemanche, Eleanor. *The "Invisible Hand" and British Fiction, 1818–1860: Adam Smith, Political Economy, and the Genre of Realism.* New York: Palgrave Macmillan, 2011.

Cowley, Malcolm. "Introduction." In *Miss Lonelyhearts*, 1–22. New York: Avon Books, 1959.

Cox, James. "*A Connecticut Yankee in King Arthur's Court*: The Machinery of Self-Preservation." In *A Connecticut Yankee in King Arthur's Court: An Authoritative Text, Backgrounds and Sources, Composition, and Publication, Criticism*, ed. Allison E. Ensor, 390–401. 1960. Reprint, New York: Norton, 1982.

Crane, Gregg D. "Dangerous Sentiments: Sympathy, Rights, and Revolution in Stowe's Antislavery Novels." *Nineteenth-Century Literature* 51.2 (1996): 176–204.

Crane, Hart. "From *The Double Dealer*, July 1921." In *Winesburg, Ohio*, 243–46. 1921. Reprint, New York: Modern Library, 2002.

Dalrymple, Theodore. "The Lessons of 'Lonelyhearts.'" *New Criterion* 23.3 (2004): 17–20.

DeVoto, Bernard. *Mark Twain's America.* Boston: Little, Brown, 1932.

Dewey, John. *The Later Works, 1925–1953. Vol. 5, 1929–1930.* Ed. Jo Ann Boydston. Carbondale: Southern Illinois University Press, 1984.

Dickstein, Morris. *Dancing in the Dark: A Cultural History of the Great Depression.* New York: Norton, 2009.

Dillon, Elizabeth Maddock. *The Gender of Freedom: Fictions of Liberalism and the Literary Public Sphere.* Stanford, Calif.: Stanford University Press, 2004.

———. "Sentimental Aesthetics." *American Literature* 76.3 (2004): 495–523.

Dos Passos, John. *U.S.A.* 1936. Reprint, New York: Library of America, 1996.

Douglas, Ann. *The Feminization of American Culture.* New York: Alfred A. Knopf, 1977.

———. "Introduction: The Art of Controversy." In *Uncle Tom's Cabin or, Life among the Lowly.* Ed. Ann Douglas, 7–34. New York: Penguin, 1981.

Douglass, Frederick. *Narrative of the Life of Frederick Douglass, an American Slave, Written by Himself.* 1845. 2nd ed. Reprint, Boston: Bedford/St. Martin's, 2003.

Doyno, Victor. "Afterword." In *Adventures of Huckleberry Finn.* Ed. Shelley Fisher Fishkin, 1–25. New York: Oxford University Press, 1996.

———. "The Composition of *Adventures of Huckleberry Finn.*" In *Adventures of Huckleberry Finn: Complete Text with Introduction, Historical Contexts, Critical Essays,* ed. Susan K. Harris, 9–17. 1996. Reprint, New Riverside Editions. Boston: Houghton Mifflin, 2000.

Dreiser, Theodore. *Sister Carrie.* 1900. Reprint, New York: Norton, 1991.

Drucker, Peter F. *The Practice of Management.* New York: Harper & Brothers, 1954.

Duffey, Bernard. "From the Chicago Renaissance in American Letters." In *The Achievement of Sherwood Anderson,* ed. Ray Lewis White, 46–59. 1954. Reprint, Chapel Hill: University of North Carolina Press, 1966.

Eagleton, Terry. *The Ideology of the Aesthetic.* 1990. Reprint, Malden, Mass.: Blackwell, 2004.

Edenbaum, Robert I. "To Kill God and Build a Church: Nathanael West's *Miss Lonelyhearts.*" In *Twentieth Century Interpretations of Miss Lonelyhearts,* ed. Thomas H. Jackson, 61–69. 1967. Reprint, Englewood Cliffs, N.J.: Prentice-Hall, 1971.

Eliot, T. S. "The Boy and the River: Without Beginning or End." In *Adventures of Huckleberry Finn: A Case Study in Critical Controversy,* ed. Gerald Graff and James Phelan, 286–90. 1950. Case Studies in Critical Controversy. Reprint, Boston: Bedford/St. Martin's, 1995.

———. "*Ulysses,* Order, and Myth." In Selected Prose of T. S. Eliot, ed. Frank Kermode, 175-178. 1923. Reprint, London: Faber, 1975.

Fernstrom, Karl D., Robert F. Elder, Wyman P. Fiske, Albert A. Schaefer, and B. Alden Thresher. *Organization and Management of a Business Enterprise.* New York: Harper, 1935.

Ferres, John H. "The Nostalgia of *Winesburg, Ohio.*" In *Winesburg, Ohio: Text and Criticism,* ed. John H. Ferres, 466–73. 1971. Reprint, New York: Penguin, 1996.

Fiedler, Leslie A. *Love and Death in the American Novel.* 1960. Reprint, Normal, Ill.: Dalkey Archive Press, 1997.

Fielding, Henry. *The History of Tom Jones a Foundling.* 1749. Reprint, Hanover, N.H.: Wesleyan University Press, 1975.

Fisher, Philip. *Hard Facts: Setting and Form in the American Novel.* New York: Oxford University Press, 1987.

Fishkin, Shelley Fisher. "Mark Twain and Women." In *The Cambridge Companion to Mark Twain,* ed. Forrest G. Robinson, 52–73. 1995. Reprint, New York: Cambridge University Press, 1999.

Fluck, Winfried. "The Power and Failure of Representation in Harriet Beecher Stowe's Uncle Tom's Cabin." *New Literary History* 23.2 (1992): 319–38.

Ford, Henry, in collaboration with Samuel Crowther. *My Life and Work.* New York: Doubleday, 1923.

Franta, Andrew. "Godwin's Handshake." *PMLA* 122.3 (2007): 696–710.

Franzen, Jonathan. "Tribute." In *Five Dials: Celebrating the Life and Work of David Foster Wallace 1962–2008, 16–17.* London: Hamish Hamilton, 2008.

Fredrickson, George M. "Uncle Tom and the Anglo-Saxons: Romantic Racialism in the North." In *Uncle Tom's Cabin: Authoritative Text, Backgrounds and Context, Criticism,* ed. Elizabeth Ammons, 429–38. 1971. Reprint, New York: Norton, 1994.

Frye, Northrop. "Varieties of Literary Utopias." In *Utopias and Utopian Thought,* ed. Frank E. Manuel, 25–49. 1965. Reprint, Boston: Houghton Mifflin, 1966.

Fussell, Edwin. "*Winesburg, Ohio*: Art and Isolation." In *The Achievement of Sherwood Anderson,* ed. Ray Lewis White, 104–13. Reprint, Chapel Hill: University of North Carolina Press, 1966.

Galambos, Louis. *The Public Image of Big Business in America, 1880–1940.* Baltimore: Johns Hopkins University Press, 1975.

Gay, Edwin F., and Leo Wolman. "Trends in Economic Organization." In *Recent Social Trends in the United States: Report of the President's Research Committee on Social Trends,* 218–67. New York: McGraw-Hill, 1932.

Giedion, Sigfried. *Mechanization Takes Command: A Contribution to Anonymous History.* New York: Oxford University Press, 1948.

Gilmore, Michael T. *American Romanticism and the Marketplace.* Chicago: University of Chicago Press, 1985.

———. *Surface and Depth: The Quest for Legibility in American Culture.* New York: Oxford University Press, 2003.

———. "*Uncle Tom's Cabin* and the American Renaissance: The Sacramental Aesthetic of Harriet Beecher Stowe." In *The Cambridge Companion to*

Harriet Beecher Stowe, ed. Cindy Weinstein, 58–76. New York: Cambridge University Press, 2004.

Goshgarian, G. M. *To Kiss the Chastening Rod: Domestic Fiction and Sexual Ideology in the American Renaissance.* Ithaca, N.Y.: Cornell University Press, 1992.

Gowin, Enoch Burton. *The Selection and Training of the Business Executive.* New York: Macmillan, 1918.

"Hand." Def.1.I.8. *Oxford English Dictionary.* 2nd ed. 1989.

The Hand Phrenologically Considered: Being a Glimpse at the Relation of the Mind with the Organisation of the Body. London: Chapman and Hall, 1848.

Hansen, Chadwick. "The Once and Future Boss: Mark Twain's Yankee." *Nineteenth-Century Fiction* 28.1 (1973): 62–73.

Harpham, Geoffrey. "The Grotesque: First Principles." *Journal of Aesthetics and Art Criticism* 34.4 (1976): 461–68.

Harris, Susan K. "Four Ways to Inscribe a Mackerel: Mark Twain and Laura Hawkins." *Studies of Novels* 21.2 (1991): 138–53.

Hawthorne, Nathaniel. *The Scarlet Letter.* Ed. Ross C. Murfin. 1850. Case Studies in Contemporary Criticism. Reprint, Boston: Bedford/St. Martin's, 1991.

Hedrick, Joan. *Harriet Beecher Stowe: A Life.* New York: Oxford University Press, 1994.

Hemingway, Ernest. *A Farewell to Arms.* 1929. Reprint, New York: Scribner, 2003.

Hendley, W. Clark. "Dear Abby, Miss Lonelyhearts, and the Eighteenth Century: The Origins of the Newspaper Advice Column." *Journal of Popular Culture* 11.2 (1977): 345–52.

Hirschman, Albert O. *The Passions and the Interests.* Princeton, N.J.: Princeton University Press, 1977.

Hoffman, Frederick J. *Freudianism and the Literary Mind.* Baton Rouge: Louisiana State University Press, 1945.

Holman, C. Hugh. "Of Everything the Unexplained and Irresponsible Specimen: Notes on How to Read American Realism." In *The Rise of Silas Lapham: An Authoritative Text, Composition and Backgrounds, Contemporary Responses, Criticism*, ed. Don L. Cook, 487–92. 1964. Reprint, New York: Norton, 1982.

Howard, June. "What Is Sentimentality?" *American Literary History* 11.1 (1999): 63–81.

Howe, Irving. "The Book of the Grotesque." In *The Achievement of Sherwood Anderson*, ed. Ray Lewis White, 90–101. 1951. Reprint, Chapel Hill: University of North Carolina Press, 1966.

Howells, W. D. "A Call for Realism." In *The Rise of Silas Lapham: An Authoritative Text, Composition and Backgrounds, Contemporary Responses, Criticism*, ed. Don L. Cook, 496–500. 1891. Reprint, New York: Norton, 1982.

Hoxie, Robert Franklin. *Scientific Management and Labor.* New York: D. Appleton, 1915.

Hutcheson, Francis. *An Essay on the Nature and Conduct of the Passions and Affections, with Illustrations on the Moral Sense.* Ed. Aaron Garrett. 1725. Reprint, Indianapolis: Liberty Fund, 2002.

Hyman, Stanley Edgar. "Nathanael West." In *Twentieth Century Interpretations of Miss Lonelyhearts*, ed. Thomas H. Jackson, 70–80. 1962. Reprint, Englewood Cliffs, N.J.: Prentice-Hall, 1971.

Irr, Caren. *The Suburb of Dissent.* Durham, N.C.: Duke University Press, 1998.

Jackson, Thomas H. "Introduction." In *Twentieth Century Interpretations of Miss Lonelyhearts*, ed. Thomas H. Jackson, 1–17. Englewood Cliffs, N.J.: Prentice-Hall, 1971.

James, William. *Varieties of Religious Experience.* 1902. Reprint, Mineola, N.Y.: Dover, 2002.

———. "What Is an Emotion?" *Mind* 9 (1884): 188–205.

Jauss, Hans Robert. "Literary History as a Challenge to Literary Theory." Trans. Elizabeth Benzinger. In *Literature in the Modern World*, ed. Dennis Walder, 67–75. 1967. Reprint, New York: Oxford University Press, 1990.

Jefferson, Mark. "What's Wrong with Sentimentality?" *Mind* 92.367 (1983): 519–29.

Kanigel, Robert. *The One Best Way: Frederick Winslow Taylor and the Enigma of Efficiency.* New York: Viking, 1997.

Kaplan, Amy. *The Social Construction of American Realism.* Chicago: University of Chicago Press, 1988.

Kazin, Alfred. *On Native Grounds.* New York: Reynal and Hitchcock, 1942.

Kete, Mary Louise. *Sentimental Collaborations: Mourning and Middle-Class Identity in Nineteenth-Century America.* Durham, N.C.: Duke University Press, 2000.

Kiskis, Michael J. "Mark Twain and the Tradition of Literary Domesticity." In *Constructing Mark Twain: New Directions in Scholarship*, ed. Laura E. Skandera Trombley and Michael J. Kiskis, 13–27. Columbia: University of Missouri Press, 2001.

Klein, Lawrence E. *Shaftesbury and the Culture of Politeness: Moral Discourse and Cultural Politics in Early Eighteenth-Century England.* Cambridge: Cambridge University Press, 1994.

Knox, Loren H. B. "Our Lost Individuality." *Atlantic* 104 (1909): 818–24.

Korobkin, Laura. *Criminal Conversations: Sentimentality and Nineteenth-Century Legal Stories of Adultery.* New York: Columbia University Press, 1998.

Krauth, Leland. *Proper Mark Twain.* Athens: University of Georgia Press, 1999.

Lang, Andrew. "The Art of Mark Twain." In *Huck Finn among the Critics: A Centennial Selection*, ed. M. Thomas Inge, 37–41. 1891. Reprint, Frederick, Md.: University Publications of America, 1985.

Larsen, Nella. *Passing.* 1929. Reprint, New York: Penguin Books, 1997.

Laurie, Bruce. *Artisans into Workers.* New York: Hill and Wang, 1989.

Lears, T. J. Jackson. "From Salvation to Self-Realization: Advertising and the Therapeutic Roots of the Consumer Culture, 1880–1930." In *The Culture of*

Consumption: Critical Essays in American History, 1880–1980, ed. Richard Wightman Fox and T. J. Jackson Lears, 3-38. New York: Pantheon Books, 1983.

———. *No Place of Grace: Antimodernism and the Transformation of American Culture 1880–1920.* New York: Pantheon Books, 1981.

Lester, Julius. "Morality and *Adventures of Huckleberry Finn.*" In *Adventures of Huckleberry Finn: A Case Study in Critical Controversy,* ed. Gerald Graff and James Phelan, 340-48. 1984. Case Studies in Critical Controversy. Reprint, Boston: Bedford/St. Martin's, 1995.

Levenson, Michael. *Modernism and the Fate of Individuality: Character and Novelistic Form from Conrad to Woolf.* New York: Cambridge University Press, 1991.

Levine, Lawrence W. *The Unpredictable Past: Explorations in American Cultural History.* New York: Oxford University Press, 1993.

Lewis, Sinclair. *Babbitt.* 1922. Reprint, New York: Modern Library, 2002.

Love, Glen A. *Babbitt: An American Life.* New York: Twayne, 1993.

———. "*Winesburg, Ohio* and the Rhetoric of Silence." *American Literature* 40.1 (1968): 38-57.

Mahoney, John J. "An Analysis of *Winesburg, Ohio.*" *Journal of Aesthetics and Art Criticism* 15.2 (1956): 245-52.

Mailloux, Steven. "The Bad-Boy Boom." In *Adventures of Huckleberry Finn: Complete Text with Introduction, Historical Contexts, Critical Essays,* ed. Susan K. Harris, 43-50. 1989. New Riverside Editions. Reprint, Boston: Houghton Mifflin, 2000.

Marchand, Roland. *Creating the Corporate Soul: The Rise of Public Relations and Corporate Imagery in American Big Business.* Berkeley: University of California Press, 1998.

Marcuse, Herbert. *Eros and Civilization.* 1955. Reprint, Boston: Beacon Press, 1966.

Margolis, Stacey. "Huckleberry Finn; or, Consequences." *PMLA* 116.2 (2001): 329-43.

Martin, Jay. *Nathanael West: The Art of His Life.* New York: Carrol and Graff, 1970.

Marx, Karl. *Capital: Volume One.* 1867. Trans. Ben Fowkes. New York: Vintage Books, 1977.

Marx, Leo. *The Machine in the Garden: Technology and the Pastoral Ideal in America.* New York: Oxford University Press, 1964.

———. "Mr. Eliot, Mr. Trilling, and *Huckleberry Finn.*" In *Adventures of Huckleberry Finn: A Case Study in Critical Controversy,* ed. Gerald Graff and James Phelan, 290-305. 1953. Case Studies in Critical Controversy. Reprint, Boston: Bedford/St. Martin's, 1995.

McCaffery, Larry. "An Interview with David Foster Wallace." *Review of Contemporary Fiction* 13.2 (1993): 127-50.

McCullers, Carson. *The Heart Is a Lonely Hunter.* 1940. Reprint, Boston: Mariner, 2000.

Melville, Herman. *Moby-Dick*. 1851. Reprint, New York: Norton, 1967.

Merish, Lori. "Sentimental Consumption: Harriet Beecher Stowe and the Aesthetics of Middle-Class Ownership." *American Literary History* 8.1 (1996): 1–33.

Michaels, Walter Benn. *The Gold Standard and the Logic of Naturalism: American Literature at the Turn of the Century*. Berkeley: University of California Press, 1987.

Michaud, Regis. *The American Novel To-Day: A Social and Psychological Study*. Boston: Little, Brown, 1931.

Milton, John. Paradise Lost. 1674. In *The Riverside Milton*, ed. Roy Flannagan. Boston: Houghton Mifflin, 1998.

Mintz, Steven, and Susan Kellogg. *Domestic Revolutions: A Social History of American Family Life*. New York: Free Press, 1988.

Mizruchi, Susan L. "Becoming Multicultural: Culture, Economy, and the Novel, 1860–1920." In *The Cambridge History of American Literature. Vol. 3, Prose Writing 1860–1920*, ed. Sacvan Bercovitch, 413–740. Cambridge: Cambridge University Press, 2005.

Montgomery, David. *Worker's Control in America*. New York: Cambridge University Press, 1979.

Morrison, Toni. "Re-Marking Twain." In *Adventures of Huckleberry Finn: Complete Text with Introduction, Historical Contexts, Critical Essays*, ed. Susan K. Harris, 374-82. 1996. New Riverside Editions. Reprint, Boston: Houghton Mifflin, 2000.

Mullan, John. *Sentiment and Sociability: The Language of Feeling in the Eighteenth Century*. Oxford: Clarendon Press, 1988.

Mumford, Lewis. *Technics and Civilization*. New York: Harcourt, Brace, 1934.

Norris, Frank. *McTeague*. 1899. Reprint, New York: Penguin, 1994.

Nuernberg, Susan M. "Stowe, the Abolition Movement, and Prevailing Theories of Race in Nineteenth-Century America." In *Approaches to Teaching Stowe's Uncle Tom's Cabin*, ed. Elizabeth Ammons and Susan Belasco, 36–45. New York: MLA, 2000.

Nussbaum, Martha C. *Upheavals of Thought: The Intelligence of Emotions*. New York: Cambridge University Press, 2001.

O'Connell, Catharine E. "'The Magic of the Real Presence of Distress': Sentimentality and Competing Rhetorics of Authority." In *The Stowe Debate: Rhetorical Strategies in Uncle Tom's Cabin*, ed. Mason I. Lowance Jr., Ellen E. Westbrook, and R. C. De Prospo, 13–36. Amherst: University of Massachusetts Press, 1994.

O'Farrell, Mary Ann. *Telling Complexions: The Nineteenth-Century English Novel and the Blush*. Durham, N.C.: Duke University Press, 1997.

Oxenhandler, Neal. "The Changing Concept of Literary Emotion: A Selective History." *New Literary History* 20.1 (1988): 105–21.

Parker, E. P. "Harriet Beecher Stowe." In *Eminent Women of the Age; Being Narratives of the Lives and Deeds of the Prominent Women of the Present*

Generation, ed. James Barton et al., 296-331. Hartford, Conn.: S. M. Betts, 1869.

"Pass." Def.6.IX.43. *Oxford English Dictionary*. 2nd ed. 1989.

Phillips, William L. "How Sherwood Anderson Wrote *Winesburg, Ohio*." In *The Achievement of Sherwood Anderson: Essays in Criticism*, ed. Ray Lewis White, 62–84. 1951. Reprint, Chapel Hill: University of North Carolina Press, 1966.

Phillipson, Nicholas. *Adam Smith: An Enlightened Life*. New Haven, Conn.: Yale University Press, 2010.

Philoponus, John [attributed to]. *On Aristotle's "On the Soul 3.1–8."* Sixth Century. Trans. William Charlton. Ithaca, N.Y.: Cornell University Press, 2000.

Pinker, Steven. *The Blank Slate: The Modern Denial of Human Nature*. New York: Penguin, 2002.

Podhoretz, Norman. "Nathanael West: A Particular Kind of Joking." In *Nathanael West: A Collection of Critical Essays*. 1957. Comp. Jay Martin, 154–60. Englewood Cliffs, N.J.: Prentice-Hall, 1971.

Raban, Jonathan. "A Surfeit of Commodities: The Novels of Nathanael West." In *The American Novel and the Nineteen Twenties*, ed. Malcolm Bradbury and David Palmer, 215–31. New York: Edward Arnold, 1971.

Railton, Stephen. "Black Slaves and White Readers." In *Approaches to Teaching Stowe's Uncle Tom's Cabin*, ed. Elizabeth Ammons and Susan Belasco, 104–10. New York: MLA, 2000.

Ransom, John Crowe. *The World's Body*. New York: Charles Scribner's Sons, 1938.

Renton, David. *Dissident Marxism*. New York: Zed Books, 2004.

Reynolds, David. *Mightier Than the Sword: Uncle Tom's Cabin and the Battle for America*. New York: Norton, 2011.

Richardson, Samuel. *Clarissa, or the History of a Young Lady*. 1748. Reprint, New York: Penguin, 1985.

Rideout, Walter B. "The Simplicity of *Winesburg, Ohio*." In *Winesburg, Ohio: Authoritative Text, Backgrounds and Contexts, Criticism*, ed. Charles E. Modlin and Ray Lewis White, 169-77. 1962. Reprint, New York: Norton, 1996.

Rigsbee, Sally Adair. "The Feminine in *Winesburg, Ohio*." In *Winesburg, Ohio: Authoritative Text, Backgrounds and Contexts, Criticism*, ed. Charles E. Modlin and Ray Lewis White, 178-88. 1981. Reprint, New York: Norton, 1996.

Robinson, Forrest G. "The Characterization of Jim in *Huckleberry Finn*." *Nineteenth-Century Literature* 43.3 (1988): 361–91.

———. "The Silences in *Huckleberry Finn*." *Nineteenth-Century Fiction* 37.1 (1982): 50–74.

Romero, Lora. "Bio-Political Resistance in Domestic Ideology and *Uncle Tom's Cabin*." *American Literary History* 1.4 (1989): 715–34.

Roodenburg, Herman. "The 'Hand of Friendship': Shaking Hands and Other Gestures in the Dutch Republic." In *A Cultural History of Gesture*, ed. Jan

Bremmer and Herman Roodenburg, 152–89. Ithaca, N.Y.: Cornell University Press, 1991.

Rothschild, Emma. *Economic Sentiments: Adam Smith, Condorcet, and the Enlightenment*. Cambridge, Mass.: Harvard University Press, 2001.

Sanchez-Eppler, Karen. "Bodily Bonds: The Intersecting Rhetorics of Feminism and Abolition." In *The Culture of Sentiment: Race, Gender, and Sentimentality in Nineteenth-Century America*, ed. Shirley Samuels, 92–114. 1988. Reprint, New York: Oxford University Press, 1992.

Sand, George. "Review of *Uncle Tom's Cabin*." In *Uncle Tom's Cabin: Authoritative Text, Backgrounds and Contexts, Criticism*, ed. Elizabeth Ammons, 459–63. 1852. Reprint, New York: Norton, 1994.

Schevill, James. "Notes on the Grotesque: Anderson, Brecht, and Williams." *Twentieth Century Literature* 23.2 (1977): 229–38.

Schmitz, Christopher J. *The Growth of Big Business in the United States and Western Europe, 1850–1963*, ed. Michael Sanderson. 1993. Reprint, Cambridge: Cambridge University Press, 1995.

Schneidau, Herbert N. *Waking Giants: The Presence of the Past in Modernism*. New York: Oxford University Press, 1991.

Shank, Barry. *A Token of My Affection: Greeting Cards and American Business Culture*. New York: Columbia University Press, 2004.

Shulman, Robert. *Social Criticism and Nineteenth-Century American Fictions*. Columbia: University of Missouri Press, 1987.

Skandera-Trombley, Laura. *Mark Twain in the Company of Women*. Philadelphia: University of Pennsylvania Press, 1994.

Sklar, Martin J. *The Corporate Reconstruction of American Capitalism, 1890–1916: The Market, the Law, and Politics*. New York: Cambridge University Press, 1988.

Smith, Adam. "The Principles Which Lead and Direct Philosophical Enquiries; as Illustrated by the History of Astronomy." 1795. In *The Essays of Adam Smith*. London: Alex Murray & Son, 1869.

———. *The Theory of Moral Sentiments*. 1759. Reprint, New York: Cambridge University Press, 2002.

———. *The Wealth of Nations*. 1776. Reprint, New York: Modern Library, 2000.

Smith, Henry Nash. *Mark Twain's Fables of Progress: Political and Economic Ideas in "A Connecticut Yankee."* New Brunswick, N.J.: Rutgers University Press, 1964.

Snyder, Thomas D. *120 Years of American Education: A Statistical Portrait*. Washington, D.C.: U.S. Department of Education, 1993.

Spangler, George M. "The Ending of the Novel." In *The Awakening: An Authoritative Text, Contexts, Criticism*, ed. Margaret Culley, 186–89. 1970. Reprint, New York: Norton, 1976.

Spencer, David A. "Braverman and the Contribution of Labour Process Analysis to the Critique of Capitalist Production Twenty-Five Years On." *Work, Employment & Society* 14.2 (2000): 223–43.

"Springfield *Republican*, March 1885." In *Adventures of Huckleberry Finn: An Authoritative Text, Contexts and Sources, Criticism*, ed. Thomas Cooley, 308. 1885. Reprint, New York: Norton, 1999.

Sterne, Laurence. *The Life and Opinions of Tristram Shandy, Gentleman.* 1759. Reprint, North Clarendon, Vt.: Everyman, 2000.

Stewart, Matthew. *The Management Myth: Debunking Modern Business Philosophy.* New York: Norton, 2009.

Stone, Albert E. "Mark Twain's Joan of Arc: The Child as Goddess." *American Literature* 31.1 (1959): 1–20.

Stoneley, Peter. *Mark Twain and the Feminine Aesthetic.* New York: Cambridge University Press, 1992.

Stouck, David. "Anderson's Expressionist Art." In *Winesburg, Ohio: Authoritative Text, Backgrounds and Contexts, Criticism*, ed. Charles E. Modlin and Ray Lewis White, 211–29. 1990. Reprint, New York: Norton, 1996.

Stowe, Harriet Beecher. "An Appeal to Women of the Free States of America, on the Present Crisis in Our Country." In *The Oxford Harriet Beecher Stowe Reader*, ed. Joan D. Hedrick, 452–56. 1854. Reprint, New York: Oxford University Press, 1999.

———. *Uncle Tom's Cabin or, Life among the Lowly.* 1852. Reprint, New York: Penguin, 1986.

Strasser, Mark Philip. "Hutcheson on the Higher and Lower Pleasures." *Journal of the History of Philosophy* 25.4 (1987): 517–31.

Sundquist, Eric J. "Introduction." In *New Essays on Uncle Tom's Cabin*, ed. Eric J. Sundquist, 1–44. New York: Cambridge University Press, 1986.

———. "Introduction: The Country of the Blue." In *American Realism: New Essays*, ed. Eric J. Sundquist, 3–24. Baltimore: Johns Hopkins University Press, 1982.

Sutton, William A. *Exit to Elsinore.* Muncie, Ind.: Ball State University Press, 1967.

Szalay, Michael. *New Deal Modernism: American Literature and the Invention of the Welfare State.* Durham, N.C.: Duke University Press, 2001.

Tanner, Michael. "Sentimentality." *Proceedings of the Aristotelian Society* 77 (1976–1977): 127–47.

Taylor, Frederick Winslow. *The Principles of Scientific Management.* 1911. Reprint, New York: Harper & Brothers, 1914.

Thomas, Brook. *Cross Examinations of Law and Literature: Cooper, Hawthorne, Stowe, and Melville.* New York: Cambridge University Press, 1987.

Thomas, Keith. "Introduction." In *A Cultural History of Gesture*, ed. Jan Bremmer and Herman Roodenburg, 1–14. Ithaca, N.Y.: Cornell University Press, 1992.

Thompson, E. P. "Time, Work-Discipline, and Industrial Capitalism." *Past & Present* 38 (December 1967): 56–97.

Thurston, Jarvis A. "Technique in *Winesburg, Ohio*." In *Winesburg, Ohio: Text and Criticism*, ed. John H. Ferres, 304–17. 1956. Reprint, New York: Penguin, 1996.

Tinker, Tony. "Spectres of Marx and Braverman in the Twilight of Postmodernist Labour Process Research." *Work, Employment, and Society* 16.2 (2002): 251–81.

Tompkins, Jane. *Sensational Designs: The Cultural Work of American Fiction 1790–1860.* New York: Oxford University Press, 1985.

Tonnies, Ferdinand. *Community and Civil Society.* 1887. Trans. Jose and Margaret Hollis Harris. Reprint, New York: Cambridge University Press, 2001.

Trachtenberg, Alan. *The Incorporation of America: Culture and Society in the Gilded Age.* New York: Hill and Wang, 1982.

Trilling, Lionel. "A Certain Formal Aptness." In *Adventures of Huckleberry Finn: A Case Study in Critical Controversy,* ed. Gerald Graff and James Phelan, 284–85. 1948. Case Studies in Critical Controversy. Reprint, Boston: Bedford/St. Martin's, 1995.

Troy, William. "Four Newer Novelists." *Nation,* June 14, 1933, Summer Book Section, 672–73.

Twain, Mark. *Adventures of Huckleberry Finn.* 1885. Ed. Gerald Graff and James Phelan. Case Studies in Critical Controversy. Reprint, Boston: Bedford/St. Martin's, 1995.

———. *The Adventures of Tom Sawyer.* 1875. Reprint, New York: Grosset and Dunlap, 1985.

———. "The Art of Authorship." In Mark Twain, *Selected Shorter Writings of Mark Twain.* Ed. Walter Blair, 225–226. Boston: Houghton Mifflin, 1980.

———. *Autobiography of Mark Twain. Vol. 1.* Ed. Harriet Elinor Smith. Berkeley: University of California Press, 2010.

———. *A Connecticut Yankee in King Arthur's Court.* 1889. Reprint, New York: Penguin, 1986.

———. "Fenimore Cooper's Literary Offenses." In Mark Twain, *Selected Shorter Writings of Mark Twain.* Ed. Walter Blair, 227–38. Boston: Houghton Mifflin, 1980.

———. "How To Tell a Story." In Mark Twain, *Selected Shorter Writings of Mark Twain.* Ed. Walter Blair, 239–43. Boston: Houghton Mifflin, 1980.

———. *Letters from the Earth.* 1939. Reprint, New York: Harper Perennial, 2004.

———. *Life on the Mississippi.* 1883. Reprint, New York: Penguin Classics, 1986.

———. *Selected Shorter Writings of Mark Twain.* Ed. Walter Blair. Boston: Houghton Mifflin, 1980.

———. *A Tramp Abroad.* 1880. Reprint, New York: Penguin Classics, 1997.

Updike, John. "Introduction." In Sherwood Anderson, *Winesburg, Ohio,* xiii–xxii. 1991. Reprint, New York: Modern Library, 2002.

Veblen, Thorstein. *The Theory of Business Enterprise.* 1904. Reprint, New York: Charles Scribner's Sons, 1937.

Veitch, Jonathan. *American Superrealism: Nathanael West and the Politics of Representation in the 1930s.* Madison: University of Wisconsin Press, 1997.

Volpe, Edmond L. "The Waste Land of Nathanael West." In *Nathanael West: A Collection of Critical Essays.* 1961. Comp. Jay Martin, 91–101. Englewood Cliffs, N.J.: Prentice-Hall, 1971.

Walker, Nancy A. "Reformers and Young Maidens: Women and Virtue in *Adventures of Huckleberry Finn.*" In *One Hundred Years of Huckleberry Finn: The Boy, His Book, and American Culture,* ed. Robert Sattelmeyer and J. Donald Crowley, 171–85. Columbia: University of Missouri Press, 1985.

Wallace, David Foster. *Infinite Jest.* Boston: Little, Brown, 1996.

Wardell, Mark, et al., eds. *Rethinking the Labor Process.* Albany, N.Y.: SUNY Press, 1999.

Warner, Charles Dudley. "*Uncle Tom's Cabin* a Half Century Later." In *Uncle Tom's Cabin: Authoritative Text, Backgrounds and Contexts, Criticism,* ed. Elizabeth Ammons, 483–88. 1896. Reprint, New York: Norton, 1994.

Warner, Susan. *The Wide, Wide World.* 1850. Reprint, New York: Feminist Press, 1987.

Warner, W. Lloyd, et al. *Social Class in America: A Manual of Procedure for the Measurement of Social Status.* Chicago: Science Research Associates, 1949.

Watt, Ian. *The Rise of the Novel.* 1951. Reprint, Berkeley: University of California Press, 2001.

Wead, Douglas. *The Compassionate Touch.* Carol Stream, Ill.: Creation House, 1977.

Weber, Max. "Max Weber on Bureaucratization in 1909." Trans. J. P. Mayer. In *Max Weber and German Politics,* ed. J. P. Mayer, 125–31. 1909. Reprint, New York: Arno Press, 1979.

———. *Max Weber on Law in Economy and Society.* Trans. Edward Shils and Max Rheinstein. Cambridge, Mass.: Harvard University Press, 1954.

———. *The Protestant Ethic and the Spirit of Capitalism.* 1920. Trans. Talcott Parsons. Ed. Richard Swedberg. New York: Norton, 2009.

Weinstein, Cindy. *The Literature of Labor and the Labors of Literature: Allegory in Nineteenth-Century American Fiction.* New York: Cambridge University Press, 1995.

Weisberg, Jacob. *The Bush Tragedy.* New York: Random House, 2008.

West, Nathanael. *Miss Lonelyhearts & The Day of the Locust.* 1933; 1939. Reprint, New York: New Directions, 1969.

———. "Some Notes on Miss L." In *Nathanael West: A Collection of Critical Essays.* 1933. Comp. Jay Martin, 66–67. Reprint, Englewood Cliffs, N.J.: Prentice-Hall, 1971.

———. "Some Notes on Violence." In *Nathanael West: A Collection of Critical Essays.* 1932. Comp. Jay Martin, 50–51. Reprint, Englewood Cliffs, N.J.: Prentice-Hall, 1971.

West, Rebecca. "From *New Statesman,* July 22, 1922." In *Winesburg, Ohio,* 235. 1922. Reprint, New York: Modern Library, 2002.

Wexelblatt, Robert. "*Miss Lonelyhearts* and the Rhetoric of Disintegration." In *Nathanael West's Miss Lonelyhearts,* ed. Harold Bloom, 99–111. Philadelphia: Chelsea House, 2005.

Wexler, Laura. "Tender Violence: Literary Eavesdropping, Domestic Fiction, and Educational Reform." In *The Culture of Sentiment: Race, Gender, and*

Sentimentality in Nineteenth-Century America, ed. Shirley Samuels, 9–38. New York: Oxford University Press, 1992.

Whalan, Mark. "Dreams of Manhood: Narrative, Gender, and History in *Winesburg, Ohio*." *Studies in American Fiction* 30.2 (2002): 229–48.

Wiebe, Robert H. *The Search for Order: 1877–1920*. New York: Hill and Wang, 1967.

Willey, Malcolm M., and Stuart Rice. "The Agencies of Communication." In *Recent Social Trends in the United States: Report of the President's Research Committee on Social Trends*, 167–217. New York: McGraw-Hill, 1932.

Williams, Raymond. *Marxism and Literature*. New York: Oxford University Press, 1977.

Wilson, Woodrow, ed. *The Public Papers of Woodrow Wilson*. Vol. 2. New York: Harper & Brothers, 1925.

Witt, John Fabian. *The Accidental Republic: Crippled Workingmen, Destitute Widows, and the Remaking of American Law*. Cambridge, Mass.: Harvard University Press, 2004.

Zandy, Janet. *Hands: Physical Labor, Class, and Cultural Work*. New Brunswick, N.J.: Rutgers University Press, 2004.

Zerubavel, Eviatar. "The Standardization of Time: A Sociohistorical Perspective." *American Journal of Sociology* 88.1 (July 1982): 1–23.

Zunz, Olivier. *Making America Corporate*. Chicago: University of Chicago Press, 1990.

Index